An OPUS book

THE LAWFUL RIGHTS OF MANKIND

The
Lawful Rights of
Mankind

*An Introduction to the International
Legal Code of Human Rights*

PAUL SIEGHART

Oxford   New York

OXFORD UNIVERSITY PRESS

1985

Oxford University Press, Walton Street, Oxford OX2 6DP

London New York Toronto
Delhi Bombay Calcutta Madras Karachi
Kuala Lumpur Singapore Hong Kong Tokyo
Nairobi Dar es Salaam Cape Town
Melbourne Auckland

and associated companies in
Beirut Berlin Ibadan Mexico City Nicosia

Oxford is a trade mark of Oxford University Press

British Library Cataloguing in Publication Data
Sieghart, Paul
The lawful rights of mankind: an introduction to
the international legal code of human rights.—
(An Opus book)
1. Civil rights (International law)
I. Title II. Series
341.4'81 K3240.4
ISBN 0-19-219190-X

Printed in Great Britain by
Billing & Sons Ltd.
Worcester

For F.A.

Preface

We hear a good deal more about human rights these days than we used to, not least from statesmen scarcely renowned for respecting them. One of the main reasons for this lies in some recent developments in the field of international law which are still far too little known, and which provide the occasion for this book.

Down to the end of the second world war, it was a matter of universally accepted doctrine in international affairs that how a state treated its own citizens was a matter entirely for its own sovereign determination, and not the legitimate concern of anyone outside its own frontiers. Had a well-meaning delegation from abroad called on Chancellor Adolf Hitler in 1936 to complain about the notorious Nürnberg laws, and the manner in which they were being applied to persecute German Jews, the Führer would probably have dismissed such an initiative with the classic phrase of 'an illegitimate interference in the internal affairs of the sovereign German State', pointing out that these laws had been enacted in full accordance with the provisions of the German Constitution, by an assembly constitutionally and legally competent to enact them, and that neither they nor their application were the concern of any meddling foreigners. And, in international law as it then stood, he would have been perfectly right—and so would Party Secretary-General Josef Stalin have been if a similar delegation had called on him at around the same time to complain about the wholesale liquidation of the kulaks in the Soviet Union.

Were such delegations to call today on some of the world's living tyrants to complain about the injustice of some of *their* laws, those protests too would doubtless be dismissed with the same phrase. But, in international law as it stands today, those tyrants would be wrong. For since Hitler's and Stalin's time there has been a change in international law so profound that it can properly be called a revolution. Today, for the first time in history, how a sovereign state treats its own citizens is no longer a matter for its own exclusive determination, but a matter of *legitimate* concern for all other states, and for their inhabitants.

The formal product of that revolution is a detailed code of international law laying down rights of individuals against the states which exercise power over them, and so making these individuals the subjects of *legal* rights under that law, and no longer the mere objects of its compassion. The code calls these rights 'human' rights. Different parts of it have come into force since the end of the second world war, but one of its main components—the twin United Nations Covenants—only entered into force in early 1976. Since then, this particular component has been extended to nearly eighty of the world's sovereign states, and that is one of the main reasons why we hear so much more about human rights today than we ever did before.

However, neither the existence nor the contents of the code itself are yet widely known beyond the practitioners of international law, diplomacy, and some other branches of government. Plainly, they should be far better known, and that is the main purpose of this book. The code consists of nine general instruments—two Declarations, two Covenants, two Conventions, and three Charters—together with about another twenty specialized treaties of various kinds. Some parts of it have already been copiously interpreted and applied by international tribunals and other competent bodies, which have generated much learning and many precedents in this new field. The bulk of that material is collected in another book of mine called *The International Law of Human Rights*, published by the Clarendon Press in February 1983. But that is a solid tome of nearly 600 pages, designed mainly as a reference work for practitioners. I would not wish upon anyone the task of trying to read it as an introduction to the subject, and I therefore readily accepted the invitation of the Oxford University Press to write this much shorter book for their OPUS series.

But this book is not only intended as an introduction for the general reader, for it may also serve to some extent as a companion to the larger work. In a reference volume of that kind, pressures of space preclude one from much discussion, and academic conventions from expressing too many views of one's own. These constraints do not operate here, and I have therefore felt free to discuss, to advance my own ideas, and to give expression to some of my own concerns—especially about the limitations and defects of the code, much as its arrival is to be welcomed. But I hope I have made it sufficiently clear where I have done this, so that readers are free to disagree, and to reach their own conclusions.

It is a commonplace that, in far too many places in the world, human rights continue to be violated, sometimes on a massive and tragic scale. Indeed, there are probably still no more than a couple of dozen or so countries where one can confidently say that they are reasonably well respected. This is no great recommendation for the new code, and may lead some to believe that it amounts to no more than a lot of useless paper. I believe that view to be profoundly mistaken. One must remember that the whole code *is* new: in the time-scale of legal history, very new indeed. We have hardly yet had time to become accustomed to its existence, let alone to become familiar enough with it to use it with any degree of confidence or authority. None the less, its first effects are beginning to become apparent. In Europe, for example, many states have already had to modify their national laws or administrative practices, following authoritative and reasoned findings by the competent international institutions in Strasbourg that they have failed to comply with their legal obligations under the European Convention on Human Rights, or the European Social Charter. Further afield, the outright rejection of international criticism as an 'illegitimate interference in the internal affairs of a sovereign state' is now heard much less often. More frequently, oppressive governments today seek to *justify* what they do within the terms of the code itself, relying on what they hope will serve them as escape clauses, such as exceptions for states of emergency, national security, public order, and the like. This is a welcome development, for it helps to confirm the acceptance of the code as binding law, in place of the earlier rejection of *any* international law in this field. After all, a plea of 'not guilty' at least presupposes acceptance of the law, and of the jurisdiction of the court.

Readers of this book will need to bear constantly in mind the important distinction between the theoretical subject of human rights, and the practical one of human rights *law*. Philosophers and others have debated for many centuries about the concept of 'rights': what they are, who has them or ought to have them, how one acquires them and loses them, against whom they are (or ought to be) exerciseable, whether they are of different kinds, whether there are some that everyone has (or ought to have), and so forth. In the course of their work, they have developed many important and complex theories about these things—including the theories about 'natural rights', 'rights of man', and 'moral rights' which were the precursors of the modern bundle of 'human rights'. Those debates still continue; indeed, they can have no final conclusion, since different starting points and different paths of reasoning will necessarily lead to different results—including those of Hitler and Stalin. It was precisely to overcome this uncertainty that the international community established its agreed legal code—much as scientists and engineers have established internationally agreed standards of measurement such as the metre and the gram, in order to short-circuit further disputes about miles, leagues, ells, pounds, ounces, and grains.

Since this book is about the new legal code, it deliberately avoids any extensive discussion about the philosophy of human rights. It is therefore not really about human rights, but only about human rights *law*—as that law now is, rather than as people might think it ought to be. So long as there is no law about some important moral issue, one's attitude to the problem—and one's conduct in relation to it—will be determined by one's personal convictions, religious, moral, ideological, or cultural; and one's opponents in debate may remain unconvinced by the most persuasive arguments, simply because their own primary convictions happen to be different. But once there *is* a law, it determines the issue for all the disputants, at least in prescribing their conduct. They may think the law is wrong and wish to have it changed; they may try to take the appropriate steps towards that end; but so long as it remains in force, they are bound by it and can only disobey it at their peril.

Because of the inherent conflicts of interest within all societies, and the inherent tensions between those who govern and those who are governed, there will always be arguments about human rights, and struggles for their protection and realization. There is no foreseeable prospect that we shall ever be able to relax, confident that all such struggles have been won for all time. Nor is it likely that the time will ever come when everyone can agree that the legal code is both right and complete, that it need never be amended, and that there are no more human rights which ought to be added to it—any more than this is likely to happen in the field of scientific or engineering standards. But at long last we now *have* a code, and it has become legally binding on many members of the international community, who have never known anything like it before. How the code squares with one ideology or another, or what were its philosophical, political, or cultural antecedents, is strictly irrelevant to its application once it has entered into legal force. What we must therefore now do is to learn to understand it, as a necessary preliminary to extending its application to those places where it is not yet being applied.

In short, if we want to know today whether someone has a particular *legal* human right, we can look objectively at the code, and hope to find the answer by investigating its precise application to the particular circumstances, and so bypassing any philosophical doubts or ideological objections. Such an investigation is necessarily legalistic, and involves poring over the precise words of every relevant text, using all the lawyer's pedantic rules for teasing out their meaning, and applying the result to the particular facts of the case. Legalism may not be a very popular attitude or activity, but in the field of human rights law it is both necessary and important, for the ultimate *legitimacy* of any government depends on the *legality* of its acts. Once a government breaks the laws by which it is itself bound, it puts at risk the legitimacy which alone entitles it to claim the allegiance of its citizens, their compliance with its commands, and the recognition of the other members of the international community. It is therefore supremely important to know whether a government does or does not comply with its legal obligations, and this can only be objectively established by the use of the lawyer's techniques. In human rights law, we now have an objective framework against which we can test whether a government is behaving justly or unjustly to its inhabitants, provided we know how to carry out such tests.

Design and arrangement

The single aim of this book is to explain how this can be done. For that purpose, no special knowledge in any particular field is needed. The book is divided into three parts. The first sets the scene, and explains what lies behind the new code. It begins with an allegory, followed by a highly selective collage of assorted items of political history, legal and constitutional history, and history of ideas. This is included only because *some* notion of *some* of these matters is necessary for an appreciation of the place of the new code in the modern world, but the reader must be warned against its manifest shortcomings, and advised against relying on it for any purpose other than getting a few rough compass bearings.

Part II explains briefly how international law is generally made, how this particular branch of it was in fact made, and how it works. Part III then summarizes and discusses what the code actually says. Because space is limited, a great deal has had to be left out. The governing texts of the code—that is, the Preambles and the substantive Articles of the nine general instruments—are reprinted in the Appendix, to which the reader is encouraged to refer. (Where quotations from texts in the book itself contain italics, these are mine: the texts themselves have none.) There are now many hundreds of decided cases on the interpretation of most of these Articles, but I have only had room to mention a few: anyone interested in the others will find them summarized in *The International Law of Human Rights*, and if their interest extends even further they should consult the original case reports which are cited there.

Like its larger companion, this book is not about the actual observance of human rights from time to time and from place to place. For that reason—and also because these things can change quite quickly, as we have seen most recently in Argentina—I have only mentioned past violations where this has been necessary to explain the genesis of the law, and I have made no specific mention of present ones, nor any criticism of the current performance in this field of any named countries, even those whose deplorable record is notorious. This is of course not to be taken as any tacit endorsement of such things, or of any lack of concern for their improvement. (Nor is the language of sober detachment which is appropriate to a book about law to be taken to suggest that there is no need for continued commitment, passion, and polemic in the cause of human rights.)

Since human rights law is now universal, and is independent of particular cultures or ideologies, it is important not to exhibit any national or ideological bias when one is writing about it. However, I have found it frankly impossible to avoid a Eurocentric, and indeed an Anglocentric, bias in sketching the historical background in Chapters 3 and 4, since it happens to be the case that the world's best-documented record of the struggle for human rights from the Middle Ages onwards starts in the history of England, and that many of the principles now enshrined in the international code had their origins here, even if their later development was carried through in France, the USA, and elsewhere. This fact alone cannot support an argument that human rights are an exclusively Western, or First World, concern: the concern is indeed universal, and human rights have been cherished and fought for wherever human beings live and work together. That their best-known formulation began in these islands may be no more than an accident of geography, climate, or political and social history, for which we may not deserve any particular credit. But it would be less than honest to try to disguise the fact.

PAUL SIEGHART

Gray's Inn,
London, England
August 1984

Acknowledgements

I should like to express my thanks to a number of friends who were kind enough to read a draft of the typescript, and whose critical comments have been most valuable: Philip Alston, Alejandro Artucio, Andrew Drzemczewski, Samuel Finer, Leah Levin, Richard Longhorne, Daniel Ravindran, Nigel Rodley, Mary Ann Sieghart, and Robert Sackville West. I am also much indebted to Alan Ryan for a number of perceptive suggestions. Needless to say, none of them bear any responsibility for the remaining errors and omissions.

Contents

Contents

Abbreviations

International instruments and international organizations tend to have very long titles. The following abbreviations are therefore used in this book:

International Covenant on Civil and Political Rights	CPR Covenant
International Covenant on Economic, Social and Cultural Rights	ESCR Covenant
International Labour Organization	ILO
Organization of American States	OAS
United Nations Economic and Social Council	ECOSOC
United Nations Educational, Scientific and Cultural Organization	UNESCO

Part I

What lies behind the code

1

An allegory

The international code of human rights law in force today is the outcome of many events, ideas, and movements over many centuries, and the resultant of many interacting forces. One cannot therefore simply pick up its governing texts and hope to understand their significance, or grasp their intricacies, without some knowledge of their antecedents and their context; how the code came to be installed; what preceded it; what is new about it; what purposes it is meant to serve; what are the rules for interpreting it; how it is meant to work; and what are its limitations. Even a general picture of these things requires at least some idea of the code's legal history, both nationally and internationally; the development of the ideas that it reflects; the long sequence of political events that ultimately led to its installation; the economic and other interests it seeks to accommodate and adjust; and the social changes that have made it both necessary and possible.

Much has been written on all those subjects. What follows in this first part is one attempt at selecting some of the central features of that material—without either going into far more detail than the non-specialist needs, or misleading the general reader by gross over-simplification—and presenting those features in some connected form, even if it is only a series of sketches.

Individuals and their needs

The view that we take of a nation or a state nowadays is that it is—or at least that it ought to be—a society founded on the consent of its members, who are broadly agreed on how their community should be governed for their common good. If we are asked how that agreement was first reached, we are apt to extrapolate backwards in time, conjure up a picture of some simple early village community, and imagine how its members might have gone about deciding how to regulate their affairs.

This is in fact as good a starting-point as any. Let us therefore begin our consideration with such an imaginary—or, more exactly, allegorical—account. But as we are particularly concerned with human rights—that is, the rights of human *individuals*—let us start our account just a shade earlier, with a single human individual. Since we are at the very beginning of our allegory, let us assume that this individual is, just for the moment, alone in the world. That being so, we do not need to distinguish him or her from any other individuals, and need not therefore give him or her any name. But even though a name is not necessary, it is certainly useful. For our own convenience, let us therefore follow a familiar tradition in naming our first human being Adam.

We know, of course, that if our newly created species is to extend beyond a single member, we shall soon need to introduce Eve. But before we do, let us just take a closer look at Adam. If he is to survive for even a few minutes, he must have air to breathe; and if that survival is to be prolonged beyond a few days, he must have water to drink and food to eat. In the Garden of Eden from which we borrowed his name he would have been able to pluck that food off abundant boughs, but anywhere else in the world he will have to gather, grow, or hunt it. He will therefore need to move about a good deal whenever he wants to. He will also need shelter from inclement weather, and refuge from predators.

Given those few basic necessities of life, there is a reasonable prospect that our Adam might survive for several years; indeed, with luck, even for a reasonable lifetime—at all events, so long as he remains fit to fend for himself. But that is as much as he can hope to achieve. Without others of his kind he cannot even procreate, let alone develop the manifold aspects of his human potential.

Human groupings

Let us therefore now quickly bring in Eve and, in order to accelerate the process, let us add their children Cain and Abel, as well as a few similar families, in order to constitute the first small village community, which we imagine as typical of such early groups at the beginning of human civilizations the world over. By adding these others to our solitary Adam, we can greatly extend his own prospects of survival, and make possible the creation of future generations, and so the long-term survival of our whole new species. But we shall also introduce some complications.

Our village community will soon discover, for example, that there are some things they can do much better together than separately. A lone hunter is unlikely to be able to catch a zebra single-handed: a band of hunters split into two co-operating groups, one of which drives the zebra into the ambush of the other, is far more likely to succeed in that enterprise. The community will also find that some of its members are more skilled at hunting, others at gathering, and yet others at raising crops or domesticating animals. Some will excel at fashioning tools and weapons, others at building huts and stores. The men cannot suckle the babies, nor can most of the women lift or drag really heavy objects. Some degree of division of labour therefore soon becomes established—and with it the beginnings of economic relationships, based first on barter, and later on more complex patterns of exchange and trade.

As that happens, the community will develop a *structure*, in which different members perform different functions. But these functions will need to be co-ordinated in some way. The hunters will therefore get together to plan their tactics, the gatherers to exchange news of what is growing where, the tillers to decide where they will plant which crops, and the domesticators to work out how many animals they can safely pasture on the available meadows. Decisions will have to be taken about where to build huts and stores. The village elders may have to be called on for advice on what to do in new or difficult circumstances, since they may have come across something similar before, and have learnt from that experience how best to deal with such problems. If all these things are to be effectively carried out, people will have to rely on each other, and promises will therefore have to be kept. But so far, in our Arcadian community, there are no rulers or ruled, no leaders or led, no landlords or serfs. As John Ball put it 600 years ago, at the outbreak of the English peasants' rebellion: 'When Adam delved, and Eve span, who was then a gentleman?'

Scarcity, claims, counterclaims, and conflicts

Perhaps it is time we gave our allegorical village a name. Let us call it Adamsville, after its founder. So long as there is enough to go round to fulfil everyone's needs for air, water, food, and shelter, all will probably be well. But let us now suppose that a real shortage develops in one of these things—perhaps in food. The rains have failed, or the zebras have moved away, or perhaps the population of the village has just grown too large for the natural resources at its command. For the first time, some members of the community are forced to go hungry—and, for the first time, they have to face the problem of the allocation of a scarce resource.

Until this shortage, there was no need for any of its members to make any claims against any of the others. In our extension of the Garden of Eden, people were content to hunt, gather, or till, to build and craft, to suckle and rear, to prepare and cook, and to do all the other things needed for their sustenance. But in the time of the shortage it was no longer so. Especially at first, everyone was making conflicting claims. Nimrod, for instance, contended that, because he and his band had killed twice as many zebras as anyone else before the crisis, they were entitled to twice as much to eat as everyone else so long as the shortage lasted ('to each according to his contribution', that was later called). Absalom maintained that, having broken his ankle when he fell out of a tree while gathering fruit, the others should feed him while his disability lasted, even though he could contribute no more for the time being towards the provision of more food ('to each according to his needs'). And as if such disputes were not enough, Cain and Abel came to blows over a bushel of grain and a sheep, and the episode proved fatal for Abel.

How will they deal with problems like these in Adamsville? In essence, they have two options: competition or co-operation. If they compete, the strongest among them will take what they need and will therefore survive; the rest will go short, fall sick, and eventually perish—unless they can combine to *force* the strong to restrain their greed. On the other hand, if they all co-operate, they will share out what there is according to some sensible scheme, and there is a reasonable prospect that all, or most of them, will survive—albeit perhaps a little emaciated. On the whole, co-operation tends to produce a better *general* pay-off than uncontrolled competition. By sharing suffering widely, its total amount can be reduced.

Let us now suppose that, in the event, our village chose co-operation and survived—though only after much bickering and many vicissitudes, and slightly reduced in numbers by the loss of Abel. The zebras returned and so did the rains. But with creditable foresight, the village elders drew an important conclusion. What had happened once could happen again. And if it did, it would be wise for Adamsville to be better prepared for such a traumatic event. Plans for crisis management, they decided, should not be made only when the crisis had arrived, but well before. In times of prosperity, people would be more ready to agree to sensible plans than in times of shortage and trouble. And so they called a village meeting to discuss some ideas.

Rules, laws, and rights

Recent events, they said, had shown that in times of crisis co-operation paid off better than raw competition. Accordingly, they proposed, the village should draw up a set of rules for the distribution of anything which ever became scarce again in the future—food, water, building materials, or anything else. They would have to decide, for instance, whether Nimrod was right, or Absalom, or perhaps both. Once agreed, these rules should then be regarded as binding on every member of the community if and when a shortage arose, so that no one could challenge them when that time came. Whatever claim anyone made to a share of the scarce commodity would then be determined by applying the agreed rules to his particular case, and giving him whatever that exercise showed him to be entitled to—no more and no less.

In the course of the discussion that followed, no one raised any serious objection to the principle of the thing, for it seemed a sensible enough idea. Instead, the debate focused on three problems:

1. What exactly were the rules going to say?
2. Who was going to apply them to the various individual claims?
3. How could one ensure that no one would break them?

The village had to hold several more meetings before they were able to answer those questions. Finally, what they decided was this:

1. The rules were to be prepared by a group consisting of a hunter, a gatherer, a tiller, a domesticator, a builder, and a mother. (Male dominance was already making its appearance.) Between them, they should try to foresee every eventuality, and make sure the rules dealt with it. They should then present

their ideas to another village meeting for amendment or approval. And when the final rules were agreed, these were to be
given a special name to mark their binding force—'laws', they
decided, was probably the best word.

2. Provided the laws were clear and detailed enough, applying
them should present no problem. Each claim could be submitted to the village elders, who would determine it according
to the laws. But to make sure they got it right, every claim
should be heard and determined in public, with all the village
entitled to be present.

3. As for enforcement, there were two options. One was for the
community to give a single one of its members the power to
ensure, if necessary by force, that everyone would comply with
the laws. The other was that if anyone was found to be breaking them, any loser could himself use force to retrieve whatever
he had lost; failing that, the village as a whole could call on
the law-breaker to make good any damage he had done; if he
refused, they could then bring collective pressures on him to
comply; if that failed too, they could as a last resort decide to
exclude him completely from the community and all its activities, and share his possessions among them. Since, at that time,
there was no one whom they were willing to trust with the first
of these options, they decided to adopt the second.

At one of the meetings, Adam asked: 'What shall we call a
claim that is entitled to succeed under our laws?' They pondered
for some time. Finally, they decided to call it a 'right'.

The feud

Meanwhile, however, another problem had arisen which threatened to destroy the entire village, even in the absence of any
natural calamity. By the time Abel was killed he had a large
family, with half a dozen sturdy sons of his own, not to mention
his wife's brothers. All of them railed against Cain, and called on
the community to punish him for the murder of Abel. But Cain
too had strong support. He was one of the leading tillers of the
soil, and though none in his group approved of what he had
done, they felt impelled by the strong sense of tillers' solidarity to
support him in adversity, as he had often helped to support one
or other of them who had had a crop failure.

So, for some time, there was deadlock. The wrong suffered by Abel's family festered unrequited, and Cain remained unpunished. After some weeks, the menfolk in Abel's family decided to take matters into their own hands. One dark night they burnt down Cain's house, and him with it. This was more than Cain's cronies could bear. In an upsurge of blind fury, they rampaged through Adamsville, seeking out any members of Abel's family they could find—men, women, or children—in order to kill them in their turn. Happily, most of them escaped by taking to the bush, but not before a few had been slaughtered.

For some time after that, Adamsville was divided between the supporters of the two factions. Life there now presented an added danger beyond those of drought, flood, earthquake, and pestilence—the risk of being killed by a member of one's own community who happened to belong to the other side of an unresolved quarrel. For the first time, people had to bar their doors and windows at night, and post watchmen. And when they went out, even in the daytime, it was seldom in groups of fewer than five or six. Yet despite these precautions, hardly a week passed without a violent death—soon followed by another, and often more than one, in retaliation.

When the village had lost a full quarter of its members in this way, the survivors began to see that here too a co-operative solution would have to be found, if the community was not to destroy itself altogether. And so, once again, village meetings were held to discuss what was to be done. Having previously decided that, in times of natural crisis, the distribution of scarce resources was to be governed by binding laws, they decided to adopt a similar solution for resolving man-made crises. Here again, they had to face the same questions as before. Who was to make the laws? How were they to be applied to particular cases? And how were they to be enforced?

By then, their previous answers to the first two questions had been shown to work well, and so they decided to follow them on this occasion too. The laws were to be drawn up in the first place by a small group representing the different interests within the community, debated and approved at a full village meeting, and thereafter applied in particular cases by the elders sitting in public. But the third question, as before, proved less tractable. What should have happened to Cain when he first killed Abel, in order to avoid the multiplied bloodshed that had followed?

The Abel faction had a simple solution. Cain should have been killed in his turn, either by Abel's kin or by someone formally nominated by the community to carry out that execution on its behalf and in its name, and that would have been the end of the matter. But the Cain faction raised several objections to this:

1. Cain should have had a chance to redeem his own life by making due reparation to Abel's family, or perhaps by turning his possessions over to them, and voluntarily leaving the village.
2. If Cain was killed, the resentment among his kinsfolk and friends was bound to lead to further trouble, whoever had done the deed.
3. If someone was deputed to carry out an official execution on behalf of the village, he would become the community's licensed killer of its own members. Could one even contemplate vesting such a terrible power in anyone?

These objections proved persuasive, especially the last; for the village was quite unwilling to invest anyone with power over their own lives and deaths. And so they adopted the following solution. If one of their members killed another, he had the option to pay full reparation for that life to the victim's family. If the amount, or the manner or time of payment, was in dispute, the village elders would determine the issues at a public hearing. If the killer paid what was due, his life was no longer in jeopardy, and peace should prevail. But if he did not, then he had put himself outside the community. Having refused to respect its laws, he was no longer entitled to their protection. The victim's family could kill him without fear of retaliation, and his possessions could be seized and distributed; in short, he would be expelled from the community altogether.

At the meeting where all this was finally agreed, Adam asked another question: 'What shall we call such a man once he is outside our law?' And it did not take long for someone to suggest the obvious answer: 'an outlaw'.

The newcomers

One day, a new family arrived in Adamsville: the Ishmaels. They spoke with a curious accent; they prepared their food differently; and they had what the villagers thought some other strange habits, particularly in matters of dress and decorum. But they seemed pleasant enough, and they brought some new skills with them, especially in trading with other villages with which Adamsville was just starting to make contact. So they were welcomed, and invited to stay and settle.

Not long after, Seth's storehouse caught fire and burned down. Under Adamsville's co-operative laws, all the other families were bound to share the burden of rebuilding it, and re-stocking it from their own stores.

This puzzled Ishmael. 'Where we come from', he said, 'we have no laws like that. The loss lies where it falls, and no one else need share it.'

'That's as may be,' said Seth, 'but here we have our own laws, and if you want to live among us you must abide by them.'

'But we weren't even here when you agreed all that', Ishmael protested. 'Why should we be bound by laws when we had no part in making them?'

The matter was brought to the village elders, who conducted a public hearing about it. Seth and Ishmael both argued their cases. But Ishmael now had another point: why should the Adamsville elders decide this question, when he had never accepted their jurisdiction, and anyway it was in their interests to rule against him? After all, any contribution he was ordered to make to Seth's new store would diminish what they would have to put in themselves. What was more, although he was of the right age and had all the other necessary qualifications, *he* had never been made an elder—probably, as he darkly hinted, because the other villagers didn't care for the cooking smells from his house, or the way the women in his family dressed.

The elders were puzzled, but they saw both points of view. They asked Ishmael whether he would accept the laws of Adamsville if he and his family were treated as full members of the community in all respects—that is, if he were made an elder, with a voice in the village council, and if there were to be full recognition and respect for all the rights of all the members of his family under those laws.

When Ishmael had had a chance to consult his family, he agreed that this would be a fair solution to the problem. And so peace and harmony again reigned in Adamsville.

2

Priests and Princes

Our allegory has served a useful purpose, in providing us with a sketch of the bare outlines of two key concepts: 'laws' as rules of conduct treated within a community as binding on all its members, and 'rights' as claims made by those members and entitled to succeed under the community's laws. We have also had a glimpse of some of the problems of making, applying, and enforcing laws. None of this can be any substitute for a rigorous analysis of these concepts, on which there exists an extensive literature in the field that used to be called jurisprudence, but is now more commonly called philosophy of law. Even the most superficial study of that subject will soon show that both 'laws' and 'rights' are far more complex and contentious notions than the simple inhabitants of Adamsville could have realized. But for our purposes here, the allegory will have to serve—provided we do not try to push it any further, lest we start to believe in its historicity.

Magic and religion

That would be decidedly dangerous, for Adamsville was no more than a fantasy, and the reality is quite different. There is no evidence that in the real world any early village communities have ever made their laws by any processes such as those we have recounted. One may wish that they had, for we like to think that laws should be rational, and made by the general consent of the people who will be ruled by them, after thorough debate, in order that they will be broadly acceptable. Indeed, that is what we try to achieve nowadays in representative democracies.

But we must face the fact that Adamsville, like the 'state of nature' which the political philosophers Locke and Rousseau invented to support the theory of a 'social contract', is only a myth unsupported by any evidence. All we know of pre-literate village communities comes from two sources: the few societies of that kind which still exist in the remoter parts of the world today, as in some parts of the South-East Asian jungles and the Amazon basin; and what we can guess at by extrapolating backwards from the vanished civilizations which became advanced enough to pass on to us their records of some of their public affairs—such as the Babylonians, Assyrians, Hittites, Egyptians, Jews, Greeks, Romans, Aztecs, Incas, Mayas, and so on.

So far as one can tell from that material, the origins of laws in primitive communities seem to have been associated far more closely with systems of magical or religious belief than with any logical reasoning or public debate. Laws were declared by the gods, or a single God, and applied and interpreted by their priests. A breach of the law was not just a transgression against a socially accepted code of conduct: it was blasphemous, an affront to the sacred deity. Crime and sin were largely synonymous. In such communities, of course, the concepts of knowledge and belief were not rigorously separated as they are in modern secular societies. The whole world was perceived as inhabited or dominated by powerful spirits, some benevolent and others malign. Magic and religion therefore covered a wide range of what we now treat as independent branches of knowledge, such as genealogy, history (including mythology), the natural sciences (including cosmology), and philosophy (including ethics)—quite apart from theology. It is therefore perhaps not surprising that law and jurisprudence were also included within their scope.

But whatever the reason for the religious origins of laws, they had some important consequences. One was the *rigidity* of laws: if the gods had made them in the first place, only the gods could change them—and, since gods are eternal, or at least work on a far longer time-scale than mere mortals, there was no particular reason why they should. If a law had been divinely propounded in the immemorial past and now no longer fitted the community's changed circumstances, that was man's fault and not the gods'. One could hardly expect them to reappear and change their laws just to suit man: it was for man, and not them, to make the necessary adaptations. The best that could be hoped for was a limited degree of progressive reinterpretation by the priests, who might mitigate the law's rigours by putting their own gloss on it, and by slow degrees alter such glosses over time.

Another, and related, consequence was the *sanctity* of laws. Forming part, as they did, of Holy Writ, they fell to be treated with the special reverence and deference due to divine pronouncements. They had about them a sacred numinousness, transcending anything that was the work of mere mortals—often symbolized by inscribing them on stone tablets like the early Romans' Twelve Tables, or on rolls of parchment like the Jewish Torah, and depositing and venerating these in the community's holy places.

A third consequence was the *power* which such sacred laws conferred on their custodians: whoever held the tablets or parchments in his custody, and interpreted and applied their provisions, somehow shared in the reverence and deference which was due to them, and which they in their turn reflected on him.

Spiritual and temporal rulers

For that reason among others, priests were important people in early communities. But they were not the only ones. Then, as now, war was an endemic disease of mankind. Factions within a village fought each other; villages fought each other; tribes comprising numbers of village communities fought each other. And in matters of warfare, as in so many others, there is great competitive benefit in having a skilled leader, and the trade or vocation of the warlord is therefore as old as that of the priest. Sometimes, he was the same man, but more often the roles were divided. Like the priest, the military leader was called by different names in different languages and different places. Today, we usually call him a general. But for many centuries, the role of supreme warlord was that of the king—the temporal, rather than the spiritual, ruler of the community.

Communities ruled by kings were of course much larger than single villages. By that time, a process of aggregation had taken place, observable almost everywhere except in a few places where geographic barriers prevented it from happening. Independent village communities may have traded with each other and their members may have intermarried, but it was usually not long before they made war on each other, to their mutual detriment. Sooner or later, a single ruler would arise who would try to put a number of them under his dominance (usually exploiting their squabbles for that purpose), and then seek to maintain peace within his extended dominion or domain. If he succeeded, the members of the previously warring communities would generally have cause to be grateful, and would therefore support—or at least tolerate—his continued rule. But sooner or later he in his turn would find himself at war with a neighbouring ruler, each of them seeking to add the other's domain to his own. Ultimately, the process tended to stabilize, at a scale again largely determined by the major features of the local geography. In islands or in mountainous country, rulers of quite small domains were able to defend themselves successfully against incursions by their neighbours. In most of the continental plains, only powerful rulers of large domains had enough strength and resources to resist their predatory rivals for any substantial time, and even then the equilibrium was frequently disturbed by frontier skirmishes, and occasionally by major wars. But on some occasions, a king might become so powerful that he was able to extend his dominions over very large territories indeed. He was then apt to call himself an emperor.

In that brief and over-simplified summary of some very complex historical processes, we have so far used the past tense. But the factors which underlie these processes do not just belong to past times: they continue with us today. Laws are still more rigid than many other social institutions; changing them still takes much time and effort; and judges constantly have to reinterpret them to fit new circumstances. They continue to exude a special odour of sanctity, and to demand reverence and deference, and so do their custodians. In many societies, priests continue to command power and influence: Iran is a current example. Communities continue to go to war with each other, and to have rulers whose power flows from military leadership—as, currently, in much of Latin America and some parts of Asia and Africa. Islands and small mountainous countries still manage to maintain their independence: Great Britain and Switzerland were among the few countries in Western Europe to escape invasion in the last world war, and Sri Lanka, Madagascar, and Nepal are still independent states, even if Tibet and Sikkim no longer are. The plains of northern Europe, northern India, and the Middle East have witnessed major wars within living memory, and armed confrontation continues there to this day. And more than one great empire still survives.

Let us now turn to look at the *internal* affairs of kingdoms and empires as they develop. Having recognized that such developments are not confined to the past, we can change our tense to the historic present. And we can also take the opportunity to choose a single generic name for temporal rulers variously called kings, emperors, tsars, moguls, maharajas, dukes, counts, barons, margraves, or whatever. The Latin word *princeps* literally means 'the first in order', and from it is derived not only our adjective 'principal', but also the noun 'Prince'. From the early Middle Ages until the end of the nineteenth century, that noun was widely used (and not only by Machiavelli) as a generic title for temporal rulers when one was discussing their functions, powers, rights, and duties, especially in the context of international law. Let us therefore now follow that precedent.

The sovereign Prince

If he is to survive in power, a Prince must maintain at least internal peace in whatever domain he controls, for that is the main condition on which its inhabitants will tolerate or support his rule, rather than try to overthrow him. In order to do that, he must first establish or acquire a *monopoly of force*: that is, the very thing which the inhabitants of Adamsville were so unwilling to confer on any single one of their members. Their only remedy for a breach of the law was self-help, or collective pressures, or as a last resort to outlaw the law-breaker by expelling him from the community. A Prince must try to do better than that, and the most effective thing he can achieve is to establish a centrally administered regime of law enforcement throughout his domain, executed by officers under his control. Such a regime will serve the twin purposes of underpinning his own power, and putting that power at the service of the inhabitants of his domain by enforcing peace among them, responding to the need for 'law and order' which all communities manifest, and so maintaining their support. Instead of vendettas, feuds, squabbles, and outlawry, all 'breaches of the peace' will be dealt with by the Prince, either personally or through his own officers. But the corollary is that only he, and they in his name, will be allowed to use force to keep the peace: the previous remedies of self-help and outlawry must be abolished, and the individual may no longer 'take the law into his own hands'.

Now a Prince bringing a number of communities within a single domain will often find that their laws differ from each other. Where they share a single religion and culture, the differences may only be slight. But as the Prince's domain expands to take in communities previously beyond its borders, these will increasingly diverge in their religions and cultures, and so probably also in their laws. Up to a point, it may be possible for the Prince's officers to enforce different laws in different parts of the domain, but this can give rise to considerable problems. As we saw in the case of Ishmael, what is to happen if an inhabitant of one of the Prince's provinces does something in another one which would be perfectly lawful where he comes from, but is unlawful where he does it? Princes therefore prefer to have a single set of laws in force throughout their domains: like the central monopoly of force, this also has the advantage of encouraging the different communities to cohere with each other as part of a single principality.

The primary motive for the establishment of a monopoly of force, and the central administration of a single legal system, is the consolidation of the Prince's power within his domain, and what Princes are least able to tolerate is any challenge to that power. Both within and outside his domain, the value that each Prince most jealously pursues and guards is his autonomy: his independence from others who might wish to impose their will on him. Later, that supreme value came to be called 'sovereignty'. Where rulers are able to exercise power within their domains, and yet are not truly independent because they are subject to interference by some even more powerful ruler, it is not infrequently their ambition to shake off that last yoke, and so become truly sovereign. Once they achieve this, their overriding aim is to maintain their sovereignty, and if possible to extend it over an even larger domain, which they can then call their empire. (In these respects, they of course display qualities which they share with many lesser mortals.)

Over time, the concept of sovereignty became central to all concepts of nationhood, statecraft, and international affairs generally. These international affairs—that is, the relationships between sovereign Princes, whether in war or in peace—also came to develop some rules of conduct, which eventually became consolidated into a single system of international law, imposing certain constraints even on sovereign Princes. But that took a long time. Meanwhile, there were other constraints, which we must now examine more closely.

3

Princes and subjects

In establishing a monopoly of force to take the place of self-help and outlawry, and developing a single set of laws to hold sway throughout his domain, our Prince has taken on a great deal. He has become the maker of laws in the place of the gods, their interpreter in the place of the priests, and their enforcer in the place of the collective community. In short, he has become the fountain-head of all law and all justice. That is precisely what happened in the Roman Empire. And it happened in many other principalities too: as late as 1655, King Louis XIV of France was still able to assert, quite correctly under the political system then still in place in his domain, '*L'Etat, c'est moi*'—'I am the State.'

Constraints on the Prince

But Princes do not live alone: they share their domains with large numbers of those over whom they rule, and whom they call their subjects. Now if *all* those subjects ever manifested a collective will to overthrow their ruler and replace him by another, there would be nothing to stop them. If he is to maintain his rule, therefore, the Prince cannot ever afford to make enemies of all his subjects, or even of a substantial majority of them, especially the more powerful. However absolute his rule, its continuance ultimately depends on at least the passive consent of his subjects, and preferably the active support of at least some of them. That means playing off different interest groups within the domain against each other, and binding at least some of them to him by making their particular interests dependent on his survival in power. Princes need to become adept at such power games, sometimes dignified by the name of statecraft. Those who develop the necessary political skills tend to survive; those who fail risk being overthrown.

Among a Prince's natural supporters are usually those who originally contributed to his installation. Where the Prince is a military leader called to power in a time of war, he will find his main support among his soldiers. Roman emperors, for example, often emerged from the army, and might be overthrown again by army units if they failed to pursue policies acceptable to them. Later, the feudal system owed its origins to the organization of agriculture and defence in flat country, where the established population, having no natural barriers behind which to emplace themselves, could only resist an invader if someone had the power to call them to arms, equip them, and lead them into battle. A feudal king was able to do this through a pyramid of devolved power: his underlings—the dukes, earls or counts, barons, and knights—held their lands directly or indirectly from him in return for their allegiance, and the obligation to raise and equip the appropriate number of soldiers from their estates whenever they received the royal command for the defence of his realm—what later became the call to fight 'for king and country'.

We saw earlier how it suited Princes to impose a single set of laws within their domains, in the place of the variety they had found there when they first acquired them. An important illustration of this process is provided by the strategies pursued by the Norman, Angevin, and early Plantagenet kings of England in the eleventh, twelfth, and thirteenth centuries of the Christian era. As Duke of Normandy, William the Conqueror had succeeded in making himself remarkably independent of the weak King of France to whom he owed nominal allegiance. When he acquired the Crown of England, he was determined not to allow his own earls and barons to do likewise. In those days, land was the principal form and source of wealth; accordingly, whoever decided disputes about land commanded great power, since he could buy support by awarding disputed estates. One of the first steps taken by King William I of England to consolidate his power was to establish royal jurisdiction over all land disputes. Such disputes were no longer to be determined by the local earl or baron, but only in the King's own court as 'royal' actions. (In Norman French, the word for 'royal' was *réal*, which is why we still speak today of 'real property' or, in North America, 'real estate'.) Indeed, for several years after his accession, King William would travel regularly throughout his English domain in order to hear and determine the local land disputes, though after some time he appointed a royal Justiciar to do this for him.

One of the main tasks of his successors was to weld together into a single legal system the diverse laws of their English domain, which were largely derived from earlier laws which Angles, Saxons, and Danes had brought with them. Because of the inherent rigidity of laws, it took even those powerful kings the best part of two centuries to achieve that end, mainly by instructing their royal justiciars (by then there were several) to apply in their travels 'on circuit' throughout the realm those laws which they found to be 'common' to its different parts, and gradually to cease to apply laws which varied from one part of the kingdom to another. And so there was painfully constructed that great legal edifice which came to be called, for this very reason, 'the common law of England'—a single set of laws centrally enforced throughout the English kings' domain, serving both to maintain them in power and to provide a focus of cohesion for all its disparate inhabitants.

Several centuries later, the dominions of the English Crown began to extend overseas, to some very distant parts of the world. But the lessons of William I and his early successors were not forgotten: wherever the English went, as settlers or as conquerors, they took their common law with them, with the result that a great many of the modern world's legal systems are still founded on it—indeed, only Roman law is a comparably important source of legal systems in the world today.

The British Empire was of course by no means unique. There had been many others before its time: in antiquity, those of Babylon and of the Egyptian Pharaohs, a Persian one under the Achaemenides, a Macedonian one under Alexander the Great, and that of Rome, the most famous of them all; then there were those of the Arabs, the Mongols, the Turks, and the Moguls; other maritime empires were established almost contemporaneously with the British one by the Portuguese, the Spaniards, and the Dutch, to be followed later by the French and the Germans; and among continental empires were those of Russia and China. What they all had in common was that they brought under the rule of a single Prince domains containing peoples whose languages, cultures, and laws were quite different from those of the Prince's homelands, and that the Prince found it necessary, in order to maintain internal peace within his dominions and with it his own power, to impose upon those peoples a single set of laws, centrally administered, and enforced through the use of a single monopoly of force.

Returning to William I of England, it was on his immediate underlings—the 'mesne [intermediate] lords'—that the power of a feudal sovereign Prince like himself primarily depended, and unless he could satisfy their interests his new throne would always be at risk. In another brilliant innovation, he tried to undermine this precarious system to his advantage. In 1086, he assembled together in Salisbury Plain all the freeholders of his realm—of all degrees, down to the yeoman farmer, and not merely the great nobles—and called on them, in the Oath of Sarum (as Salisbury was then called), to swear their feudal allegiance direct to him, rather than to their mesne lords.

But such attempts at undermining the power of feudal nobles by going over their heads did not always succeed for long. If the nobles were able to sink their own differences for long enough to present a united front against the king, they were often still able to extract considerable concessions from him, as in the case of the famous Magna Carta which King John of England was forced to grant them in 1215, and which his successors were several times called upon to confirm, with or without improvements. We shall return to that document shortly, but first we must look at some constraints on the absolute power of Princes which the priests of the medieval Latin Church continued to be able to apply.

'*An unjust law is not a law*'

Since one of the functions of law is to regulate the exercise of power, there is in theory no reason why laws should not be used to regulate even the powers of a sovereign Prince. But there is a practical problem: so long as the Prince is himself the supreme maker, interpreter, and enforcer of all laws, why should he voluntarily make any law to constrain his own powers? And even if he does, who will interpret and enforce such a law, and how can the Prince be prevented from evading or even abrogating it whenever it suits him? In short, can we find any set of rules of such high standing and authority that they will bind even sovereign Princes?

So long as laws remained closely associated with religious belief systems, the problem was not so great, for even the Prince ranked below the divinity, and was therefore subject to divine law. In Greek antiquity, for a secular ruler to defy the laws of the gods was a form of *hubris*, which *nemesis* would punish in its appointed

time. Old Testamentary prophets regularly castigated their temporal rulers for failing to carry out God's law. In later Roman
times, the *jus gentium*—that is, those laws which the Romans
found to be common to the legal systems of their different subject
peoples—commanded high respect as reflecting some universal
values. Later still, in the Middle Ages, the European sovereigns
were all Christian Princes, and their installation was not complete
until they had been formally crowned, and also religiously
anointed, at a ceremony which included their taking an oath to
rule under God, and in accordance with his law.

The interpretation of that divine law remained a task for the
Church, and the Church therefore claimed the right to determine
the ultimate boundaries of the Prince's law-making powers.
Indeed, in the eleventh and twelfth centuries the canon lawyers
in the new universities of Paris and Bologna made great advances
in this field. Basing themselves on divine law (later to be identified
by St Thomas Aquinas with 'natural law', descended from the
Roman concept of *ius naturale*, which was itself derived from the
jus gentium and the work of the Stoic philosophers), they asserted
a legal maxim of immense significance: *lex injusta non est lex*—
an unjust law is not a law.

Legality, justice, and legitimacy

That maxim is pregnant with several concepts of high importance,
and we must therefore pause to look at it more closely. People
have always insisted on *legality*: once there is a law, it should be
obeyed; lawful conduct is good, and unlawful conduct is bad.
Moreover, any conduct that is likely to have important effects on
others *should* be regulated by law, so that we may know what is
lawful and what is not, and be able to base our own conduct on
our expectation of the lawful conduct of others. But here, for the
first time, we are offered the startling proposition that a law may
not be a law at all—not because it has not been made in due form,
or duly promulgated, or because it is vitiated by some procedural
defect, but because it fails to conform to some other, and superior,
standard: the standard of *justice*. What the maxim tells us is that,
while a law may appear to be *legal*, it may at the same time not
be *legitimate*, and that such a defect will be fatal to it.

Now legitimacy lies at the very root of all government. If a
Prince is not legitimately in power, he is a mere usurper and

may lawfully be overthrown: indeed, his lack of legitimacy itself confers legitimacy on attempts to overthrow him, and on those who undertake such ventures. And here the Church tells us that, if a Prince makes unjust laws, they are not laws at all and we need therefore not obey them—a subversive proposition which undermines the very foundation of a Prince's rule.

But what exactly is an 'unjust' law? To the canonists who first coined the maxim, it was a law that failed to conform with divine law. But the concept of justice extends far beyond divine justice: it is a deeply ingrained human value, applicable to a very wide range of transactions between human beings. *Justum* in Latin means 'righteous', and justice therefore implies such things as uprightness, rectitude, propriety, integrity, impartiality, fairness, equity, even-handedness, proportionality, and a good many other similar things. Even today we still perceive it as the ultimate test of whether any given law is a good law or a bad law: if it leads to a palpably unjust result in a particular case, we are apt to condemn it and call for its reform.

So, according to those medieval canonists, once we can agree on what is just we shall have a test for determining the legitimacy of a Prince's laws, and with it ultimately of his rule. And ever since, the search has gone on for agreement on what is just.

The liberties of the subject

It may be that the barons who extracted Magna Carta from King John in 1215 were less concerned with the justice of laws than with their own interests. But those interests seem to have included a concern for the rights and liberties of a good many others of the Prince's subjects too, as well as for legality and the administration of the laws. For instance, one of the Great Charter's provisions was that

'No freeman shall be taken or imprisoned, or be disseized [deprived] of his liberties, or free customs, or outlawed, or exiled, or any other wise destroyed; nor will we pass upon him, nor condemn him, but by the lawful judgment of his peers, or by the law of the land.'

Then again,

'We will sell to no man, we will not deny or defer to any man, either justice or right.'

And when King Edward III reaffirmed the Charter in 1354, he undertook that no man, of whatever estate or condition, should be harmed except '*per due process de ley*', so introducing the great concept of 'due process of law'—undoubtedly one of the central concerns of justice—which was later to become one of the cornerstones of the edifice of human rights.

By the time we come to the end of the Middle Ages in Europe, we arrive at a turning-point in the power of both Princes and priests, and so in the future political structures of nations. The single Western Christian faith, universally held for many centuries, finally fragmented with the Reformation. Just before, the Renaissance had instigated a major ferment in secular thought. Profiting from all this, Princes were increasingly able to defy the Church. Henry VIII of England, for instance, not only made laws to suit himself, but assumed the position of sole arbiter of their justice by the simple expedient of installing himself at the head of a church of his own.

But by 1581, a group of the Netherlands subjects of King Philip II of Spain, assembled in their States-General, was able to assert an even more revolutionary proposition, namely

'that God did not create the subjects for the benefit of the Prince, to do his bidding in all things whether godly or ungodly, right or wrong, and to serve him as slaves, but the Prince for the benefit of the subjects, *without which he is no Prince.*'

Clearly, the statecraft of Philip II had failed in his Flemish domains. But that Act of Abjuration was more than a complaint of some dissatisfied interest group: it was a challenge by the Prince's own subjects to the very legitimacy of his rule. And that challenge did not take long to spread. One of the places in which it was put to the test was again England where, in the following century, a combination of religious, economic, and social factors led to a civil war, the beheading of a sovereign Prince by the authority of an assembly of his own subjects, and the final rejection of the 'divine right of kings' which he and his Stuart family had consistently claimed as the lawful foundation of their rule.

This was a true revolution, on two levels. The Prince's subjects had tried their strength with him, and had won—not only on the battlefield, but in their own hearts and minds. True, they installed another Prince to rule over them, but this time, and from then on, only by their own choice and at their own sufferance. In another important document, the English Bill of Rights of 1688, those victorious subjects spelt out, much like King John's barons in 1215, their 'ancient rights and liberties' which their Princes were henceforth to maintain sacrosanct, and not to infringe. That document explicitly founded its case on the illegitimacy of the previous Prince's ostensible legality. 'The pretended power of suspending of laws and the execution of laws by regal authority without the consent of Parliament', it said, '*is illegal*'; so is 'dispending with laws', setting up irregular courts, failing to empanel juries, imposing excessive bail or fines, and inflicting 'cruel and unusual punishment'.

And so the ground was laid for the next stage. Whether laws were just, and so whether a Prince's rule was legitimate, could henceforth be determined by his own subjects, who claimed the right even to replace him—and had shown that if they had the will, they also had the power to do it. Sovereignty was beginning to pass from the Prince to the people.

4

Subjects and states

The following century, the eighteenth, saw the flowering of the Age of Reason and the Enlightenment. Encouraged by the advances of natural science and the consequent further liberation of thought from long-established dogmas, the ferment which had begun in the Renaissance and had been increased by the Reformation came to its full maturity. The English revolution, and the ideas of its principal philosopher John Locke, attracted a great deal of interest—not least in France, where Louis XIV's successors still claimed to rule by divine right. There, Jean Jacques Rousseau developed even more extreme revolutionary political theories, based on the idea (derived from Locke and Hugo Grotius, the father of modern international law) that a ruler could only derive his powers from a 'social contract' with his subjects, which imposed obligations on him as well as granting him rights. According to Rousseau, the will of the sovereign could only be the 'general will' of the people. Another Frenchman, Montesquieu, studied the new English—strictly, now British—political system, and in *L'Esprit des lois* derived from it an analysis of political institutions which included the novel idea of a 'separation of powers' between the three important functions of government with which we have been familiar ever since Adamsville—that is, making, applying, and enforcing laws. Each of these functions, he argued, should be carried out by a separate institution—a Legislature, a Judiciary, and an Executive—and these should all be independent of each other. As it happened, this analysis did not accurately reflect the real position in Britain at that time, but it had an enormous influence on the events that were to follow towards the end of that century.

The American and French revolutions

Those events were the near-contemporaneous American and French revolutions, each of which substituted a republic ruled by elected representatives for the previous rule of a hereditary Prince. But that was not the only novelty. There had been earlier republics: in the Greek city states, and indeed in Rome itself, in antiquity; and in Switzerland, Venice, and the Netherlands more recently. What had never been done before was to enshrine the entire foundation of the new state in a single document called a Constitution, from which all governmental powers and functions—duly separated in accordance with the Montesquieu doctrine—were thenceforth to flow. That example was to be followed over the next century by many other states; even those which retained hereditary Princes as their nominal rulers began to try to constrain their powers by extracting written constitutions from them, and so reducing their status to that of constitutional monarchs. Today, there are not many absolute Princes left, at all events in constitutional theory: the modern nation state has taken most of their places.

But the American and French revolutions produced another innovation, even more important for our purposes: the first formal enumerations and definitions of the rights and freedoms of individuals within the state, incorporated into the very foundations of the new state itself. In France, this took the form of the *Déclaration des droits de l'homme et du citoyen*—'Declaration of the Rights of Man and the Citizen'—of 1789; in the USA, of the Bill of Rights added to the Constitution in 1791. Between them, these included such things as equality before the law, due process of law, freedom from arbitrary arrest and imprisonment, freedom from unreasonable searches and seizures, the presumption of innocence, fair trial, freedom of assembly, speech, conscience, and religion—and the right to own property. These two documents, the first of their kind in history, came to exert a pervasive influence over the later development of the theory of human rights, and the practice of ensuring respect for them.

The Rights of Man

But both these revolutions needed a new theory of the proper legal relationships between the individual and the community. So long as divine law could provide a universally accepted frame of reference for the justice (and so the legitimacy) of any given secular law, the only matter fit for dispute was the precise content and interpretation of the divine law. That was a familiar procedure, well worked out by the canonists. True, there could be disagreement, but at least the disputants started from common premises. But as the Renaissance and the Reformation moved into the Age of Reason, these common premises crumbled, and a new test for the justice of laws came to be looked for. Once again, natural law was prayed in aid, revived by the work of Grotius and Locke. But this now took the form of 'the Law of Nature', to be looked for not so much in divine revelation as in the world around us, and to be discerned by the new discipline which was variously called natural history, natural science, or natural philosophy.

The search was intense, and pursued for a long time by many people. But in a dispassionate study of the material world it is difficult to find any evidence for a moral dimension, or for any laws of nature, analogous to those of physics, as to what is right or just. So, when the draftsmen of the American Declaration of Independence wrestled with that problem, they found themselves still falling back on God: 'All men', they asserted, 'are created equal, [and] are endowed *by their Creator* with certain unalienable rights . . .'. But they introduced that assertion, with engaging candour, by the admission that 'We hold these truths to be self-evident'—that is, we firmly believe in them; we are deeply convinced that they are true; but we cannot actually derive them from any independently ascertainable prior facts. (Thomas Jefferson, in his original draft, would have preferred the rights to have been 'sacred and undeniable', rather than to invoke the Creator by name.) The French too made their Declaration 'in the presence and under the auspices of the Supreme Being', invoking that authority for the proposition that 'Men are born and remain free and equal in respect of rights.'

But however shaky their premises, the texts of the great documents of the American and French revolutions differed in one fundamental respect from all that had gone before, including Magna Carta and the English Bill of Rights. These were no longer concessions extracted from an unwilling Prince, reflecting struggles between different interest groups. They were, for the first time, coherent catalogues of fundamental rights and freedoms, by then called the Rights of Man, and regarded as 'inhering' in all human individuals in virtue of their humanity alone, and as 'inalienable'—that is, as universal rights and freedoms which it lay in no one's power either to give or to take away. That was the biggest single step in the development of the concept of human rights, and once taken it proved to be irreversible.

National human rights law

Both the Americans and the French 'entrenched' their catalogues in the very foundations of their new states, by including them in the written constitution which stood supreme over everything and everyone else—including the laws made by the newly created legislature. In this respect, in the new secular age, the constitution took the place of divine law or natural law as the test whether an ordinary law was 'just' and therefore legitimate: the legislature only had power to make such laws as the constitution allowed it to make. Instead of being illegitimate if it was *injusta*, a law was illegitimate if it was unconstitutional. And, instead of leaving the Church to decide the former question, the constitution assigned the latter to a judicial tribunal—in the United States, the Supreme Court.

During the following century, many other countries followed that example. As they acquired written constitutions, they included in them their own catalogues of the Rights of Man, variously adapted to their local circumstances, and established constitutional or supreme courts to test their laws for constitutionality. And so, through those constitutions, the detailed laws made under their authority, and the interpretation of both by the national courts, there began to develop in many countries a new corpus of law, variously called by names such as the law of civil rights or of civil liberties, and in fact concerned with the fundamental legal relationships between the state and the individual. Today, this may suitably be called national (as opposed to international) human rights law. In that sense, the US Supreme Court was the world's first human rights tribunal.

Socialism

One important factor which had led first to the English, and then to the American and French, revolutions was the 'rise of the bourgeoisie': the gradual acquisition of economic power by a new class of people who accumulated their wealth not from owning land, but from trade—and, later, from manufacture. In those revolutions, the members of that class were of course primarily concerned to enlarge and entrench *their* rights. But, like King John's barons, that was not their only concern, for they claimed the new freedoms not only for themselves, but for all citizens (although that concept then still excluded slaves in the United

States, and women in France). During the nineteenth century, the industrial revolution spread through much of Europe, and wrought economic changes even more profound than those that had gone before. Although it greatly increased the total wealth of communities, it did so very unequally, at least at first. During that phase, some of its social effects, especially in the exploitation of individuals for their labour, were nothing less than scandalous, and were graphically described in the England of their time by Engels, Dickens, and others. They led to the development of a new political approach, that of socialism, to which Proudhon in France and Marx in England made major contributions.

In a sense, the pendulum was beginning to swing back: where the liberals of the seventeenth and eighteenth centuries had been concerned to shake themselves free of the yoke of absolute rulers, and had therefore articulated their demands as claims to non-intervention—that is, in essence, claims to be left alone by government—the socialists of the nineteenth century were demanding the precise opposite, namely that government should intervene actively to redress social or economic injustices. In Europe at least, following many struggles which included the unsuccessful revolutions of 1848 and the ultimately successful fight of trade unions for legal recognition, their demands were gradually met—first in the form of factory legislation and other labour laws, and in our own century increasingly through schemes for health care, state pensions, unemployment benefit, and social security payments. The success of these struggles owed much to the solidarity of those who fought them, often making great individual sacrifices for the sake of the collective enterprise which they sought to advance. Indeed, 'collectivism' was from the start a salient feature of socialism. And the first avowedly socialist, and fully collectivist, state was established under Lenin's leadership in Soviet Russia in 1917.

Meanwhile, as the recognition of the evils of the unrestricted exploitation of human beings in the productive process grew during that whole period—not least through the influence of Pope Leo XIII's encyclical *rerum novarum* in 1891—many countries which were not in the least socialist in any formal sense also expanded their constitutional catalogues to include rights which were claims on the intervention, rather than the mere non-intervention, of the public authorities of the state.

Utilitarianism and positivism

And so, gradually, the notion of 'fundamental' rights and freedoms, enjoying a status above the ordinary laws and furnishing a test for their justice and legitimacy, gained some ground. By the early part of the twentieth century, it had become well established among many of the world's sovereign states—at least in their constitutional theory, even though not yet often implemented in their colonies, or sometimes even at home. But it was not without its critics, who were sceptical of its shaky theoretical foundations.

Utilitarian philosophers, for example, held that the common good lay in the achievement of the greatest happiness for the greatest number, and that this furnished the only valid test for the rightness of social policies. Accordingly, they had little time for the idea of 'rights' derived from 'natural law'. In the view of Jeremy Bentham, for example, 'natural' rights were simple nonsense, and 'natural and imprescriptible' (that is, inalienable) rights were rhetorical nonsense, 'nonsense upon stilts'. There was also a vogue for 'positivism', both in general philosophy and the philosophy of law, a later version of which held that it was literally meaningless to discuss anything that could not be empirically demonstrated to exist in the external world. So, according to that doctrine, the only rights of which one could properly speak were those which could be enforced in practice: if a particular court gave you a remedy, then you had a right in that place; if it did not, then it was simply meaningless to say that you had any right at all. The proponents of that view had at least one valid point: so long as one needs to base one's support for human rights on God, or nature, or moral principle, or self-evidence, one is bound to be on tenuous ground if one is debating with someone who does not believe in God, has found no Rights of Man embedded in the natural world, bases his morality on a different set of principles, and denies the self-evidence of any propositions that are not either tautological or trivial.

In fact, neither utilitarians nor positivists denied moral claims, nor did they deny that, in proper cases, such claims *ought* to be transformed into legal rights. But they questioned whether, until that had happened, it was legitimate to use the word 'rights' for such claims. As we shall see, others later exploited that doubt for their own advantage, in combination with the doctrine of national sovereignty.

National sovereignty

The development of the nation state in the nineteenth century was accompanied by a parallel development in the doctrine of national sovereignty. That doctrine, as we have seen, had its roots in the desire of Princes for autonomy. Just as subjects claim the right to be left alone in their private affairs by their neighbours— and even by their Princes or their states—so Princes claim the right to be left alone by other Princes. True, they constantly have to deal with them, just as subjects have to deal with other subjects; and these constant dealings lead, over time, to rules of conduct which eventually become formalized as international law. But, like their subjects, Princes will brook no interference from each other when it comes to their internal affairs. As against all other Princes, each Prince claims absolute sovereignty in his own domain. And since that suits all Princes, they are very willing to concede it to each other, and so it soon becomes part of 'international custom'—the first source from which international law was derived, and with which we shall deal in more detail in Part II.

Legal theory eventually divided the concept of princely sovereignty into two components. The first was called territorial sovereignty, and signified the Prince's exclusive control over his physical domain. The second, called his personal sovereignty, signified his exclusive control over his own subjects, within or without his domain. So, for example, a subject who tried to accomplish his Prince's overthrow would be guilty of treason even though all his acts were committed outside the Prince's domain— so conferring on the Prince, by the consent of his fellow Princes and in the interests of them all, a degree of extra-territorial jurisdiction. By parity of reasoning, if one Prince inflicted an injury on the subject of another, that was an affront to the personal sovereignty of the other Prince, giving him a right to complain and seek recompense—not for the injury to his subject, but for the injury to himself. It followed that the 'subjects' of international law—that is, the entities to whom that law applied, and who had rights and obligations under it—were Princes, and their later successors the nation states, but no one else. Ordinary human beings could only be the subjects of Princes and states, and of their national laws; they could not be the subjects of international law, or claim any rights under that system for themselves.

As these concepts developed, they led to some important consequences. Once it was granted that a Prince could exercise jurisdiction over acts committed outside his own domain, the stage was set for what came to be called 'crimes under international law'—that is, crimes punishable by Princes other than those in whose domain they had been committed. An obvious candidate for that status was piracy on the high seas, committed in the 'public domain' and therefore punishable wherever the pirate might be apprehended. (That status has since been extended by what has come to be called the Nürnberg principle to war crimes and crimes against humanity, and by subsequent international treaties to genocide, apartheid, the kidnapping of diplomats, the hijacking of aeroplanes, and most recently offences in connection with nuclear materials.)

Again, the notion that injury to a Prince's subject entailed an injury to the Prince himself led, over time, to the development of an internationally recognized set of minimum standards for the treatment of *aliens*, requiring the protection of their lives, liberty, and property, and their proper treatment before courts of justice, by every sovereign Prince under his domestic laws. This produced the curious result that Princes were obliged, in international law, to respect at least some of what are today called human rights in the case of aliens, at a time when they were under no such obligation to respect any for their own citizens.

In short, for centuries it remained the undisputed doctrine that, while one Prince might have to answer to another for his treatment of that other's subjects, how any Prince treated *his own* subjects was a matter for his own exclusive sovereign determination, and any attempt to influence what he did to them could be rightly rejected as an attempt to infringe his personal sovereignty—an 'illegitimate interference in the internal affairs of a sovereign Prince'.

Humanitarian affairs

None the less, by small degrees the international community did begin to concern itself with the affairs, not only of Princes, but of some of their subjects. There was, for example, the problem of slavery, an institution which had been regarded as perfectly respectable in antiquity, having even been recognized without any explicit condemnation by St Paul. It was widely practised in the

British colonies of North America and the West Indies, as well as in other empires, but towards the end of the eighteenth and the beginning of the nineteenth centuries public opinion began to swing against it. In *Sommersett's case* in 1772, Lord Mansfield declared that slavery did not exist in England, and that any slave became free as soon as he set foot on English soil. Mainly under the influence of the English campaigner William Wilberforce, the British Parliament in 1807 abolished the slave trade, and in 1833 the institution of slavery itself, throughout the Empire. But despite the self-evident truth of 1776 that all men are born equal, it was not abolished in the USA until nearly a century after that, and then only after a bloody civil war had been fought over it. (The diatribe against it in Thomas Jefferson's original draft had not managed to find its way into the final version of the Declaration of Independence.)

All that, of course, did not happen at the level of international law, but of national or domestic law—though, given the size of the British Empire at that time, a substantial fraction of the world's inhabitants were subject to what was more or less a single legal system. At the truly international level, it was not until 1885 that a Conference on Central Africa held in Berlin was willing to affirm, in its General Act to which all the states represented subscribed, that 'trading in slaves is forbidden in conformity with the principles of international law'. But that affirmation related only to an international trade, with which the community of sovereign Princes could be legitimately concerned because much of it took place *between* their domains, and not to the domestic institution of slavery, which was excluded from such concerns because it could exist only *within* them. Not until 1926 did the sovereign states go further by adopting an international Slavery Convention, requiring those states which chose to become parties to it to abolish the institution itself within their own territories. Even so, and despite the absolute prohibition of the institution by the modern international code of human rights law since 1945, the last state to abolish it formally—Muscat and Oman—only did so in 1970.

Meanwhile, in the nineteenth century, the internal affairs of the Ottoman Empire provided another cause for international concern with the treatment of a Prince's own subjects within his domain. In the 1820s, Lord Byron lent his support to the campaign to enlist public sympathy for the Greeks in their struggle for independence; in the 1850s, there were problems over the Holy Places and the treatment of Christians in Palestine; in 1860–1 there was widespread concern in France about events in Syria and the Lebanon; and in 1877 Gladstone stirred up British Parliamentary and public feeling about the slaughter of around 12,000 Christians, by irregular Ottoman troops, in what is now Bulgaria. Formally, all these events took place within the domains of the sovereign Turkish Sultan, and should therefore have been no one else's affair. But because they were events which 'shocked the conscience of mankind', they were said to justify acts of 'humanitarian intervention', so beginning to undermine the previously absolute doctrine of state sovereignty in such matters.

At about the same time, the Red Cross movement which Henri Dunant had founded in neutral Switzerland began to promote reforms in the laws of war, which had been one of the major concerns of international law from its beginnings, in order to make warfare more humane. This led to the Hague Conventions, and ultimately the Geneva Conventions, designed to limit the suffering caused by wars, and to regulate the treatment of prisoners of war.

Another problem area at the beginning of our present century was the pay, conditions of work, health, and safety of industrial workers. By then, several of the more advanced industrialized countries were quite willing to improve these, but not at the cost of losing their trade to countries which were not. Here too, therefore, there was scope for international agreements, and the International Labour Organization (the ILO), established in Geneva in 1919, took the lead in proposing and negotiating these. Even before its formal establishment, two multilateral labour conventions were adopted in Berne in 1906: one directed against night work by women, the other against the use of poisonous white phosphorus in the manufacture of matches.

Versailles and after

One of the consequences of the first world war was the re-creation of Poland as an independent state. But its frontiers were so drawn as to include substantial German and Czech speaking minorities, and specific protections for these were included in the Treaty of Versailles of 1919, and the Polish–German Upper Silesia Treaty of 1922, guaranteeing them the right to establish schools and religious institutions, and to use their own languages for publications, at public meetings, and before the courts.

But these treaties went rather further, for they also guaranteed the rights to life, liberty, and the free exercise of religion *for all inhabitants*; and equal treatment before the law, and the same civil and political rights, *for all nationals*. Apart perhaps from the ILO conventions, this was the first occasion on which any sovereign state bound itself, by treaty, as to the manner in which it could treat its own citizens, and this proved later to be a precedent of far-reaching importance—especially as the second treaty also established an *international* Arbitration Tribunal in which, for the first time in legal history, both citizens and aliens were entitled to establish individual rights against a sovereign nation state. And so, in 1927, an otherwise unknown Pole called Steiner and a Czech called Gross (that is, one citizen and one alien) became the first private individuals to sue a state before an international tribunal, claiming compensation for the loss of their tobacco business because of the Polish state's tobacco monopoly, and asserting rights conferred on them by *international* law.

Cataclysms

And then, at almost the same time, there came some cataclysmic reversals to all this apparent progress. In the 1930s, Josef Stalin's attempts to establish full Marxist-Leninist collectivist socialism in the Soviet Union led to unparalleled suffering, in which at least four million people, and possibly several times that number, are now believed to have perished. At the same time, the National Socialists under the leadership of Adolf Hitler, basing their political philosophy at least in part on the ideas of Nietzsche, and no less collectivist in their policies than Stalin, came to power in Germany. There, and later in the neighbouring countries which they invaded, they proceeded to perpetrate atrocities of a kind, and on a scale, never seen before, claiming over six million Jewish victims alone. And in the second world war which they unleashed, and in which Japan later joined them, more than another twenty million perished on the battlefields and as prisoners of war, and so did at least another fifteen million civilians.

Those events 'shocked the conscience of mankind' more profoundly than anything that had ever gone before. Clearly, something had to be done in order to prevent such things from happening again. But there was a disturbing difficulty. Hitler and Stalin were scarcely utilitarians, but they had gratefully adopted the position that natural rights were 'nonsense upon stilts'. In their systems, *they* decided what constituted the greatest happiness for the greatest number, without any sensitive regard for the breaking of a few—or even very many—heads in the process. And they were supreme legal positivists: the only rights that existed for them were those they allowed to be enforced in their own countries. For a brief but disastrous spell, they re-established themselves in the position of absolute Princes, but without the embarrassment of having to bow to priests holding uncomfortable views about justice or legitimacy. And if meddling foreigners came along to protest, they saw them off sharply with the doctrine of national sovereignty in its crudest form.

Now in strict international law as it then stood, there was no way of judging whether the actions of Hitler and Stalin were legitimate. If they claimed—as indeed they did—that their actions were perfectly lawful under the domestic laws of their respective sovereign states, no one outside those states was in any position to controvert their claims, since all other states were bound in international law not to infringe either their territorial or their personal sovereignties. In short, *national* human rights law had failed as a safeguard against tyranny, since the national tyrant could himself override and even abolish it, and there was no law superior to his which could render that exercise illegitimate, or to which outsiders could even appeal. True, under the doctrine of humanitarian intervention other sovereign states might arguably have sent their troops in—if they had been strong enough—to rescue Hitler's Jews or Stalin's kulaks; but that would not have been founded on a formal challenge to the legitimacy of those tyrants' rule, let alone of their laws. In fact it was Hitler and Stalin, following their unholy and mercifully short-lived alliance, who both chose to send *their* troops into the sovereign territory of Poland, and it was only in fulfilment of the solemn guarantees of the integrity of that state, and not on the ground of any humanitarian intervention, that Britain and France finally declared war on Germany.

On any view, this was an intolerable state of affairs. In international law, there was then not even a generally binding prohibition against the launching of aggressive wars, let alone of anything called 'war crimes' or 'crimes against humanity'. That gap was filled after the event, but only by the decidedly dubious means of trying Hitler's ministers and generals, on those charges, before a tribunal convened specially for the purpose and composed entirely of representatives of the victors. Since that trial took place at Nürnberg, it is this 'Nürnberg principle' which is now the authority for the proposition that the waging of aggressive wars, and the commission of war crimes and crimes against humanity, constitute crimes under international law.

One of the minor ironies generated by those cataclysms is that Nürnberg was the place where there had been enacted, in 1936, the National Socialist laws which legalized first the persecution of Germany's Jews, and later their wholesale slaughter. But a much greater irony lies in the fact that, today, we have to thank Hitler and Stalin for the installation of the new international code of human rights law—for, without them, the modern secular world might never have rediscovered the need, forgotten since the Reformation, for a set of universal standards, superior to the sovereign will of any Prince or state, which can place external constraints on their relationships with their own subjects.

5

Modern human rights law

We have now come to the end of our series of selected sketches, marking various steps in the progression from allegorical Adamsville, through priests and Princes, Renaissance, Reformation, Enlightenment, revolutions, and cataclysms, to the modern sovereign nation state and its subjects. In fact, two strands of political and legal theory run through that progression: a strand of absolutism, and a strand of constraints on it. The strand of absolutism is exemplified not only by the Roman emperor as the fountain-head of all law and justice, or later Princes set by divine right over their peoples as the repositories of all sovereignty: it runs through the eighteenth-century doctrine of the absolute sovereignty of the people, and even the nineteenth-century individualistic one of utilitarianism, right down to the extremes of modern nationalistic fascism and the collective socialist dogmas of the dictatorship of the proletariat and the leading role of the Party. The strand of constraints drew its inspiration partly from natural law, derived by the Romans from the *jus gentium*, developed by the Stoics, and identified by St Thomas Aquinas with divine law as the law of right reason; and partly from the idea of a social contract, looking back to the Athenian city state of the fifth century BC, later exemplified in the mutual rights and obligations assumed by feudal lords and their vassals, and eventually united with a revived theory of natural law by Grotius and Locke.

Today, we have to deal with the modern nation state—remembering that this entity has no concrete reality, but is only an abstraction designed to reflect the relationships of individuals with the land and other tangible objects over which they exercise control, and to regulate and legitimate the powers which those individuals exercise over each other. Within each such state, there will already be laws governing the relationships of the official power-holders with the state's other inhabitants. But the events preceding and precipitating the second world war made it plain that the international community constituted by all those states could not afford to continue to leave it to each of them to choose alone, in the exercise of its unfettered sovereignty, between the absolutist strand and the strand of constraints: a superior and external set of constraints had to be imposed on each of them, in the interests of all. And so, from 1945 onwards, that community installed an overriding code of *international* human rights law, at which we shall look in more detail in Parts II and III of this book. But before we do, we must first look at some general features of this new code.

Features of the international code

The code starts from the premises that in human societies some people will always exercise some powers over others; that the rulers' views and interests will necessarily differ from those of the ruled; that these conflicting views and interests can only be adjusted by national laws; but that these laws must conform to certain standards which are of international concern.

Starting from those premises, the new code displays the following salient features:

1. It rests entirely on the consent of the international community—reflecting, at last, international agreement between sovereign states on what laws are just. This agreement therefore now replaces the previous shaky ground of a Creator in whom many no longer believe, a Law of Nature which consistently eludes empirical observation, or moral principles on which people may sincerely but profoundly differ. The code does not depend on any prior theory of 'divine', 'moral', 'natural', or any other kind of rights. Instead, just as scientists and engineers have got together to agree on international standards such as the metre and the gram in order to avoid further disputes about miles, leagues, ells, pounds, ounces, and grains, so the nations have now simply agreed on international legal standards of human rights, thereby creating positive law among themselves.

2. These standards are deliberately designed to be culturally and ideologically neutral: they are not specifically liberal or socialist, Eastern or Western, Northern or Southern, developed or developing, Christian, Buddhist, Islamic, or Hindu.

3. Nor are they naïve, starry-eyed, or idealistic, either about states or about their subjects. On the contrary, they are sober and

pragmatic. Starting from the realistic assumption that there will always be tensions and conflicts between rulers and ruled, the code displays a practical respect for both, and sets out to strike a workable balance between them.

4. That balance is achieved by a set of sometimes quite intricate rules for weighing and adjusting a variety of closely defined individual values and social interests, in such a way as to enhance their constructive interaction. And this is no longer done in the vague language of aspirations which used to prevail in this field of discourse: at least in the operative part of the code the values, the interests, and the rules are all defined with considerable precision.

5. The entire code emphasizes both the role of law and the rule of law in the striking of these balances, and so provides objective tests for assessing the legitimacy of the exercise of the power of rulers. The code therefore now constitutes the highest rank of safeguards against tyranny—including what Alexis de Tocqueville called the 'tyranny of the majority'.

Inherent, inalienable, and equal

The individual values which the code defines, and which it balances against each other as well as against the defined social interests, might have been expressed in a variety of ways. However, for the historical reasons which have been sketched earlier, their definition takes the form of a catalogue of 'human rights and fundamental freedoms' which the code obliges the member states of the international community to ensure and respect. These rights and freedoms are all of the kind to which are ascribed the particular characteristics of being 'inherent', 'inalienable', and 'equal', and these concepts merit a moment's reflection.

Most of our legal rights come to us because we have acquired them in the course of some transaction. My right to live in my house, and to exclude others from it, derives from the fact that I have bought or leased it, or inherited it, from someone else. If I ever acquire a right to sue someone for personal injuries, it will be because he has run me over in the street. And it is open to me at any time to 'alienate' such rights—that is, to transfer them to someone else by sale or gift, or to mortgage them, or to forfeit them altogether. Moreover, different individuals may have such rights in different measure: you may have a larger house than mine, and if you earn more than I do you will get larger damages than I will if we are each put out of work as the result of a road accident.

But none of this applies to 'human' rights. We do not need to acquire them by purchase, or by gift or grant from the Prince or the state, or as the result of any other transaction: the code simply treats us as coming into the world with them. Nor can the Prince or the state ever take them away from us, whatever we do wrong; nor can we sell them, mortgage them, or forfeit them. (As we shall see later, this means that the legal boundaries of the human rights included in the code need to be very carefully defined: an unqualified human right to 'liberty', for example, would mean that no convicted criminal could ever be sentenced to imprisonment, even after a fair trial by a competent court.)

As for equality, the code is not so naïve as to found itself on the notion that all human beings are equivalent or interchangeable. Far from it: what makes them human, and lies at the very foundation of the principle that they should all be treated with equal dignity and respect, is precisely the fact that they are all so different from each other as to be unique. But in order to allow their unique potentials to flower, it is essential that we should not arbitrarily cripple their development—as by killing them, imprisoning them, torturing them, exiling them, starving them of food, shelter, or education, letting them die of curable diseases, strangling their private lives or their personal relationships, or preventing them from communicating or associating with others. And so, *as to their 'fundamental' human rights and freedoms*, we must treat them equally. Whatever may be the differences between us in other rights, we are all taken to have our *human* rights in the same measure, whether we are male or female, old or young, black or white, rich or poor, strong or weak, clever or stupid, conformist or dissenting.

These are the considerations which found the code's clear bias in favour of the kind of society that displays a specific coherent set of civilized values: tolerance of diversity; plurality of belief, ideas, and culture; reasonableness and rationality; the peaceable resolution of conflicts under the rule of law; and, above all, respect for the dignity, autonomy, and integrity of every single one of its individual members. If the code reflects an ideology, these are its values. They may have a familiar ring for Western liberals, but they lie at the roots of many other cultures, and they have now been endorsed by a majority of the world's nations, of many different traditions and political and economic systems.

But the code fully accepts that these values are fragile, and may not survive if they cannot be defended against their enemies: the intolerant, the bigoted, the fanatic, the violent, the oppressive, the arrogant. It therefore leaves open the necessary means for their defence. But it also tries to ensure that these means will not be abused, and that in using them such a society will not find itself in the end destroying the very values which it is seeking to protect.

Rights and duties

The three characteristics of inherence, inalienability, and equality are what essentially distinguish the 'human' rights of the code from other, ordinary, legal rights. But there is another distinction too. In all legal theory and practice, rights and duties are symmetrical. It is a popular fallacy to believe that this symmetry applies within the same individual: that if I have a right, *I* must also have a correlative duty. This is not so: if I have a right, *someone else* must have a correlative duty; if I have a duty, *someone else* must have a corresponding right. Your duty to pay the agreed price for what you have bought from me founds my right to withhold it from you until you do, and to sue you if you do not pay at the agreed time. Your right to walk across the street unharmed founds my duty to drive with care, and to compensate you for any injuries I inflict on you if I do not. Our mutual rights and duties arise from the mutuality of our interests.

So it is, too, with human rights—but with one important difference. All human rights are, by their very nature, vested in individuals. But the protection which they are intended to confer is protection by the one entity which, in a sovereign state, has the power to give it—that is, the sovereign state itself, and its public authorities. If I am to be protected from the strong who seek to abuse their powers over me, only the state is in a position, by enacting and enforcing appropriate laws, to limit and constrain those powers. And the supreme power is that of the state itself, and it is therefore from this that I need the most effective protection of all. Accordingly, for human rights, *all* the correlative duties fall on the state: it has to try to protect me from everyone, *including itself*.

This creates some apparent anomalies, to which we shall return in later chapters. But it also creates an asymmetry of interest, for it is against the inherent interests of rulers to constrain their own powers over those whom they govern. Rulers have few incentives to enact laws to protect their subjects from them. That is, of course, precisely why such constraints must ultimately be imposed on the state at some level superior (or at least external) to itself— and the only such level that we have is that of the international community. However, as we shall see in Part II, the international community is decidedly deficient in mechanisms for enforcing its own laws—rather like our allegorical Adamsville. This is the principal reason why, despite all the international law that is now in place, we continue to witness some quite horrific, and unpunished, breaches of it.

There lies the rub, and we shall need to return to it later. But meanwhile, it is time to look at how the code was made, and how it works. For, in various ways, it *does* work: if it did not exist, there would today be far more violations of human rights than there already are.

Part II

How the code was made, and how it works

6

Making international law

We need to begin this part of our enquiry by looking a little more closely at the way international law is made; what forms it takes; how it comes to bind those who are its subjects; and how it is interpreted and applied. We shall leave to Chapters 9 and 10 the question of how it can be enforced.

The international community

As we have seen, laws are binding rules which govern the conduct of the members of a particular community—such as the population of our allegorical Adamsville, or all the subjects of a particular Prince, or all the inhabitants of the territory of a modern nation state—by classifying that conduct into what is lawful and what is not, and prescribing the consequences for each. When international law first came to be recognized as having any existence and content, the members of the international community to whom it applied were sovereign Princes. Today, these members are the sovereign nation states—regarded as legal entities having legal rights and duties much as corporations and companies do in domestic law—together with certain intergovernmental organizations brought into existence by the states which take part in them, such as the United Nations and its specialized agencies, or regional associations like the Council of Europe, the Organization of American States, or the Organization of African Unity.

In many respects, therefore, international law mirrors national law. But the analogy cannot be pressed too far, for there are two important differences.

The first is that the international legal system has no formal institutional law-maker or legislature. There is no single super-sovereign Prince who can decree what laws shall bind the members of the international community, nor do the sovereign nation states have an elected assembly competent to enact laws that will bind them all. Secondly, there is no institution in the international community with a monopoly of force to ensure compliance with the law: no international policeman to arrest a wrongdoing state and bring it before a court; no bailiff to seize its assets to satisfy the judgment of such a court—indeed, not even an international court with compulsory jurisdiction over all sovereign states.

In these two respects at least, the international community is still at a stage of development corresponding to Adamsville. The only laws that bind its members are those by which they have consented to be bound, and the only means of enforcing them are self-help, collective sanctions, and in the last resort outlawry. This is why some people still describe international law as being at a 'primitive' stage of evolution, despite the fact that its *content* is very advanced indeed, for it deals today with many complex matters in a highly sophisticated fashion.

Customary international law

Like their analogues in Adamsville, the members of the international community also face the problem of the new arrival who claims that he is not bound by any of the existing laws, since he has never expressly consented to them. That problem is resolved much as it was in Adamsville: once a law appears to command a sufficiently wide measure of assent, it is regarded as binding on all, even if some of them have never *expressly* consented to it. Indeed, for a long time this was the main source of all international law. In order to discover what it was, one looked to the international custom of civilized Princes, as evidence of the general practice which they accepted as law. So if civilized Princes constantly sent their enemies' ambassadors home with a safe conduct on the outbreak of war, and publicly declared that this was what their enemies must also do, that came to be regarded as a general rule of international law binding on all Princes. In effect, international law was rather like the ancient Romans' *jus gentium*: those rules which seemed to be common to everyone, whatever their other differences.

The important concepts here are 'constant' and 'civilized', and they merit a moment's reflection. 'Constant' was not always construed too strictly. The occasional lapse from a general practice, even by a most civilized Prince, was not regarded as fatal to the rule, provided that the lapse was generally regarded as a breach of the law. But the word 'civilized' for a long time performed a very useful function, since it provided scope for the reform and improvement of international law by enabling what one might call 'the best practice of Princes' to set standards which others would then follow, in order to avoid the risk of being relegated to the outer circle of the uncivilized. Today, the phrase 'civilized Princes', even with the word 'states' or 'nations' substituted for 'Princes', has fallen somewhat out of fashion—largely because the European powers in the nineteenth century used it too often to distinguish themselves from the African and Asian 'natives' whom they regarded as uncivilized, if not positively savage, and the concept still carries those associations among some of the new nation states which have since emerged from colonial rule. That is of course quite understandable, and yet it must still be regretted. For the concept of civilization is an important one, by no means confined to Western cultures, and in at least some of its aspects it has made substantial contributions to improvements in the rules of international law.

None the less, the 'international custom of [civilized] nations', including their public declarations, remains an important source of international law. But today it is becoming rather less important than it was in the past, for virtually all *new* international law is now made by the *explicit* consent of sovereign states, and it is to the formal procedures through which that consent is given that we must now turn.

Legislation by contract

Every national legal system has a law of contract based on the general principle that promises should be kept, and regulating such questions as how legally binding agreements are made, what obligations they impose, how these are discharged, what happens if they are not performed, how contracts come to an end, and so on. In international law, there is likewise a general law of contract regulating all these things for agreements entered into between sovereign states. Until very recently, that law too was all customary, and therefore only to be found in the textbooks written by learned jurists or 'publicists', whose writings (known in French as *la doctrine*) form the most authoritative source of knowledge about 'the general practices accepted as law by civilized nations'. But the international law of contract has now been codified in the form of what is itself an international contract: the Vienna Convention on the Law of Treaties, which was drafted in 1969 and became effective in January 1980.

Now there is one respect in which contracts between sovereign states can achieve something which contracts between private individuals never can: they can themselves make new law. A contract between two sovereigns, like a contract between two private individuals, only constitutes a *lex specialis*—a special law—for the two contracting parties, that is to say a set of binding rules which will govern their conduct towards each other. A multi-lateral treaty will then operate as such a special law for all the states which are parties to it, and the more such parties there are, the more of them will be governed by the special law.

In the absence of a law-maker or a legislative assembly, we are once more back in Adamsville, where laws can only be made by the assent of the entire village community. But, as in Adamsville, once the special law of a particular treaty, directly binding only on those states that are parties to it, becomes a 'general practice accepted as law' by the international community, what started as a special law binding only on the parties will become a general law binding on everyone. So, over time, 'law-making treaties' can make new *general* law.

Adoption and ratification

Rulers, like others, cannot live in a vacuum. However sovereign they may be within their own territories, they have to live with each other. And so, for as long as there have been rulers, they have made agreements with each other for the regulation of a wide range of aspects of their mutual relationships. Defensive or aggressive alliances for war; the exchange of ambassadors, hostages, or prisoners; the regulation of trade, tolls, and customs duties—all these and many others have been the subjects of agreements between rulers over many centuries, and have reflected the very essence of international relations. In the increasingly interdependent world of today, such agreements cover a very wide range indeed. And they may be called by many different names—charters, pacts, covenants, conventions, etc.—but the generic term for all of them is 'treaties', and this is the term that will be used throughout the rest of this book.

Like all agreements, a treaty is of no value to any of the parties unless they can have some confidence that the others will abide by it. And so, from the first, international law has adopted the fundamental principle of private law that promises must be kept (*pacta sunt servanda*), that they must be performed in good faith (*bona fide*), and that a state's internal arrangements—even its own national constitution—cannot excuse the non-performance of its binding international promises.

As in the case of private contracts, a treaty between Princes would often be preceded by a long period of detailed negotiation. But Princes did not often meet face to face except on rare state visits of brief duration, and the negotiations therefore had to be carried out by someone else on their behalf. The usual practice was for one of the negotiating Princes to send to the other's court a special envoy, equipped with full negotiating powers (*pleins pouvoirs*), and therefore called a plenipotentiary. He would negotiate with the other Prince, his chancellor, his secretary, his ministers, and his other officials, until he had achieved the best bargain he could, and one he was willing to recommend to his own sovereign. In the days of Princes, communications were poor, and in order to present the outcome of his negotiations to his sovereign, the plenipotentiary had to return to his own court. But by then that sovereign's position might have changed: he might have formed different alliances with other Princes, or run into domestic problems, and so no longer wish to conclude this particular bargain. For these reasons the standard procedure was this: when the plenipotentiary had negotiated all the details, the proposed treaty between the two Princes was written out in duplicate, and either signed or initialled by the plenipotentiary and his opposite number to authenticate the text; the plenipotentiary would then go home with his own copy and submit it to his sovereign with his recommendations; the sovereign would ponder, consult his nobles and other advisers, and ponder again; if he decided to accept the bargain he would send a message to the other Prince that he 'ratified' what his plenipotentiary had signed or initialled; if by then the other sovereign was still minded to do the deal, he would send back an equivalent message of ratification—and only at that point, when both the principals had ratified what their agents had provisionally agreed, did the bargain become a binding one; then and only then did the treaty enter into force.

Despite the improvements in modern communications, this traditional procedure is still adhered to. Ambassadors and other plenipotentiaries will negotiate face to face, by correspondence, by telex, or over the telephone. Throughout that process, they will of course consult the governments they serve. They may even initial or sign the final agreed text, but until their governments have formally ratified those texts the treaty will not enter into force.

Bilateral treaties—that is, treaties to which only two sovereign states are parties—continue to be made all over the world. But as that world gets smaller and the volume of international transactions increases, more and more treaties are made today between a larger number of states, sometimes embracing almost the whole of the international community. And particularly in the field of human rights, it is through these multilateral treaties that new international law is made.

Here the process of negotiation is necessarily different. Instead of an individual plenipotentiary being despatched to the foreign court, the plenipotentiaries of all the negotiating states meet in a common forum. This may be a special conference such as the one which produced the Vienna Convention on the Law of Treaties, or it may be the standing forum of an intergovernmental organization such as the United Nations, or one of its specialized agencies, or an organization of common interest like the International Telecommunications Union, or a regional organization like the Council of Europe, the Organization of American States, or the Organization of African Unity. First, one of the participating states may present a draft text, or a secretariat may be instructed to prepare one. That text will then be discussed and debated, clause by clause. The assembled plenipotentiaries will make speeches and interventions, propose amendments, and form alliances for mutual support, or for mutual opposition to some other state or group. They will consult their home governments, report on the current state of the game, tender advice, and receive instructions. The whole process may take years. But because the governments concerned all decided in the first place to conduct such a multilateral negotiation with the object of reaching some agreement, there will always be powerful pressures to agree something, even though it will not suit everyone equally and will necessarily involve concessions and compromises. If the process becomes deadlocked over some issue, different drafts will be left in square brackets until a later session, and the meeting will move on to discuss another clause. From time to time the conference will go into recess, and the plenipotentiaries will return home for further advice and instructions. Meanwhile, governments may come and go, and the policies of some of the states concerned may change. Surprisingly rarely, the process fails altogether. Much more often, something is eventually achieved, even if only after a very long time.

What is finally achieved is the text of a treaty to which all the states represented are in principle, however reluctantly, willing to agree. When that moment at last arrives, the formal event is that this text is 'adopted' by the meeting, often without the taking of a formal vote, but 'by consensus' or 'by acclamation'. Following that adoption, the text is formally opened for signature; that is, the plenipotentiaries, or their instructing ministers, will sign the text on behalf of the governments concerned.

At this point, the innocent bystander might be forgiven for believing that the governments which had signed the treaty were now bound by it. But, as we have seen, that is not so. For the inveterate practice persists that, however long they have spent in negotiating over every comma, and however many opportunities they have had for deliberating amongst themselves what they would be willing to agree to, governments are not bound by treaties until they have ratified them. And many of the world's governments have, in their time, signed many treaties which, for one reason or another, they have subsequently failed to ratify, and by which they therefore never became bound at all—unless, much later, the special rules laid down by those treaties eventually became part of general customary law.

There are in fact some very good reasons even today for requiring ratification before a state enters into binding international obligations. Negotiations of this kind are invariably carried out by governments, and not by parliaments. Yet a treaty, once it enters into force, may impose very important obligations on the state which, in their turn, may have all sorts of consequences for its inhabitants. For example, the performance of the new international obligation may entail changes in the state's domestic laws. It is therefore at least prudent for the negotiating government to consult its own people, or their representatives in the domestic parliament, before finally binding the nation to the terms of a new formal treaty; indeed, under the constitutions of many countries this *has* to be done as a matter of domestic law. A prominent example is the USA, where treaties automatically become part of the law of the land—but not until the Senate has agreed to ratification by a two-thirds majority. The US Senate has therefore been understandably cautious about giving a consent which could affect the laws of all the fifty States of the Union—with the result that the USA, despite its championship of human rights elsewhere, has still not ratified any of the global or regional human rights treaties.

A common feature of modern multilateral treaties is the appointment, by the treaty, of a central 'depositary' with whom instruments of ratification, as well as any other formal notices which may need to be given, will be deposited. This avoids the need for every ratifying state to deliver a formal instrument of ratification to every other state that has signed the treaty: instead, it deposits just one such instrument with the depositary, who then notifies the others that he has received it. Where the forum in which the treaty was negotiated is an intergovernmental organization, its Secretary-General will usually be appointed as the depositary.

Entry into force

Suppose now that, say, all the twenty-one member states of the Council of Europe have formally adopted the text of a new treaty and that, say, eighteen of them have signed it. It cannot enter into force when the first one ratifies, for it takes at least two to agree to anything. If nothing more were said, it would therefore enter into force when the second state ratified it, at which moment it would become binding on those two alone. That might have some odd and unintended consequences if none of the others ever ratified, and such multilateral treaties therefore today almost invariably contain a clause saying that they will only enter into force when they have been ratified by some minimum number of states. In our example, this might be, say, ten; and what would then trigger the entry into force of the new treaty would be the deposit of the tenth instrument of ratification with the Secretary-General of the Council of Europe. When he receives that document—or, if the treaty so provides, after some further fixed period from then—the treaty finally enters into force, binding the state which has delivered it as well as the other nine which delivered theirs before. From that point onwards, every newly ratifying

state becomes bound when it deposits its instrument of ratification, unless again the treaty provides some additional period
after that event.

Accession and adherence

Like many others, the international community continues to
grow. New nations are added to it, most frequently upon attaining
their independence from colonial or trusteeship status. By necessity, they can have taken no part in the negotiation of the texts of
any treaties then already in force. Nor could they have joined in
adopting their texts, or in signing them when they were first
opened for signature. Other existing states may have chosen not
to sign at that stage, but may later change their minds, perhaps
after a change of government. Since 'ratification' technically
means confirming and validating something that has already been
done for one by someone else, there is, in strictness, nothing any
of these can ratify in respect of such a treaty. And so, in order to
respect such legal technicalities, they must use a slightly different
terminology if they wish to become bound by it: instead of ratifying it, they are said to accede to it. They will do that by precisely
the same procedure as in the case of ratification: that is, they will
deposit an instrument with the appropriate depositary, usually
the Secretary-General of the intergovernmental organization in
whose forum the treaty was originally negotiated. But instead of
using the language of ratification, the instrument will use the
language of accession, and that will be the only difference. Once
the document is deposited, the new state will become bound by
the treaty exactly as if it had ratified it.

And once a state has become bound by a treaty—whether by
ratification or accession—it is said to have adhered to it, and so
to have become a [state] party to it.

Reservations

It sometimes happens that a particular state, much as it would
like to adopt the text of a treaty, sign it, or even ratify it or accede
to it, jibs at some provision in that text which it simply cannot
swallow. What such a state commonly does in such circumstances
is to make a formal 'reservation' to the treaty, specifying the
particular provision which it feels it cannot accept, and usually
explaining why. Provided the reservation goes only to some detail

and not to the heart of the treaty, the other states concerned are usually content to accept it: they would rather have the reserving state bound by most of the instrument than by none of it at all. But if the reservation goes to the very substance of the treaty so that adherence to it, subject to the reservation, would for all practical purposes be a sham, the other state parties, or the depositary on their behalf, may say that they reject the ratification or accession in that form. An intermediate possibility is for one or more states to notify objections to a reservation by another. If that happens, some rather technical provisions come into play which are a happy hunting ground for international lawyers. Broadly speaking, the result is that the reserving state and the objecting state or states do not become bound by the treaty (or at all events those parts of it to which the reservation relates) *to each other*, though they do become bound to all the other states which are parties to it.

Denunciation

In a changing world, nothing can last for ever. One might therefore ask how a state, having adhered to a treaty, can be released from it again if it no longer wishes to be bound by it, perhaps in the light of changing circumstances. Except for a few specific situations which cannot arise in the case of treaties about human rights, the simple answer in international law is that no party to a treaty can achieve such a release without the consent of all the other parties—either at the critical time, or because the treaty itself provides in advance for unilateral 'denunciation'. As in any other law of contract, the rule is that mutual promises can only be mutually dissolved.

Denunciation needs to be distinguished from derogation, with which we shall deal under the heading of 'Emergencies' in Chapter 8.

Other instruments

Apart from formal treaties, the members of the international community are given to producing other kinds of texts, such as declarations, resolutions, or recommendations. The preparation of these often follows a similar pattern to that of treaties: first drafted by a state or by a secretariat, discussed, debated, and amended, and finally adopted. The main difference is that the adoption of such a text does not, in general, create a legally binding obligation for any state: it is nothing more than an expression of general policy or intent. But these texts are often the precursors of treaties: having created a general climate of opinion favourable towards a particular policy, and found words, phrases, and clauses suitable for expressing it, this preliminary work can then be used for the construction of an appropriate treaty. But even if no formal treaty ever follows, a mere declaration or resolution can, over time, eventually become binding international law if its provisions can at some later stage be shown to have become a general practice accepted by states—perhaps because they constantly cite it in public as if they accepted it as law. As we shall see in the next chapter, this is of particular importance in international human rights law, because of the status of the Universal Declaration of Human Rights.

All such texts—declarations, resolutions, recommendations, as well as treaties by any name—are generically called 'instruments'. So, the rule is that all *treaties* are legally binding; and some other *instruments* may eventually become binding even if they are not treaties.

Interpretation and application

If two parties disagree about the precise interpretation of some piece of national law in its application to a particular case which concerns them, they will often get opinions from their lawyers. Being trained in the same discipline, the lawyers are less likely to disagree than their clients. But if they do, the matter can only be settled authoritatively by a competent national court, and that court will normally have *compulsory* jurisdiction—that is, if one of the parties asks it for a ruling, the ruling will be binding on the other party even if he never agreed to the proceedings being started, has taken no active part in them, and has done nothing to recognize the competence of the court; provided, of course, that he had proper notice of the proceedings, and an adequate opportunity to put his case forward if he wanted to.

Here again, international law is similar, but only up to a point. If two states disagree about some matter of interpretation, they will get opinions from their international lawyers, who may include distinguished and learned contributors to *la doctrine*. But even these may quite legitimately differ. When that happens, there is a problem, for as we have seen the whole of the international legal system depends on consent, and the world's nations have never yet consented to accepting the compulsory jurisdiction of any court—not even the International Court of Justice at The Hague, whose judges are drawn from the world's most eminent jurists. Accordingly, there can only be an authoritative ruling on a disputed point of international law—what the French call *la jurisprudence*—if the states concerned *both* (or all, if the dispute involves more than two) agree to submit it to the International Court, or to some other special tribunal of their choice, and to be bound by the outcome.

Because of this problem, some treaties lay down a special procedure, and even create a special tribunal, for the resolution of disputes between the state parties about its particular provisions. But even then, there are always special arrangements to ensure that no state can be brought before such a tribunal without its explicit consent, either to the tribunal's general jurisdiction under the treaty, or in the particular case. There are several such tribunals and procedures under the human rights treaties, which are briefly mentioned in the next chapter, and more fully described in Chapter 10.

7

Components of the code

Let us now see what components make up the modern code of
international human rights law. Like other branches of international law, this one has two possible sources: custom and
treaties. Since it is of very recent origin, most of it is still only
found in treaty law, but at least some of it can already be said to
be customary.

The treaties can be roughly divided into three categories: global,
regional, and specialized. There are three global treaties: the Charter of the United Nations; and the two UN Covenants on Economic, Social and Cultural Rights, and on Civil and Political
Rights respectively, which we shall call 'the ESCR Covenant' and
'the CPR Covenant' in the rest of this book. There are four
regional treaties: the European Convention for the Protection of
Human Rights and Fundamental Freedoms, the European Social
Charter, the American Convention on Human Rights, and the
African Charter on Human and Peoples' Rights (which has been
adopted but has not yet entered into force). And there are two
Declarations, one global and one regional: the Universal Declaration of Human Rights, and the American Declaration of the
Rights and Duties of Man. (The substantive Articles of all these
nine instruments are reprinted in the Appendix to this book, to
which the reader can refer for their exact texts; a Table at the
end of the book shows which states were bound by which of
the general treaties on 1 January 1984.) Depending on where
one draws the line between human rights law and other kinds
of international law, there are also twenty or more specialized
treaties now in force in this field, which are listed in the Table of
Instruments at the end of this book.

In this chapter we shall take a general look at all this law, in
order to see where its different parts fit in with each other, before
we look at it in more detail in later chapters.

Customary law

The most authoritative institution competent to declare what
rules of international law are or are not binding *by custom* is the

International Court of Justice at The Hague. But that Court has only had few occasions to lay down the law about human rights, and then only on the outskirts of some other question which it has been asked to decide, or on which it has been asked for advice. Lacking such final authority, one therefore has to look for the content of customary international human rights law largely to *la doctrine*, the practice (including the public declarations) of states, and the occasional judgment of another international or national court which has had to decide a relevant question of international law in the context of some dispute.

Against this background, there are only four human rights which one can say with some confidence are now already protected by customary international law: freedom from slavery, freedom from genocide, freedom from racial discrimination, and freedom from torture.

Freedom from slavery goes back to the last century: we have already traced the sequence of events in Chapter 4. In the nearly sixty years since the first Slavery Convention was adopted in 1926, every state in the world has gone on public record to condemn slavery and the slave trade, and has formally prohibited them in its domestic legislation. Certainly none has been heard to support them in public—even though it is known that, as a fact, several still tolerate them at home. In those circumstances, one can say with some confidence that both slavery and the slave trade are today prohibited by customary international law for all states, and not merely for the ninety-odd parties to the Slavery Conventions.

Genocide is the subject of another specialized treaty, the Genocide Convention, which was adopted in 1948 and entered into force in 1951. Its purpose is often misunderstood, for it was not designed (as many still believe) to forbid genocide itself by treaty. Instead, its main purpose was to make genocide a 'crime under international law'—that is, to extend the criminal jurisdiction of individual states beyond their own territories, so that they could try and convict individuals who had taken part in a genocidal activity, even if the state's own courts would normally not have had any jurisdiction because the activity had not been committed within the the state's own territory, or by or against its nationals. The objective was to make it increasingly difficult for such individuals to find safe havens to which to escape after perpetrating such atrocities. Eight states—Bulgaria, Byelorussia, Czecho-slovakia, the Philippines, Poland, Romania, the Ukraine, and the USSR—tried to make a total of eighteen reservations to this treaty when they ratified it, to which several other states then objected. This created a good deal of confusion, and eventually the UN General Assembly asked the International Court of Justice for an advisory opinion. In delivering that opinion, the majority of the Court said that 'the principles underlying this Convention are principles which are recognized by civilized nations as binding on states, even without any conventional obligation'. That statement was admittedly by way of an aside, but despite this it is probably now safe to say that acts aimed at the deliberate destruction of all or part of a national, ethnic, racial, or religious group (which is how genocide is generally defined) are today prohibited by customary international law, independently of any treaty obligations.

In another aside in the *Barcelona Traction* case almost twenty years later, the Court discussed the obligations which a state might have 'towards the international community as a whole', and said that these included not only the outlawing of genocide, but also 'the principles and rules concerning the basic rights of the human person, including protection from slavery *and racial discrimination*'—so perhaps adding this last freedom to the growing group of human rights protected under customary international law.

As for torture, that obscene practice did not become formally condemned on the international plane until the Universal Declaration of Human Rights in 1948, the wording of which has been followed in all the relevant global and regional treaties which have entered into force since then. But here there is an interesting decision, in June 1980, of the US Federal Court of Appeals for the Second Circuit, called *Filartiga* v. *Pena-Irala*. In 1976, a 17-year-old boy was tortured and killed by the police in Paraguay. His father, Mr Filartiga, tried to bring criminal proceedings there against the torturer, Inspector-General of Police Mr Pena-Irala, but without success. Later, he found him in the United States, so he and his daughter tried to sue him there. Under the US Alien Tort Statute, the US federal courts have jurisdiction to entertain actions brought by aliens for wrongs committed against them 'in violation of the law of nations'. In order to enable the court to accept jurisdiction, the father therefore had to show that, in having his son tortured, the State of Paraguay had acted in violation of international law. After a full analysis of the legal position, the Court ruled that 'deliberate torture perpetrated under the colour of official authority violates *universally* accepted norms of the international law of human rights'—in other words, that torture was now clearly and unambiguously prohibited by *customary* international law.

The UN Charter

The first multilateral treaty to deal with the whole broad spectrum of human rights was the Charter, adopted in San Francisco on 26 June 1945, of the United Nations Organization. This was of course a great event. The second world war, with all its horrors, was coming to an end. Germany had already capitulated, and Japan was soon to do likewise—though only a few then knew that the further horrors of Hiroshima and Nagasaki were to be interposed before she did. At all events, the victorious allies were determined to institute a new world order, especially in international law. Four years before, in the Atlantic Charter of 14 August 1941, they had called for 'freedom from fear and want'. On 1 January 1942, the twenty-six of them then fighting the Axis powers, already calling themselves 'the United Nations', had declared that 'complete victory over their enemies is essential to defend life, liberty, independence and religious freedom, and to preserve human rights and justice *in their own lands as well as in other lands*'. And in 1944 they had proposed, at Dumbarton Oaks, the establishment of a United Nations Organization which would, among other things, 'promote respect for human rights and fundamental freedoms'.

So the movement was already well under way towards the formal recognition of the new principle that human rights 'in their own lands as well as in other lands' were no longer to be the exclusive concern of each sovereign state, but a matter for the legitimate concern of the whole of the international community. And the UN Charter of 1945, a multilateral treaty which forms the constituent statute of the United Nations as an intergovernmental organization, several times uses the Dumbarton Oaks phrase about promoting 'respect for human rights and fundamental freedoms', but always adds to it the vital words 'for all, without distinction as to race, sex, language or religion'.

Nor is this only declared as one of the 'purposes' of the new organization: while Article 55 of the Charter says that 'the United Nations' shall do this, Article 56 then adds the crucial words that 'all *members* pledge themselves to take joint *and separate* action, in cooperation with the organization, for the achievement of the purposes set forth in Article 55'. These are clear words of obligation, and it is therefore now beyond dispute that every state which is a member of the UN—and only very few sovereign states today are not—is bound by these two Articles of its Charter, as a matter of international law, to respect and observe human rights and fundamental freedoms for all, without distinction as to race, sex, language, or religion.

So far, so good. This is a clear legal obligation binding today on almost all the sovereign states constituting the international community. It lacks only one thing: it altogether fails to define what *are* the human rights and fundamental freedoms concerned.

The Universal Declaration of Human Rights

That was the United Nations' next task, and it took them a little over three years to complete it, in the form of the now famous Universal Declaration of Human Rights. This instrument was adopted when the UN General Assembly met in Paris on 10 December 1948, and the anniversary of that adoption is still recalled on 10 December of every year as Human Rights Day.

The adoption was not by consensus, but by vote. At that time the UN had fifty-six members: forty-eight voted in favour, none voted against, but eight thought it prudent to abstain: Byelorussia, Czechoslovakia, Poland, Saudi Arabia, South Africa, Ukraine, the USSR, and Yugoslavia. And ever since, the Universal Declaration has stood as the first complete and detailed catalogue of human rights and fundamental freedoms to be recognized and solemnly declared by the international community of sovereign states.

The Declaration contains 30 Articles. The first says that 'All human beings are born free and equal in dignity and rights. They are endowed with reason and conscience and should act towards one another in a spirit of brotherhood.' There are still echoes here of the language of the eighteenth century, but there is no mention of either God or nature: references to both were deleted from the draft at the last moment. The secular age had finally arrived.

Article 2 goes on to say that 'Everyone is entitled to all the rights and freedoms set forth in this Declaration, without distinction of any kind such as race, colour, sex, language, religion, political or other opinion, national or social origin, property, birth or other status.' This is an Article of general application; it governs all that follows. And it will be noted that the catalogue of forbidden grounds of discrimination has grown, from the four in the UN Charter, to twelve.

The next twenty-six Articles enumerate and describe the rights and freedoms concerned, without ranking them in any order of priority, or dividing them into categories such as civil, political, economic, social, or cultural. The Declaration then concludes with an Article on duties and limitations, and another on abuse (see Chapter 8).

Resounding and eminently quotable though it is, the Universal Declaration is *not* a treaty. Indeed, its own Preamble describes it 'as a common standard of achievement for all peoples and all nations', and calls on 'every individual and every organ of society' to 'strive by teaching and education to promote respect for these rights and freedoms and by progressive measures, national and international, to secure their universal and effective recognition and observance'. However great its moral authority, therefore, it is clear that the Declaration was not intended, by itself, to impose legally binding obligations on the states that adopted it in 1948.

But that was more than a generation ago, and several important things have happened since then. For a start, not only do the UN and its specialized agencies keep citing it in official documents of one kind or another, but so do many individual states. Between 1958 and 1972 alone, for instance, twenty-five new national constitutions included references to it. Whatever their actual performance, sovereign states are never heard to denounce it in public: on the contrary, they constantly quote it with approval—especially when it suits their interests to accuse some other state of violating it. On grounds such as these, it is therefore now strongly arguable that the Universal Declaration is becoming, if it has not already become, part of customary international law, and so binding on all states, regardless of any treaty obligations.

Another important event was an international conference on human rights convened by the United Nations in Tehran in 1968 'to review the progress made in the twenty years since the adoption of the Universal Declaration of Human Rights and to formulate a programme for the future'. By then, the UN membership had already grown substantially, and eighty-four states attended. At the end of the conference, they adopted a solemn Proclamation which said that the Universal Declaration 'constitutes an *obligation* for the members of the international community'. This too, goes some way towards supporting the status of the Declaration as part of binding international law, at least for all the members of the UN.

Finally, there is another argument. The UN Charter, it will be recalled, contains a 'pledge' for all the member states to take action to achieve 'universal respect for, and observance of, human rights and fundamental freedoms'. What rights and what freedoms? Well, the same UN has duly adopted a catalogue, namely that set out in the Universal Declaration. And this Declaration in its own Preamble refers back specifically to this 'pledge', and immediately goes on to say that 'a common understanding of these rights and freedoms is of the greatest importance for the full realization of this pledge'. Any lawyer will tell you that, where one document refers to another, you are entitled—and indeed often bound—to look at the second in order to interpret the first. If your railway ticket says that it is 'issued subject to the regulations and byelaws of the railway', then those are the conditions by which both you and the railway are bound when they carry you, even if you have never seen them. And so it is strongly arguable on this ground that the human rights and fundamental freedoms which every member state of the United Nations is, by its Charter, bound to respect and observe are, and can only be, precisely those rights and freedoms which are enumerated in the Universal Declaration.

The linkage between these two instruments has in fact been recognized by the International Court of Justice, which observed in the *Iranian Hostages case* that 'wrongfully to deprive human beings of their freedom and to subject them to physical constraint in conditions of hardship is itself manifestly incompatible with the principles of the Charter of the United Nations, as well as with the fundamental principles enunciated in the Universal Declaration of Human Rights'.

The UN Covenants

However that may be today, a generation ago the member states of the United Nations did not rest content with a mere Decla-

ration, but decided to make some comprehensive treaty law
about human rights. Unfortunately, by then the euphoria of their
joint victory over the forces of evil that they saw represented by
the Axis powers was fast receding and, as so often happens, they
were beginning to fall out among themselves. Tensions between
East and West were increasing, to culminate soon after in the
confrontations of the cold war. Where it had taken a mere three
years to adopt a Declaration, it took nearly another twenty to
adopt the treaty texts, and yet another ten to bring them into
force. Nor was it possible to reach agreement on a single treaty,
because the Eastern bloc attached prime importance to 'economic, social and cultural rights', while the Western powers insisted
on 'civil and political' ones. The rights and freedoms listed in the
Universal Declaration were therefore distributed between two
treaties—on this occasion called Covenants—dealing separately
with each of these two groups, and imposing different kinds of
obligation on their respective state parties (see Chapter 8).

The texts of the Covenants were eventually adopted in 1966,
but it was a condition that they should not enter into force until
they had been ratified by thirty-five nations, and this did not
happen for another ten years. The total tally of ratifications and
accessions has since risen to over eighty, with more still coming
in. Among them are the whole of the Soviet bloc (but not the
USA), and others of every continent, every economic system,
every stage of economic development, every political complexion,
and every record in the observance of human rights, ranging from
the excellent to the frankly appalling. This may not say much for
the instant effect of the Covenants upon the performance of the
governments which have bound themselves to abide by them. But
what is crucial is that, where this performance still falls short of
the promise, the shortfall is no longer merely regrettable or even
deplorable: for those states it is now incontrovertibly *illegal*. Once
any state has become bound, through ratification or accession,
by such a treaty, any violation of any relevant human right for
which it is responsible is no longer merely immoral: it is a breach
by the government currently in power in that state of its *legal*
obligations under international law.

Moreover, if one takes the view that the provisions of the
Universal Declaration are retrospectively incorporated into the
UN Charter, then this is the case for *all* the members of the UN,

whether or not they have adhered to the Covenants. And if one goes even further and says that the Universal Declaration is now part of customary international law, then it binds also those few remaining states which are not members of the UN.

The European regional instruments

Europe had experienced at first hand the horrors and atrocities of the second world war, and of the period immediately preceding it. Indeed, many of them had been perpetrated by one of its own nations, not long before regarded as one of the most civilized states in the world. And the countries of Western Europe had enjoyed over many centuries a common history, a common culture, and many common traditions. Unlike the far more disparate members of the United Nations, therefore, it took the members of the Council of Europe less than two years after the adoption of the Universal Declaration to adopt their own treaty text in the form of a Convention for the Protection of Human Rights and Fundamental Freedoms, and less than another three years to bring it into force through the collection of the first ten ratifications—since increased to all the twenty-one sovereign states of non-communist Europe other than Finland, the Holy See, Monaco, and San Marino. The Convention and its later Protocols cover only civil and political rights, but a parallel European Social Charter, adopted in 1961 and entering into force in 1965, covers a wide range of economic, social, and cultural rights.

What is even more remarkable about the European Convention than the speed with which it was adopted and brought into force is the mechanism for interpreting, applying, and enforcing—yes, enforcing—it. When one recalls the jealousy with which, throughout all previous history, sovereigns in Europe and elsewhere—and not only absolute rulers but even the most democratic of sovereign states—had insisted on their complete and unfettered right to treat their own citizens as they pleased, it seems nothing short of miraculous that the sovereign member states of the Council of Europe were willing, in such a short time, to set up wholly independent institutions—a European Commission of Human Rights and a European Court of Human Rights, both sitting in Strasbourg—outside the political or administrative control of any of them, which would have the competence and the power to sit in judgment on them over precisely these issues. More remarkable still, proceedings before these institutions can be begun not only by other states, but by *individuals* against any state that has made an appropriate declaration recognizing the competence of the Commission to entertain such proceedings. And the European Court of Human Rights, to which cases may be referred after the Commission has investigated them, has express power to deliver binding judgments against the states concerned in the proceedings. All this amounts to a substantial retreat from the previously sacred principle of national sovereignty, as a necessary price for at long last including human rights in the area of *legitimate* international concern. As we shall see in Chapter 10, this system has proved remarkably effective, and has made an immense contribution to the interpretation and application of international human rights law.

Unlike the UN Covenants, both the European Convention and the European Social Charter allow a state party to 'denounce' them—that is, to notify the other parties that it will no longer be bound by them—by giving six months' notice after the first five years. In fact, this once happened: having been found guilty of gross violations of the Convention by the European Commission of Human Rights, and being threatened in consequence with expulsion from the Council of Europe, the Greek 'regime of the colonels' withdrew from the Council in 1969, so automatically denouncing the Convention. Not long after, it was overthrown, and its successor government rejoined the system in 1974.

The American regional instruments

While the United Nations were drafting their Universal Declaration, the Organization of American States (OAS) was engaged on a parallel exercise. It beat the UN by a short head, for its American Declaration of the Rights and Duties of Man was adopted just a few months before the Universal Declaration, to which it bears a close resemblance. Like the Universal Declaration, it was not intended to be a treaty. Yet despite that, it *has* since then achieved a legal status, but by a route quite different from that of the Universal Declaration.

As in the case of Europe, the member states of the OAS, sharing certain common historical and cultural traditions, decided to move on to the next stage of a regional human rights *treaty*. But this proved to take a great deal longer than it did in Europe.

Drafting did not begin until 1959, adoption took another ten years, and the American Convention on Human Rights only entered into force in July 1978. (By 1 January 1984, it had seventeen state parties.) Meanwhile, however, the OAS had already set up its own Inter-American Commission on Human Rights, with a mandate to investigate the state of affairs in that field within its member states. Lacking a binding treaty at that time, the OAS empowered the Commission to apply the provisions of the American *Declaration*, and this remains the position for those American states which have not yet ratified the American *Convention*. The same Commission, as well as a new Inter-American Court of Human Rights, now also has a mandate under the Convention to receive and investigate complaints from other state parties, or from individuals. So, when the Commission investigates human rights matters in an American state that has ratified the Convention, it applies the provisions of that treaty; but if the state has not yet ratified the Convention, it will apply the provisions of the Declaration instead. Here then is another way in which a mere declaration can effectively become part of international human rights law, and the work of the Commission and the Court are now also making an important contribution to the interpretation and application of that law.

Like the European Convention, the American one deals with civil and political rights, but it also mentions (in Article 26) the 'rights implicit in the economic, social, educational, scientific and cultural standards set forth' in the Charter of the OAS. In fact, the American states (other than the USA) also adopted an Inter-American Charter of Social Guarantees in 1948, setting out in considerable detail the social rights of workers and their families. However, this instrument has never got beyond the status of a declaration.

The American Convention also allows for denunciation, by one year's notice expiring on the fifth anniversary of its entry into force. In fact, none of the state parties has availed itself of that opportunity.

The African Charter

The African Charter on Human and Peoples' Rights is the latest of the regional human rights treaties, adopted by the Organization of African Unity in 1981. It will enter into force when a majority of the member states of that Organization, of which there are currently fifty (or fifty-one, if one includes the Sahrawi Arab Democratic Republic, alias the Polisario Front), have ratified it. It is unique in several respects. Unlike all the other general treaties, it covers civil, political, economic, social, and cultural rights, all in a single text, and imposes the same state obligations for all of them. Like the American Declaration, but unlike any of the other treaties, it includes a catalogue of duties imposed on individuals, as well as another imposed on states. And it also includes a list of what it calls 'peoples' rights' (as to which, see Chapter 18).

As in the case of the European and American systems, there will be an institution—the African Commission on Human and Peoples' Rights—competent to interpret and apply the treaty, and to receive complaints from both state parties and individuals, in this case without any prior declaration of competence by the state against which the complaint is made. But this will be the only institution: there will not be a separate Court.

Specialized treaties

All the nine instruments mentioned so far deal, singly or in complementary pairs, with the full catalogue of human rights. They impose various obligations on states in respect of those human rights, but they do not specify in any detail *how* those states are to perform their obligations. This must clearly vary for different rights and freedoms. If you want to make sure that employers will recognize trade unions, the steps you will take will be rather different from those which will ensure that policemen do not torture their suspects, or that discrimination against women is eliminated. For some of these rights—though by no means all—there are separate treaties which lay down more detailed rules. Because they only deal with one right, or a small cluster of related rights, they may be called 'specialized' treaties, to distinguish them from the general ones. The specific obligations they impose on their state parties are usually more precise, and whether a particular state party has complied with them in any particular case is therefore often less open to argument.

There are now a good many of these specialized treaties, of which around twenty fall squarely within the area of international *human rights* law. Some of the UN specialized agencies—and particularly the International Labour Organization—have been active in promoting some of them. There are also quite a few more, especially in the 'humanitarian' field—such as the Geneva Conventions on the laws of war, and their two Protocols—which are adjacent to this area, or partly overlap with it.

The Helsinki Final Act

In international practice, the formal end of a war is usually marked by the conclusion of a peace treaty, but no single comprehensive treaty was ever concluded to bring the second world war to a formal end. Instead, at a time when *détente* was the order of the day, all the sovereign states of Eastern and Western Europe (with the single exception of Albania), together with the USA and Canada, met for two years in a Conference on Security and Co-operation in Europe. The upshot was a lengthy document called a Final Act, signed with a great flourish by the respective heads of government in Helsinki on 1 August 1975, and dealing with a wide range of subject-matters. The participating states all agreed to publish the text of that document to their own populations, and 'to disseminate it and make it known as widely as possible', which in fact most of them did—on both sides of the Iron Curtain. Because of that publicity, this document is now very well known, and widely thought of as a human rights *treaty*. In fact it is not: it has no legal effect at all. But its political effect has been considerable.

Amongst much else, the Helsinki Final Act declares ten Principles. Principle VII says that the participating states 'will respect human rights and fundamental freedoms', and 'will also fulfil their obligations as set forth in the international declarations and agreements in this field . . . *by which they may be bound*'. Only a few months later, the UN Covenants entered into force, ratified by all the Eastern bloc countries and some of those in the West, most of whom were already parties to one or both of the European treaties. Today, out of all those thirty-five participating states, only four are not bound by any of the global or regional human rights treaties: the Holy See, Monaco, San Marino—and the USA.

However, whenever one of the participating states accuses another of failing to comply with Principle VII, the other is apt to retort with Principle VI: 'The participating states will refrain from any intervention, direct or indirect . . . in the internal . . .

affairs falling within the domestic jurisdiction of another participating state . . .' That principle of course reflects the great doctrine of national sovereignty, also preserved in Article 2(7) of the UN Charter: 'Nothing contained in the present Charter shall authorize *the United Nations* to intervene in matters which are essentially within the domestic jurisdiction of any state.' But today this line of defence is fundamentally fallacious: quite apart from the fact that public criticism is not 'intervention', it has always been clear that any failure by a state to comply with its *legal* obligations must be a matter for the *legitimate* concern of other states (quite apart from the UN as an intergovernmental organization)—even if, nowadays, the obligation may relate to the way in which the state treats its own subjects within its own territory.

Perhaps most important, though so far least discussed, is Principle X: 'In exercising their sovereign rights, *including the right to determine their laws and regulations*, they [the participating states] will conform with their legal obligations under international law . . .' There, in black and white, after two years of protracted negotiations, is an unqualified acceptance by all the parties of the fact that international law nowadays can limit even the sovereign right of states to legislate as they please.

8

Operation of the code

We now need to look at the techniques which the instruments use—some of them quite intricate—in order to see how they function. What they are all trying to do is to impose *obligations* on sovereign states in respect of the rights and freedoms of the individuals whom they have within their power; to make some *general* provisions about *all* those rights and freedoms; and to define *each* of the rights and freedoms concerned with an appropriate degree of precision. Let us therefore see how this is done.

State obligations

As neither the Universal Declaration nor the American Declaration was intended to be a legally binding instrument when it was first adopted, neither of them contains a clause imposing specific obligations on any state. Such declarations, as we have seen in Chapter 7, can only impose obligations (if at all) as the result of subsequent events.

The treaties, on the other hand, are specifically intended to create obligations for their state parties. One must therefore look first at the precise wording of the obligations they create, and one finds that there are two quite clearly distinguishable categories of state obligation: one which may be described as absolute and immediate, and the other as relative and progressive. The second is to be found only in the ESCR Covenant and the European Social Charter. The obligations under all the other global and regional treaties are absolute and immediate: that is, the obligation comes fully into force for each state from the moment that it becomes bound by the treaty, and is not dependent in any way on the resources available to the state. A typical formulation is that of Article 2(1) of the CPR Covenant:

'Each State Party to the present Covenant *undertakes to respect and to ensure* to all individuals within its territory and subject to its jurisdiction the rights recognized in the present Covenant . . .'

To make it clear that this obligation overrides the hitherto universally recognized principle of international law that the domestic legislation of a sovereign state is a matter for its own sovereignty and can never be the concern of anyone else, paragraph 2 of the same Article continues with an express undertaking by the state parties 'to adopt such legislative or other measures as may be necessary to give effect to the rights recognized in the present Covenant', where the laws of the state concerned do not already make the required provisions.

Accordingly, where any state has, without some relevant reservation, ratified or acceded to one of the treaties which imposes absolute and immediate obligations, it is now possible to verify *objectively* whether the rights protected by that treaty are adequately respected by that state. One looks first at the state's laws and administrative procedures to see whether they sufficiently protect the right concerned. One looks next to see whether those laws and procedures are properly applied and enforced in practice. To any extent to which this proves not to be the case, that state will be in breach of its international legal obligations.

But where the obligation is relative and progressive, the position is rather different. Here is a typical formulation, to be found in Article 2(1) of the parallel ESCR Covenant:

'Each State Party to the present Covenant undertakes *to take steps*, individually and through international assistance and cooperation, especially economic and technical, *to the maximum of its available resources, with a view to achieving progressively* the full realization of the rights recognized in the present Covenant by all appropriate means, including particularly the adoption of legislative measures.'

Here, too, the test is objective. But in applying it one needs to look further than the state's internal law, and its application and enforcement: one has to assess the state's available resources, and judge whether it has used them to the maximum extent, and made progress at the best rate it can.

The obligation under the European Social Charter seems to be hybrid. In Part I, the state parties follow the phraseology of the ESCR Covenant. They 'accept as the aim of their policy, to be pursued by all appropriate means, both national and international in character, the attainment of conditions in which the following rights and principles may be effectively realized'. But then they go on, in Part II, to 'undertake . . . to consider themselves bound by the obligations laid down in the following Articles and para-graphs', a phrase which has no overtones of either relativity or progression, but rather the ring of absolute and immediate language.

But whatever the precise form of these obligations, all of them constitute a substantial sacrifice of the old 'personal sovereignty' of states, imposing rules about what they may do to their in-habitants in the interests of an agreed new international order in this field.

Non-discrimination

The distinguishing characteristic of all human rights is that they are universal: as we have already seen in Chapter 5, they 'inhere' in all human beings by virtue of their humanity alone, and they are 'inalienable'. Logically, it must follow that one cannot dis-criminate between different individuals in respect of their human rights: no special characteristic of any individual entitles him or her to any more or any fewer human rights than anyone else.

Strictly speaking, therefore, once the instruments have said that 'everyone' has the rights they enumerate, it should not be necessary for them to forbid discrimination explicitly. But in prac-tice, most of the worst violations of human rights which have been perpetrated in the past have been discriminatory: that is, directed against the members of particular groups because of some characteristic shared by them, such as the colour of their skins, their religion, their language, their caste or class, their sex, or their political opinions. For this reason, both the Declarations and all the treaties (with the sole exception of the European Social Charter) contain a specific non-discrimination Article, stipulating in the clearest terms that there must be no distinction of any kind, or discrimination on any ground, between different individuals in their enjoyment of the rights and freedoms with which the treaty deals, and adding, with a few minor variations between the dif-ferent treaties, a standard catalogue of forbidden grounds of dis-crimination which include race, colour, sex, language, religion, political or other opinion, national or social origin, property, birth, or other status.

This Article is of quite crucial importance for each of the treat-ies in which it appears, and for the international code generally. As we have already seen in Chapter 5, it is not just a pious sentiment such as 'all human beings are equal'. It is a legal provision of great power since, together with the Article that imposes the state obligations, it governs the whole of the substantive content of the treaty. This is particularly important in the case of those rights for which the corresponding state obligation is relative and progressive. Take, for example, the much discussed 'right to work' declared by Article 6 of the ESCR Covenant, and dealt with in more detail in Chapter 13 of this book. Clearly, not even the richest state can ensure that every single one of its inhabitants will always have precisely the job that he or she wants. That is why the state obligation for this right is not absolute and immediate, but only to 'take steps . . . to the maximum of its available resources, with a view to achieving progressively the full realization' of this right. But if one finds, for example, that a state pursues policies designed to ensure that all the more responsible, interesting, and better-paid jobs go to people whose skin is of one colour, while the hard, boring, and badly paid manual labour is performed by people whose skin is of another, this would be a clear breach of that state's legal obligations if it is a party to this Covenant—because it is discriminating on the grounds of colour in the matter of the right to work. And exactly the same conclusion would follow in the case of a country which, for example, restricted employment or promotion to individuals who were members of a particular political party, or were otherwise regarded as politically reliable.

But the general non-discrimination Article is not only important in its application to rights where the state obligation is relative and progressive. The Strasbourg institutions, for example, have applied it over the years to every single one of the substantive rights protected by the European Convention, which imposes absolute and immediate obligations on its state parties. In the course of this development, those institutions have forged a powerful tool for the application and interpretation of the provisions of the Convention.

There is also scope for the application of the non-discrimination Article where the right concerned is circumscribed by restrictions or limitations, permissible in the specified circumstances laid down by the treaty (see below). If, for example, a state limits the exercise of a particular right, allegedly in conformity with the treaty, but in fact in such a way that one group of people is unjustifiably discriminated against, the state concerned will be in breach of its treaty obligation. But here one begins to approach the limit of the applicability of the principle of non-discrimination, for there must be some circumstances in which discrimination is in fact legitimate. For instance, if one imprisons people who are found guilty of committing violent crimes, one is depriving them of their human right to liberty, and human rights law would be wholly unrealistic if it then allowed them to regain their liberty by successfully pleading that they had been discriminated against. Again, someone who cannot read or write can hardly complain of adverse discrimination if he or she is not appointed to the post of a schoolteacher. And such justified discrimination may extend not only to people's activities or aptitudes, but even into areas where discrimination is expressly forbidden by the treaties, such as religion or race. A Jewish community can hardly be expected to appoint a Catholic as its rabbi, nor could one expect a black girl to be chosen as a photographic model for advertising the virtues of a sun-tan lotion, or a white man to play the lead in a film about the life and work of Martin Luther King.

The problem of where to draw the line between justified and unjustified discrimination has occupied many courts in their time—at the national level, especially the Supreme Courts of the United States and of India, because of anti-discrimination provisions in their respective constitutions; and at the international level, the Strasbourg institutions. Broadly speaking, they have all come to much the same conclusions. The distinction drawn must be *objective*; it must have an *aim* which is *rationally defensible*; and there must be *reasonable proportionality* between the means employed and the aim sought to be realized.

To all this, there are only two explicit exceptions in the code: Article 2(3) of the ESCR Covenant allows 'developing' countries to discriminate against 'non-nationals' in respect of their economic (but not their social or cultural) rights, 'with due regard to human rights and their national economy'; and Article 16 of the European Convention allows its state parties to restrict the political activities of aliens.

Discrimination is also the subject of two specialized treaties: the Convention on the Elimination of All Forms of Racial Discrimination, and the Convention on the Elimination of All Forms

of Discrimination against Women. Under each of these, a special
Committee has been installed to supervise its performance.

Emergencies

Another Article of general application is one that is found in all
the treaties except the ESCR Covenant and the African Charter
(though not in either of the Declarations). This is an Article which
allows the state parties to 'derogate' from some of the provisions
of the treaties, in the event of war or other public emergency
threatening the life of the nation. Derogation here simply means
that, within the limits set by the treaties, the state concerned will
in such cases be temporarily excused from compliance with the
provisions concerned. But the limits are very strict. First, whether
there is a war or a public emergency threatening the life of the
nation is a matter which can be objectively verified. For instance,
the 'regime of the colonels' which took power in Greece in 1967
claimed that there was a public emergency threatening the life of
the nation, and that this excused their subsequent violations of
many of the human rights protected by the European Convention
to which Greece was a state party. But the European Commission,
after a full investigation, determined that there was in fact no
such emergency. Then again, the measures taken which derogate
from the human rights obligations must be limited 'to the extent
strictly required by the exigencies of the situation', and this too is
objectively verifiable. Finally, no derogation of any kind is allowed at any time for some of the protected rights, in particular
the right to life, the freedom from torture and other ill-treatment,
the freedom from slavery and servitude, and the imposition of
retroactive penal laws. These rights can therefore be described as
'non-derogable'.

It seems curious that the ESCR Covenant contains no derogation clause. Both it and the parallel CPR Covenant protect
trade union rights. A state which has ratified both these
Covenants—and only very few have ratified one and not
the other—would therefore apparently be unable to introduce
measures derogating from trade union rights in a public emergency. For, although the CPR Covenant allows this, the ESCR
Covenant does not. It is also interesting to note that the African
Charter—the most modern of all these treaties—has no provisions for derogation at all.

Boundaries of the rights and freedoms

It is a commonplace that the exercise of one man's freedom may constitute the violation of another's. As a piece of United States judicial folklore graphically puts it, 'Your right to swing your arm ends just where the other man's nose begins.' For every right and freedom, clear boundaries must therefore be drawn. And indeed, the very attempt to define a right or freedom necessarily entails the drawing of its boundaries, for one cannot logically define anything except by its differences from other things in the same universe.

Several techniques are available for the definition of the boundaries of rights. One frequently used in the constitutions of socialist countries is to prescribe duties as well as rights, so that the limits of the rights will then be set by the duties. One may, for example, say that 'everyone has the right to free speech', and then say elsewhere 'everyone has the duty not to slander the State'. Another technique is through the concept of 'abuse' of rights. Here one would first declare everyone's rights, and then go on to say that no one must abuse his own rights in such a way as to deprive others of theirs. And finally, one can try either to draw general boundaries around all the rights, or to draw specific boundaries around specific rights, defining as precisely as one can where or why the exercise of each right must stop.

The international code uses all these techniques, but in different ways. The Universal and American Declarations are unique in that they do not use the last technique at all: none of the definitions of any of the rights contains any *specific* limitations or exceptions. But each of them has one paragraph about duties, and another of *general* limitations. Article 29 of the Universal Declaration, for instance, runs as follows:

'(1) Everyone has duties to the community in which alone the free and full development of his personality is possible.

(2) In the exercise of his rights and freedoms, everyone shall be subject only to such limitations as are determined by law solely for the purpose of securing due recognition and respect for the rights and freedoms of others and of meeting the just requirements of morality, public order and the general welfare in a democratic society.'

Of the treaties, only the American Convention and the African Charter follow this pattern. In the Covenants, duties are only mentioned in the Preambles. The ESCR Covenant also has an Article 4 which broadly follows the language of general limitation of Article 29(2) of the Universal Declaration.

By way of a belt added to the braces, the Universal Declaration and all the treaties (other than the ESCR Covenant and the African Charter) have an Article prohibiting the abuse of rights, for which the model is Article 30 of the Universal Declaration:

'Nothing in this Declaration may be interpreted as implying for any state, group or person any right to engage in any activity or to perform any act aimed at the destruction of any of the rights and freedoms set forth herein.'

To this, the treaties add 'or at their limitation to a greater extent than is provided for' in the treaty.

For a few rights like the freedom from torture, or from slavery, that is all there is, even in the treaties. But for many of the other rights, the treaties prefer the more precise technique of *specifically* defining the boundaries for each right. For this, they use a formulation which has three independent and equally important components:

1. The restriction or limitation must be 'provided by law'; that is, the principle of legality must be preserved.
2. That law must be 'necessary'; that is, not merely useful, reasonable or desirable. (Usually the treaties add here 'in a democratic society'.)
3. It must serve to protect one or more of a strictly limited set of public interests, which will vary from right to right, but usually includes such things as national security, public safety, public order, public health, public morals, and the rights and freedoms of others.

This formulation needs to be considered in the context of a fundamental principle of the interpretation of legal texts: namely that—to translate an ancient Roman maxim—the words of such a text must always be construed *against* the interests of anyone who seeks to rely upon them. So, if one of the texts in the international code declares a right, but adds that a state party may restrict this right by laws that are necessary in a democratic society to protect, say, public health, it is not enough for the state concerned to assert simply that this is what it has done. The burden is cast upon it to produce the exact law, show that such a law would be *necessary* in any democratic society, and demonstrate that this law *in fact* serves to protect public health—all to the satisfaction of some independent tribunal. In looking at these clauses of specific restriction or limitation, it is essential always to bear in mind the strictness and narrowness with which they will be construed, since one might otherwise come away with the quite fallacious impression that the limitation clause takes away with one hand all that the principal clause has given with the other. But this is in fact not so, as has now been confirmed by many decisions of the competent international bodies, and especially the European Commission and Court of Human Rights at Strasbourg, which have also given authoritative interpretations of expressions like national security, public order, public health, and so on.

Classifications of human rights

Taken all together, the entire international code lists something like forty or fifty distinct rights and freedoms. Human beings are inveterate classifiers; they are seldom content merely to wonder at an object for the qualities that render it unique. Rather, in each object qualities must be discovered which it has in common with some others, in order that it may be included in some class or category to which they all belong. And, as with objects, so also with human constructs, including human rights. Neither lawyers, nor philosophers, nor politicians appear to be content to regard each human right on its own: they seem chronically impelled to invent categories into which all such rights can be conveniently divided.

The division most commonly adopted is that between the 'civil and political' rights dealt with by the CPR Covenant and the European and American Conventions; and the 'economic, social, and cultural' rights dealt with by the ESCR Covenant and the European Social Charter. So long as one is only dealing with these treaties, the distinction is convenient enough. But it would not be legitimate to derive from this division any valid conclusion about a fundamental difference between the rights concerned: what it largely reflects are the divisions of the cold war during which the UN Covenants were negotiated—and, regrettably, the continuing divisions between the world's two major ideologies which like to describe themselves respectively as 'liberal' and 'socialist', but prefer to call each other 'bourgeois' and 'communist'; the former terms being used with pride, the latter with contempt. In fact, the distinction between these treaties is quite arbitrary: some of the same rights are protected by treaties in both categories—as, for example, trade union rights and protection for the family.

None the less, it is sometimes argued that the division reflects a true distinction between rights to positive intervention and rights to be left alone; or between rights which it is 'costly' for a state to grant, and others which are 'cost-free'. But on closer analysis this too turns out to be unfounded. Some of the traditional 'civil and political' rights entail substantial state intervention and can cost a great deal in money and resources: for example, in order to protect the individual's freedom from arbitrary arrest and detention, and his right to a fair trial before a competent, independent, and impartial court, the state must recruit, train, and pay police officers, public prosecutors, and judges to a very high level. By contrast, it requires no intervention and costs the state nothing to allow trade unions to establish national federations, or to allow everyone to take part in cultural life—yet both of these are classified as 'economic, social, and cultural' rights. In so far as there is a distinction related to costs, it lies rather in the different categories of *obligation* which the two Covenants impose.

Other distinctions too have been tried. Some of the items in the code, for example, are expressed positively as rights, and others negatively as freedoms. This is sometimes thought to reflect a distinction drawn by philosophers of law between 'rights' and 'immunities'. But again, on closer analysis, the apparent differences in the instruments generally turn out to be no more than accidents of language. One might, for example, say either that 'Everyone shall have the right not to be tortured' or, with the same effect, that 'Everyone shall have freedom from torture.' In fact, none of the instruments use either of these formulations; they simply say 'No one shall be subjected to torture.' And sometimes they even conflate rights and freedoms in the same phrase, as in 'Everyone has the right to freedom of expression.'

While it may be intellectually stimulating to attempt such distinctions, one must be constantly aware of the danger of seeking to *rank* human rights in some kind of order of importance, reflecting one's own political or ideological prejudices. That was of course one of the reasons why there were two Covenants and not one: the socialist countries insisted on the pre-eminence of economic, social, and cultural rights ('human rights begin after breakfast'), while the West continued to insist on the pre-eminence of civil and political rights ('human rights begin at the police station'). But though the two Covenants are separate instruments imposing different kinds of obligation, they are of equal status, and neither of them enjoys any formal or substantive priority over the other. (Indeed, each admits in its Preamble that the rights dealt with by the other are on a par with its own.) Besides, neither of the oldest instruments (the Universal Declaration and the American Declaration), nor the youngest one (the African Charter), draw any distinction at all between categories of human rights—not even as to the quality of the corresponding state obligation.

Only by taking all human rights together can one avoid such interesting theoretical questions as 'What does it serve a starving man to be free?'; 'Is a slave with a full belly not content?'; or 'Is it worse to be starved to death by a rapacious landlord, or beaten to death for offending the Head of State?' And equality of status is as important for human rights as it is for human beings, for once one begins to rank human rights in any order of importance, the way is wide open to abuse. Governments are constantly tempted, for all sorts of motives, to abridge human rights, and if they are once allowed to establish their own pecking order for them, it will not be long before the more inconvenient ones are ranked below those which cause less trouble—only to find themselves soon afterwards cut down in content as well as in status, for the alleged benefit of the 'prior' rights. Such ranking must therefore be avoided at all costs, and so should any classification which could lead to it. Now that the sterile debates over drafting are long past, the texts have been agreed, the code is in full force, and the UN General Assembly has said ever since 1950—and most recently in its Resolution 32/130 of 16 December 1977— that all human rights are 'interdependent and indivisible', it is far better to leave all these scholastic disputations behind. Instead, for each right, one should look carefully at the texts themselves and ask oneself: What exactly does this right or freedom comprise? What are the state's obligations in respect of it? May it be derogated from in time of war or public emergency? Where are its boundaries? What restrictions or limitations may a state legitimately place on it?

Provision of remedies

That will be the approach of Part III of this book, but before we get to it there is one more important matter to be considered. The Universal Declaration, the CPR Covenant, and three of the regional treaties—the European and American Conventions and the African Charter, but not the ESCR Covenant or the European Social Charter—all require states to ensure that everyone whose human rights or freedoms have been violated shall have an 'effective remedy', notwithstanding that the violation has been committed by one of the state's own officials or agents; and that, if such a remedy has been granted, the state's competent authorities will enforce it. This is of course enormously important, for unless there are such remedies the rights and freedoms guaranteed by the instruments will only be protected on paper. We must therefore now look at remedies, on both the national and the international planes.

9

National remedies

Legal positivists, it will be recalled, say that it is meaningless to speak of a right unless it can be enforced. In this, they follow the ancient Roman maxim *ubi remedium ibi jus*—[only] where there is a remedy, there is a right. In fact, this view has always been disputed: another school of Roman lawyers maintained that *ubi jus ibi remedium*—where there is a right, there [must be] a remedy. But whichever of these views one prefers, the fact remains that a right for which there is no remedy at all is of no practical use to anyone, and whether or not it is meaningless to discuss it will only be of interest to philosophers. That is of course why the international code contains provisions requiring each state to provide its inhabitants with an 'effective' remedy for violations of the rights which it defines.

Hierarchies of laws

In effect, this is a requirement for a complete and working system of human rights law at the *national* level of each state. Having undertaken to respect and observe the rights and freedoms concerned, the state must now also provide a remedy if they are not respected or observed, and the most effective way of doing that is by having appropriate laws, and a system for enforcing them.

How any particular state does this will depend on its particular constitutional and legal system. Almost everywhere nowadays, national laws are arrayed in hierarchies of layers. At the very top stands the constitution, from which all the national institutions derive their competence, functions, and powers. This includes the legislature, whose law-making powers will derive from, and be constrained by, the constitution: the legislature can only make those laws which the constitution allows it to make, and if it tries to go beyond that, the law concerned will be unconstitutional, and therefore void. Below that level, there will be more detailed regulations, often made by administrative authorities under powers conferred on them by some law. But here again, the regulation-making power is limited by what that law allows: a regulation which goes beyond this will be *ultra vires*—beyond the powers of—the regulation-maker, and therefore void. In deciding whether one law occupies a superior level to another, one has to ask whether the first can constrain the content of the second. If it can, it will be superior.

So, for example, a Road Traffic Act may confer on a government minister the power to make detailed regulations about the construction and use of motor vehicles; how many lights they should carry at the front and the back, and what colours these should be; on which side of the road they should be driven; what should be the minimum age for driving them; and so on. But if the minister then tries to use the Motor Vehicles (Construction and Use) Regulations to prescribe the maximum fares to be charged on the railways, that provision will be void, because it will be beyond the powers conferred on him by the Act.

In all the countries that have written constitutions, the same principle will apply to Acts of Parliament. So, if the constitution confers power on the legislature to make laws (generally called 'ordinary' laws to distinguish them from the superior law of the constitution itself) to regulate, say, matters of transport within the state, that will be the source of the legislature's competence to pass a Road Traffic Act. But if this Act then provides, say, that people of a particular religion, or skin colour, shall not be allowed to drive motor cars, or if it confers on the minister a power to make regulations about the religion or skin colour of drivers, one has to look at the constitution to see whether this lies within the legislature's powers. If the constitution says something like 'The laws of Ruritania shall not discriminate on the grounds of religion or colour', such a provision in the Road Traffic Act, or in the regulations made under it, will be unconstitutional, and therefore void. If the constitution says nothing like that, then, *as a matter of Ruritanian law*, the discriminatory Act or regulation may well be valid.

Constitutional law is therefore the best place for a state to anchor its human rights law, for this will prevent even the democratically elected legislature from making laws which will violate the human rights of its inhabitants. And that *can* happen, especially in countries which contain unpopular minorities whose votes are of no great value for most candidates in parliamentary elections, who are therefore more concerned to woo the favours of the majority group. Democracy may be a powerful safeguard against individual tyrants, but it provides no inherent protection against the 'tyranny of the majority'.

Dualism and monism

Let us now suppose that Ruritania has ratified one or more of the international treaties on human rights. What effect will this have on Ruritanian law? The answer will depend on where the Ruritanian legal system stands on another question on which legal theorists may take two different views, namely the relationship between international and national law.

One of these schools of thought—the dualists—holds that these are two distinct and separate kinds of law: they arise from different sources, govern different relationships, and differ in substance. Within a state, dualists maintain, the supreme or governing law is always national law, and international law can only become part of it if and when the constitution or the legislature has expressly said so. On the other side stand the monists, who hold that there can only be one system of law, and that national and international law are no more than two different aspects of it, both of which govern the same things, are equally binding, and are merely different manifestations of the single concept of legality. International law, they maintain, represents this single system's highest level, and is therefore superior to national law, and even to national constitutions.

In states where the dualist view prevails, international law will not be applied automatically. This is the position, for example, in the United Kingdom, in whose legal system an international treaty has no effect at all unless Parliament has passed an Act saying that it should have. Where the monist view prevails, on the other hand—as for instance in France and the USA—a treaty becomes part of the law of the land as soon as the state becomes bound by it, and those of its provisions that are sufficiently explicit and precise thereupon become 'self-executing'—that is, directly enforceable.

How this difference in theory and practice affects the performance by any particular state of its obligations under an international treaty depends on whether one looks at it from the international or the national plane. Viewed from the international plane, whether the state adopts a dualist or a monist view is quite irrelevant: having undertaken a binding obligation, it must perform it, and it is well settled in international law that none of a state's internal arrangements—not even its national constitution—will serve as an excuse for not performing its international obligations. However, viewed from the national plane, whether the state's own legal system takes a dualist or a monist view will make a great deal of difference. In the first case, the new international obligation will have an immediate effect; in the second, it will have no effect at all until the legislature has incorporated or transformed it into national law.

The Rule of Law

One of two things will therefore happen in Ruritania when it becomes bound by one of the international human rights instruments. If it has a monist legal system, those of the provisions of the instrument which are sufficiently explicit and precise will immediately become directly enforceable in Ruritania; if it has a dualist one, they will have to be made enforceable by a new law, to be enacted by the Ruritanian Parliament—unless, of course, Ruritania can truthfully say that all the human rights and freedoms which the instrument requires it to observe and respect are already sufficiently protected by Ruritanian national law as it stands. But whatever the procedure, Ruritania will only comply with its new international obligations if and when all its inhabitants have an effective remedy for the violation of any of the rights and freedoms which the instrument sets out to protect. Unless and until they do, Ruritania will not have performed what it has promised.

Now the most powerful entity in any community, and therefore the greatest potential violator of human rights, is the state itself, through its public authorities, and its officials and agents. What the Ruritanian state is therefore obliged to do is to create—if it does not already have it—a system which will provide remedies for its inhabitants *even against itself*. That may be a lot to expect, but then Ruritania has freely chosen to adhere to the treaty, and once it has done this international law requires it to perform its new obligations 'in good faith'. It must therefore now have laws which protect the rights and freedoms concerned, a law which enables individuals to obtain remedies for any violations, and a system which will ensure, in law and in fact, that those remedies will be enforced—even against the state itself.

This is what is meant by a working system of national human rights law. Take, as an example, the prohibition against torture. Once Ruritania becomes bound by that prohibition, it must have a law which forbids torture; administrative and disciplinary arrangements within its police and armed forces, and in its prisons and other places of detention, to ensure that torture is not inflicted; courts to which persons in detention can complain if, none the less, it is; and a system which will ensure that any compensation awarded by those courts will be duly and promptly paid, and that any public official who is found guilty, after a fair and public trial, of having inflicted torture will be duly punished.

All this necessarily brings in what is often called the Rule of Law: the principle of legality which requires that there should be laws which lay down what the state may or may not do, and by which one can test whether any power which it claims, or any particular exercise of such a power, is legitimate; and a system of courts, *independent of every other institution of the state, including the legislature and the executive*, which interprets and applies those laws. The total independence of the judiciary from everyone else is central to the entire concept of the Rule of Law, for the whole point about a law is that it must be upheld impartially, and that no one must therefore be a judge in a cause in which he has any personal interest, or if he is open to illegitimate pressures behind the scenes from the friends of either of the parties—especially if one of them is the state, or one of its public authorities. No less important is an independent legal profession which has nothing to fear from appearing against the state on behalf of unpopular clients. Sir Thomas Erskine expressed this in resounding language as long ago as 1792, when he was answering a scurrilous campaign against him for accepting the brief for the defence of Tom Paine, who was being prosecuted for publishing a tract called *The Rights of Man*:

'From the moment that any advocate can be permitted to say that he will or will not stand between the Crown and the subject arraigned in the court where he daily sits to practise, from that moment the liberties of England are at an end.'

And for so long as either judges or lawyers are subject to pressures from the state, the Rule of Law cannot prevail.

'Drittwirkung'

So the state must provide effective remedies against itself, its public authorities, and its officials and agents. But is it also obliged to provide effective remedies against others who may violate its inhabitants' human rights and freedoms, but who do not form any part of the state's own apparatus? Suppose, for example, I am tortured in Ruritania by my sadistic uncle, or thrown out of my job because I belong (or refuse to belong) to a trade union, or my privacy is infringed by a privately owned newspaper. What is Ruritania obliged to do about that?

This is a much debated question, for which there is no short English label. But in West Germany, where similar questions arise in relation to the 'basic rights' guaranteed by the national constitution, they call it *Drittwirkung der Grundrechte*—third-party effect of basic rights—and *Drittwirkung* will therefore have to do until we can think of something better.

Broadly speaking, the answer to the question is that there is, within limits, some *Drittwirkung*—that is, the state must, in general, provide effective remedies for violations of human rights perpetrated by anyone, and not only by the state itself. So Ruritanian law must forbid torture by anyone, and not only its own agents, and give me a remedy in the form of an action in its courts for compensation against my uncle, and enforce that court's judgment if it goes in my favour. Likewise, there must be a law which prevents *all* employers, and not only the state, from sacking me merely because I belong to a trade union, since otherwise my freedom to belong to a union, guaranteed by the treaty, would be violated. When it comes to my freedom *not* to join a particular union, the matter is more difficult. But in the case of *Young, James and Webster* v. *United Kingdom*, the European Court of Human Rights has held that a state does not comply with its obligation to respect the right to freedom of association if, under its laws, an employer may sack me with impunity merely because he has agreed with a particular union, long after he employed me in the first place, that he will henceforth only employ its members, and the result is that, unless I now join that union, I cannot find another job in the same industry in which I can exercise my particular skills. If that happens, and the national law is such that I have no 'effective remedy' against the employer or the union, then the state has failed to perform its obligation under the treaty, and *it* must therefore compensate me.

At the same time, there are limits to *Drittwirkung*. So, for example, there is a human right to life, but this does not mean that the state is obliged to provide every one of its inhabitants with a permanent bodyguard. What it is bound to do is not itself to kill people, to have in place an effective law against murder, and to do whatever it reasonably can to protect people from other *avoidable* risks to their lives—and so concern itself, for example, with infant mortality and the safety of drugs.

These, then, are the obligations of states within their own national legal systems. But then comes the question of monitoring their compliance. Some states may claim that they have done all they are obliged to do, but in fact they have not. Others may genuinely believe that they have done all that is required of them, but in fact there are gaps or loopholes which they have not noticed. For reasons such as these, there must also be systems of supervision on the international level, competent to determine whether any given state, in any given case, has or has not complied with its international legal obligations. We must consider these next.

10

International remedies

Regrettably, states differ a great deal in the 'good faith' with which they perform their international legal obligations in the field of human rights. A few are excellent, and will not even ratify such a treaty until *after* they have passed all the necessary legislation, and made all the other necessary internal arrangements, to ensure that they will comply fully as soon as they become bound. At the opposite extreme, there are states which adhere to every treaty in sight, and then do nothing at all towards performing their legally binding promises.

Incentives and sanctions

In other areas of international law, this can happen too, but nothing like so often or so much. The reason is that most other international treaties are more like commercial contracts, involving some exchange from which both (or all) the state parties will benefit. As in the case of commercial contracts, it suits everyone to perform these—for, if one of them does not, the others will not perform their parts either, and the original non-performer will therefore suffer. If you do not pay the agreed price, I will simply not deliver the goods, and that is your main incentive—and my main sanction—for payment. (There may be another, if there is also a court which can *force* you to pay.)

In the case of human rights treaties, there are no such 'commercial' incentives or sanctions. If Ruritania and Ecuamba enter into such a treaty, neither of them is likely to suffer any immediate loss if the other fails to perform it, nor does either of them usually obtain any benefit from the other's performance. Worse, the *governments* of both these states may feel that they suffer a loss—at all events, in their powers over their own subjects—if they do perform. Although it is the governments of states which enter into these treaties, the trouble is that the beneficiaries are not those governments but their subjects, who are not themselves parties to the treaty. It is as if two sets of parents whose children are about to marry each other were to agree to buy them a house to live in, and then decided to change their minds and to spend the money on something else. None of the parents has anything to lose by breaking the bargain, and the children may have no remedy, because they were not parties to the agreement.

Why then do governments enter into such treaties at all? There may be several reasons. Some governments are genuinely concerned to improve conditions within their own territories, especially if they are democratically elected and that is what their voters want. Some have an interest in improving conditions in other countries—again, perhaps because there is strong public concern about this among their own voters, or in the pursuit of their own enlightened self-interest, because they hope that this will improve their relations with those countries. Some governments continue to believe that respect for human rights contributes to a peaceful world. But for many, the principal incentive is a cosmetic one: they wish to improve their image in the eye of public opinion, both national and international. That may not be the most laudable incentive, but it is becoming increasingly powerful. As the world shrinks, as nations become more and more interdependent, communications improve, and the power of the media becomes ever greater, so the force of international public opinion is becoming more and more palpable. Even superpowers can no longer afford to ignore it altogether, as the ending of the US involvement in Vietnam demonstrated—though the Soviet invasion of Afghanistan furnished a contradictory example. But for lesser powers it is becoming an increasingly important factor affecting, and constraining, their internal policies. Few nations today believe that they can safely risk becoming outright international pariahs because of the way they treat their own citizens.

However, the risk is still not as high as perhaps one might wish. Nations must continue to live with each other, however they conduct themselves at home. If there is only one butcher in my village, the fact that he beats his wife may not be enough to persuade me to go to the expense of travelling several miles to buy my meat elsewhere. If my principal ally against my enemies is someone who bullies his children, I may find it prudent to overlook that unlovable characteristic until I can find a more humane supporter. I might even be tempted, in rationalizing such decisions, to say that other people's domestic affairs are none of my business.

And so, regrettable though it might appear, it is perhaps understandable that governments are not often seen in the forefront of concern about human rights in other countries—unless it happens to suit their particular foreign policy interests. Even if they belong to political complexions which habitually denounce each other in public, they may frequently be seen to maintain a surprising silence about each other's domestic human rights records, until one realizes that they are heavily dependent on each other in some important commodity trade, or some part of the world's strategic alliances. And this is perfectly understandable, for if you are a foreign office official your single concern will be to protect and advance your own nation's external interests, and you may not feel that your job requires you to put those interests at risk by criticizing the internal human rights record of some government with which it is important, at all events for the moment, to maintain a trade or strategic relationship.

For all these reasons, governments cannot be relied on to make a public pariah of every government that flouts its international human rights obligations. But a pariah is one thing; a law-breaker is another. *If* such things are matters for international law, and *if* there are independent international tribunals which can sit in judgment on the performance of legal obligations, the matter stands very differently, for two reasons: the injured individual may, in this way, be given a remedy which he ought to get, but cannot get, at home; and what will now be put at risk is not merely the offending government's public image, but its very legitimacy. And that is a risk which, in the long run, no government dare take. For once it ceases to be a legitimate government, it becomes legitimate for everyone else to procure its downfall: foreign enemies as well as internal opponents. The outlaw, after all, is beyond the legal pale, and has no claim for support or protection on any other member of the community. And the fact that outlawry can be a powerful sanction was well illustrated by the fall of the Greek colonels' regime in 1974. By then, the whole basis of their legitimacy had been gravely undermined by their effective expulsion in December 1969 from the Council of Europe, following findings of massive violations of human rights on their part, constituting breaches of their *legal* obligations under the European Convention. This made the task of their internal opponents much easier, and swung the pendulum of legitimacy crucially to their side. And the loss of legitimacy in the international forum, based at least in part on a deplorable record in the field of human rights, has in recent times contributed to the downfall of several similar regimes, like those of the Emperor Bokassa of Central Africa, the Shah of Iran, General Amin of Uganda, President Somoza of Nicaragua, President Macias of Equatorial Guinea, and the Argentinian military junta.

In order to determine whether any member of the international community is a law-breaker, there has to be some procedure for an independent assessment of the performance of its legal obligations. This is why all the international human rights treaties contain some provision for their supervision, interpretation, application—and in two cases even enforcement—by *international* institutions of various kinds, including some genuinely independent international tribunals, competent to hand down judgments which will bind states. These are the institutions which we must now examine.

The UN system

One of the organs of the UN is ECOSOC, its Economic and Social Council. This consists of fifty-four of the UN's member states, elected by the General Assembly. Human rights fall within its terms of reference, but as it is made up entirely of governmental representatives, it has done rather less about them than one might have expected of it. It has established a Commission on Human Rights, and a Sub-Commission on Prevention of Discrimination and Protection of Minorities. The members of the Commission are also representatives of their governments, and it too has therefore achieved rather less than it might have done. Its principal contribution to international human rights law has been as a first forum for the drafting of new treaties—including the twin Covenants—which it then passes on through ECOSOC to Committees of the General Assembly, and ultimately the General Assembly itself, for final negotiation and ultimate adoption.

Under three successive ECOSOC resolutions—No. 728F adopted in 1959, No. 1235 in 1967, and No. 1503 in 1970—the Commission is also competent to look at the thousands of complaints about violations of human rights which are sent to the UN every year, by victims who nourish the fond hope that this great organization may be able to do something about them. For a full twenty years after its establishment, the Commission took the view that it had no power to take any action about these. More recently, it has changed its policy: it will now look at them, but only if they appear to reveal 'a consistent pattern of gross and reliably attested violations of human rights and fundamental freedoms' in a 'particular situation'. If they do, the Commission can decide to undertake either a 'thorough study', or even an 'investigation' of them, followed by 'reports and recommendations'—not to the government concerned, but to the Commission's intergovernmental parent ECOSOC. All such studies, investigations, reports, and recommendations must be conducted in strict confidence. In fact, although a good many such 'particular situations' have been drawn to the Commission's attention over the years, the only ones about which it has so far done anything publicly have been Equatorial Guinea and Malawi.

The Sub-Commission is rather a different body, since its members sit 'in their personal capacities' as experts, and not as their governments' official representatives. Consequently, it is subject to rather fewer constraints—but in the end all it can do is to report its findings to the Commission, and that is often the last that is heard of them.

However, between them these two bodies do manage to keep a general eye—increasingly through Working Groups or Special Rapporteurs—on general problems such as slavery, the human rights of people in prison or detention, summary or arbitrary executions, 'disappearances', and the problems of indigenous peoples, as well as on a few selected countries which have no powerful friends. In these ways, their work undoubtedly has some value.

ECOSOC has another function in the human rights field: it is the supervisory organ for the ESCR Covenant. Under Article 16 of that treaty, its state parties must send in periodic reports on 'the measures which they have adopted and the progress made in achieving the observance of the rights recognized' by the Covenant. ECOSOC may then refer these reports to the Commission for study, and may make 'recommendations of a general nature' about them to the General Assembly. So far, ECOSOC has done neither of these things, although the Covenant entered into force in January 1976 and many of these 'country reports' have since been submitted to it. However, under Article 18 of the Covenant the UN's specialized agencies are also competent to comment. One of these is the International Labour Organization which has a great deal of expertise in these matters, and its Committee of Experts on the Application of Conventions and Recommendations—a truly independent body—has sent to ECOSOC some very helpful interpretations of some of the Covenant's provisions.

Under the CPR Covenant, the position is very different. Here, the supervisory organ is the Human Rights Committee—unlike the Commission, a body of independent experts required by the Covenant to be 'persons of high moral character and recognized competence in the field of human rights', preferably with legal experience. This body too studies reports submitted by the state parties about the 'measures they have adopted which give effect to the rights recognized' by that Covenant (including any difficulties they have encountered), and may make 'general comments'. But unlike ECOSOC, this Committee invites every state that submits a report to be present when it is discussed, and its representatives can then be subjected to a searching public examination by some very well-briefed Committee members. Few nations get an easy passage on that occasion. Moreover, the Committee has not been shy in expressing its 'general comments'.

The Committee has another, and even more important function. Under the Covenant itself, state parties can complain against each other about breaches of its provisions, provided they have made an appropriate declaration. But there is also an Optional Protocol to it, and the states that adhere to this accept the jurisdiction of the Committee to investigate complaints *from individuals*—technically called 'communications', in order not to offend anybody—about alleged violations of their human rights or freedoms protected by the Covenant. There are only three pre-conditions for that procedure: the complaint must come from, or on behalf of, a victim of the violation; he must first have exhausted any domestic remedy available to him in the state against which he complains; and the same matter must not be pending before another international institution. Over thirty states have now ratified this Optional Protocol, and as a result the Committee has had a substantial case-load of complaints. Its decisions on these are published, and are now making an important contribution to the international 'jurisprudence' about human rights—that is, the authoritative interpretation of the international code. And at least three states have already decided to change their laws or practices as a result of the Committee's adverse decisions—Canada to allow a tribal Indian to return to her reserve after the dissolution of her marriage to a non-Indian (following the *Lovelace* case); Finland in the area of religious education in schools (the *Hartikainen* case); and Mauritius to give alien husbands of its citizens the same rights as alien wives (the *Aumeeruddy-Cziffra* case).

Other independent Committees have recently been set up to supervise two specialized treaties: the Convention on racial discrimination, and the Convention on discrimination against women.

All these organs are serviced by the Centre for (previously the Division of) Human Rights of the UN's Secretariat, located in Geneva.

The European system

This is the oldest, and still by far the most effective, of all the international systems. Supervision does not amount to much: under Article 57 of the European Convention on Human Rights and Fundamental Freedoms, the Secretary-General of the Council of Europe may request 'country reports' from any state party on 'the manner in which its internal law ensures the effective implementation of any of the provisions' of the Convention, and just occasionally he does. But there is no provision for him to do any more about it after that.

By contrast, the procedures for complaints (on this occasion, politely called 'petitions') can be very effective indeed. The Convention establishes both a Commission and a Court, each composed of nationals of the different state parties—that is, twenty-one in all. All of them sit in their personal capacities; none as representatives of their governments. The commissioners are appointed for at least six years, the judges of the Court for at least nine. Complaints go initially to the Commission. They may come from a state party, or from an individual, but in the latter case only if the state against which it is directed has made a general declaration recognizing the competence of the Commission to receive such complaints. (Most of the state parties have now done this.)

To be admissible, an individual complaint must come from a victim, be made within six months after he has exhausted all available domestic remedies, and not be pending elsewhere. It must also not be 'manifestly ill-founded', and the Commission's decisions on that question provide one of the principal sources of its jurisprudence. If the Commission decides that the complaint is admissible, it will investigate it. When it has established all the facts it can, it will try to promote a 'friendly settlement'. If that fails, it will draw up a report, and these constitute another source of its jurisprudence. After that, either the state concerned, or the state whose nationality the victim holds, or the Commission itself, can refer the case to the Court, where it will be fully argued and a final judgment rendered. That judgment will be binding, and the state concerned must abide by it.

Since these institutions were established, they have dealt with many cases. A few have been complaints by one state against another, as in the case of the complaint by Denmark, Norway, Sweden, and the Netherlands against Greece under the colonels, or the complaint by Ireland against the United Kingdom about the interrogation techniques used in Northern Ireland in 1971. But the overwhelming majority, now well over 10,000, have come from individuals. The Commission has published many reports, and over 1,000 decisions on admissibility, and the Court has rendered around fifty fully reasoned judgments. As a result of these, many individuals have found redress or compensation for their grievances, and many of the state parties have had to change their national laws, or their administrative practices, in order to comply with the Convention as interpreted and applied by its own competent international institutions. The Court's decisions in particular have been of exceptional importance in the interpretation and application of the various provisions of the Convention— and, since these provisions are very similar to those of the other general human rights treaties, of great importance in interpreting those other treaties also.

This system is of course still far from perfect. The European Convention and its Protocols still protect rather fewer rights than the CPR Covenant, and some of them are hedged round with even more restrictions. The procedure takes a long time and costs money, though not as much as most other litigation: legal aid is available in some cases. The Strasbourg institutions have made it clear that they are not courts of appeal from national courts: they can only intervene when a state is in breach of one of its obligations under the Convention, and their jurisdiction is therefore only supervisory. In their early days, they also exhibited an understandable degree of caution: they were new and in many ways revolutionary institutions, and they needed to build up respect and trust from the governments which had it in their power to abolish them again. So they developed some doctrines which seemed rather less than courageous—a doctrine of 'governmental margin of appreciation', for example, and another of 'inherent limitations', both going beyond the express terms of the Convention itself. But as their experience and standing has grown, so has the strength of their jurisprudence, and with all its defects this system is today by far the most effective one on the international plane.

The European Social Charter too has provision for interpretation by an independent institution, in the shape of a Committee of Experts which scrutinizes periodic 'country reports' and publishes its comments on them. These too have had a substantial effect on the domestic laws of several of the states concerned.

The American system

This closely resembles the European system, but with two differences. Under the American Convention on Human Rights, there is also a Commission and a Court, appointed and functioning in very similar fashion. But in this case a declaration of competence is needed only for the Commission to receive complaints from other states, not from individuals: the exact reverse of the European position. Here too, there is a growing jurisprudence from the Commission, and the Court is just beginning to consider cases referred to it.

But the Commission also has a separate jurisdiction, as a 'principal organ' of the Organization of American States, over the human rights situation in member states of that organization which have not yet become bound by the American Convention. For this purpose, its governing text cannot of course be the Convention; instead, it is directed by its Statute to apply the American Declaration of the Rights and Duties of Man, so giving that instrument, although it is not a treaty and was never intended to have binding force, an indirect legal effect. Under this part of its jurisdiction, the Commission examines and conducts *ad hoc* investigations of individual cases and the general situation of human rights in various American countries, and publishes reports on them. These reports too are a fruitful source of jurisprudence.

The African system

The African Charter will only enter into force when a majority— that is, currently, twenty-six—of the member states of the Organization of African Unity have ratified it. But when it does, that continent too will have an international institution to interpret and apply the provisions of its Charter, in the form of a Commission. This will have eleven members, all serving in their personal capacities for six-year terms of office, who must be 'African personalities of the highest reputation, known for their high morality, integrity, impartiality and competence in matters of human and peoples' rights', again preferably with legal experience.

Here too, either states or individuals will be able to make complaints, but neither of these will require any prior declaration of competence, nor need they come from a victim of the alleged violation. They must be made within 'a reasonable period', and not a fixed period of six months as in Europe and the Americas; domestic remedies must have been exhausted; and they must not have been 'settled', rather than not be pending, elsewhere. The Commission's powers of investigation will be very wide; although it may not accept a complaint which is 'based exclusively on news disseminated through the mass media', it 'may resort to any appropriate method of investigation' and 'may hear from any . . . person capable of enlightening it', and not only from the parties. It may also 'draw inspiration' from a wide variety of sources, though the Charter understandably exhibits a strong bias in favour of African ones.

Once this Commission is established, it too will doubtless make an important contribution to the international jurisprudence on human rights law.

The ILO system

The ILO—the International Labour Organization—is the oldest of the UN's specialized agencies, having been founded as long ago as 1919. Its main concern is social justice, and the human rights most important for that objective—that is, mainly economic and social rights, but also of course the right to freedom of association. It functions in a unique tripartite fashion: its main organs are all composed of equal numbers of employers' and workers' representatives, in addition to the governmental ones. Its record in international law-making is unique, for it has promoted more than 150 conventions which are now in force, and which between them have received around 5,000 ratifications, some from over 100 states.

The ILO has several procedures for superintending all this treaty law. There is a supervision procedure, under which each state submits reports 'on the measures it has taken to give effect to the provisions of conventions to which it is a party'. These are studied by the ILO's tripartite Committee of Experts on the Application of Conventions and Recommendations, which can address confidential 'requests' to state parties, or publish 'observations'. There is a procedure for 'representations', and a special procedure—installed jointly with ECOSOC—for complaints about infringements of trade union rights. Each of these may be activated by associations of employers or of workers. Another 'complaints' procedure may be initiated by member states of the ILO against each other. Different tripartite Committees or Commissions of the ILO consider these, and report their conclusions to the organization's governing body.

We have also seen above how the ILO is able to play a role in the supervision procedure for the ESCR Covenant.

The UNESCO system

The United Nations Educational, Scientific and Cultural Organization (UNESCO) is another of the UN's specialized agencies, and among the human rights within its special field of concern are the rights to education, freedom of opinion and expression, and culture, arts, and science. It has been responsible for one specialized treaty in this field, the Convention Against Discrimination in Education, adopted in 1962 and now ratified by over seventy states. Under a Protocol to that Convention, there is an independent UNESCO Conciliation and Good Offices Commission, available to state parties who seek an amicable settlement of disputes between them in this field, but this procedure has not yet been invoked.

Like the UN Commission on Human Rights, UNESCO originally took the view that it had no competence to take any action on individual complaints directed to it about violations of human rights, even those within its special concern. However, in 1978 it installed a new procedure for investigating such 'communications' through a Committee on Conventions and Recommendations, 'with a view to helping to bring about a friendly solution'. The procedure may be invoked by anyone who 'can be reasonably presumed' to be a victim of a violation of one of the human rights falling within UNESCO's competence. It is confidential, and discussion in public is only allowed if the communication testifies to 'questions of massive, systematic or flagrant violations of human rights and fundamental freedoms'. So far, UNESCO has not made public any use of this procedure, or any results which it may have achieved; its future currently seems uncertain.

Non-governmental organizations

Out of all these procedures designed to provide remedies on the international plane for violations of human rights in breach of a state's obligations under international law, clearly only a few can be said to be really 'effective'. The Human Rights Committee is composed of independent, knowledgeable, and well-briefed experts, and its attempts to supervise compliance with the CPR Covenant are impressive, as are its reports on individual complaints under the Optional Protocol. But its only powers are those of public condemnation, for even under the Optional Protocol the state parties have not undertaken any obligation to accept, let alone act on, the Committee's views. Some of the other procedures suffer from at least two defects: ECOSOC's supervision of the ESCR Covenant, and the work of the UN Commission on Human Rights, are both performed by governmental representatives, whose concern for human rights in other countries may be severely constrained by their own nations' foreign policy objectives; and the Commission's general procedure, like that of UNESCO, is confidential, and so cannot even expose the offending state to the pressures of international public opinion.

The only procedures which have so far been able to provide effective remedies are those of the two Commissions and Courts of Human Rights established under the European and American Conventions, and those operating under the ILO's Constitution: these are the only entities composed of independent experts rather than governmental representatives, under treaties which effectively force the state parties to give effect to the determinations made by the competent organs.

This is why the greatest pressures on states still come from the non-governmental organizations—the NGOs—which are active in this field. Without the unremitting efforts of voluntary societies such as the International Committee of the Red Cross, Amnesty International, the International Commission of Jurists, the World Council of Churches, and hundreds if not thousands of similar national and international organizations, human rights all over the world would be respected far less than they now are. Many of these organizations have been indefatigable in protesting, calling for improvements, promoting new treaties, pressing governments to ratify them when they have been adopted, scrutinizing their performance, helping complainants under the different procedures, and briefing the members of the various supervisory institutions. Even the international community of states recognizes their value, in giving some of them 'consultative status' with ECOSOC, UN specialized agencies, and other intergovernmental organizations.

Without the handicaps suffered by governmental representatives, the NGOs can move more quickly, and can exert their pressures more freely. Some of them run considerable risks in the process, and all of them are chronically short of money, and of volunteers to help in their work. They deserve every support, and they are perhaps the single most effective way in which the ordinary person who cares about human rights can help to promote greater respect for them, both at home and abroad.

Part III

What the code says

11

Freedom of the body

Having now seen how the code was made, and how it works, we can at last look at what it actually *says*. The text of all the substantive Articles of the nine general instruments, global and regional, are set out in the Appendix, and on any disputed question they need to be read with care: as in all legal documents, every word matters. A Table at the end of the book also shows which of the world's states had become parties to which of the general treaties by 1 January 1984. What follows here is a commentary on the different rights with which these instruments deal, and how they deal with them.

Once more, we are faced with the problem of 'ranking' human rights. How shall we group the rights for discussion here, and in what order shall we take them? Once we give the impression, even if only to ourselves, that some are more important than others, the way is open for the sacrifice of one human right for the alleged benefit of another, and that is a dangerous path. But some order there must be: let us therefore take the order in which the need for human rights might present itself to our aboriginal Adam, as his life develops from mere solitary subsistence to more complex things.

The first needs that Adam will feel are for what one might call the 'physical' rights and freedoms in the international code—that is, those whose violations directly affect his body. These are the rights to life, liberty, and security; the freedom from torture and other ill-treatment; and the freedom of movement, including the right (such as it is) to find a place safe from danger.

The right to life

One might be forgiven for expecting that the right to life would have some kind of primacy in the international code; that in some way it would be ranked before the others. After all, to have *any* human rights one must be a living individual: the dead themselves have no use for rights, human or any other. But in fact one finds nothing of the kind. The right to life is like any other human

right. Like others, it has its own particular characteristics—the
state obligation is absolute and immediate, for instance, and there
can be no derogation from it even in times of war or public
emergency—but it enjoys no special pre-eminence. Indeed, in its
treaty formulations it even admits of quite a few exceptions.

At first sight, that may seem odd. But then one is recalled to
the realities of biology. After all, no one can live for ever: we must
all die in the end. When that finally happens, could we complain
that our human right to life has been infringed? Who has violated
it? Against whom would we claim a remedy, and what would it
be? Besides, life is full of risks. We may fall fatally ill, drown in a
treacherous current, fall off a mountain—or be run over by a bus.
In the last case at least, our dependants may be able to sue the
bus-driver or his employers for compensation, but could they
really argue that he has violated our *human* right to life—that is,
a right which is primarily directed against the state and its public
authorities?

But in that case, why have a 'human' right to life at all? To
answer that question, let us apply for the first time a legal rule
which we shall use again in later chapters. This rule says that, in
order to understand the purpose of a law, one should look at the
'mischief' against which it is directed, and ask oneself: 'What
exactly is this law trying to prevent? What was it that was going
wrong in the community which induced the legislature to intervene?' Once one knows the answer to this, one is better equipped
to interpret and apply the law so that it will fulfil the purpose for
which it was intended.

Now the mischief which has evoked the human right to life was
quite simply the murder by governments of those whom, for one
reason or another, they disliked or found a nuisance. After all, if
you have an official licence to do it, killing those who get in your
way is by far the simplest and cheapest way of getting rid of
them—whether in Hitler's gas chambers, or by the equally brutal
means still used for what are today politely called 'extra-judicial
executions'. The human right to life is therefore designed in
the first instance as a safeguard against wanton killing by
governments.

At the same time, an *absolute* human right to life would make
nonsense of human rights law. All over the world, tens of millions
of people die every year, most of them from natural causes. One

clearly cannot treat every state in the world, even the most benevolent, as a permanent human rights violator, simply because it
has not been able to stop its inhabitants from dying: a state can
only be held liable either where its own agents have directly caused
the death, or where there has been some other culpable act or
omission on the state's own part. So, for instance, a state that
fails to have a law against murder, or deliberately fails to enforce
it, or exempts its own agents from it, or applies it arbitrarily,
might well be held guilty of violating its inhabitants' right to life.
The Inter-American Commission has already expressed this view
where individuals have 'disappeared', but the government concerned has refused to provide any information about them, or
about the progress of any investigation to discover their where-
abouts. And the Human Rights Committee has said that states
must do what they can to minimize infant mortality. But that is
as far as it goes.

Admittedly, this can produce some apparently anomalous results. For instance, if a member of a government's security forces
kills a suspected terrorist, that is a prima-facie violation of his
human right to life: like everyone else, he is entitled not to be
punished until he has been convicted of a known crime by a
competent and impartial court. But if a terrorist kills a member
of the security forces (or indeed anyone else), the state cannot be
held responsible for a violation of the human right to life, so long
as its government has taken whatever steps it reasonably can to
minimize terrorism and to protect its agents (and indeed all its
people) from terrorists. But the anomaly is a necessary consequence of the particular characteristics of human, as opposed to
other, rights. These are, after all, designed primarily to protect
the citizen from the acts or neglects of his public authorities, not
from those of his fellow citizens. The latter is the function of
ordinary law, not human rights law, and if the state can be held
responsible for them at all, it can only be through *Drittwirkung*
(see Chapter 9).

All this is reflected in the language of the instruments. True,
the Universal Declaration (Article 3) sonorously declares that
'everyone has the right to life', and says no more. But the treaties
are more circumspect. What they require is that this right 'shall
be protected by law', and that no one shall be 'arbitrarily' (or, in
the case of the European Convention, 'intentionally') deprived of

his life—save in certain specified cases. Among these, all the treaties make an exception for the death penalty; in addition, the European Convention (Article 2(2)) includes 'the use of force which is no more than absolutely necessary' for defence against violence, lawful arrest, preventing the escape of prisoners, or 'quelling riots or insurrections'. Note that the reason for these exceptions is that human rights are inalienable: one cannot therefore simply argue that a murderer, by taking someone else's life, forfeits his own. Human rights cannot be forfeited: if you want to preserve the death penalty, you have to create a special exception for it from the human right to life.

Since the adoption of the Universal Declaration in 1948, and of the European Convention in 1950, the death penalty has begun to go out of fashion. Both the CPR Covenant (Article 6, adopted in 1966) and the American Convention (Article 4, adopted in 1969) already contain some restrictions on it: for instance, it can be imposed only for 'the most serious crimes', by the 'final judgment' of a 'competent court', under a law that was in force when the crime was committed. It may not be imposed on persons under 18 (or, under the American Convention, over 70), nor carried out on pregnant women. There must be a right to apply for (but without any right to receive) pardon or commutation of the sentence, and both these treaties encourage abolition, though they do not actually require it.

Meanwhile, Europe too has moved on, and the death penalty has now been largely abolished in most of the member states of the Council of Europe. A Sixth Protocol to the European Convention, requiring its complete abolition (except in times of war) was therefore adopted in April 1983, and will enter into force when it has been ratified by five of the member states. A similar Protocol is now also being considered by the UN General Assembly.

Surprisingly few contentious cases have been taken to the international tribunals about the right to life; perhaps less surprisingly, many of the ones that have surfaced there have been about abortion. Here, the American Convention alone says in terms (Article 4(1)) that the right to respect for life shall be protected 'in general, from the moment of conception'. (With its distinct anti-clerical tradition, Mexico has found it necessary to enter a reservation about this provision.) But there are no such guiding words in the other treaties, and the European Commission of Human Rights has not yet finally made up its mind on the issue.

Liberty and security; arrest and detention

Though the international code may not have much to say about human life as a state or condition, it has a great deal to say about the *quality* of that life while it is being lived. Indeed, in a sense this is what the whole code is all about. It may not be able to stop people from dying, but it can at least try to ensure that, so long as they are alive, their sufferings will not be unnecessarily increased by avoidable oppression, persecution, exploitation, and deprivation.

There is precious little quality to life in prison; moreover, one of the classical ways of disposing of people who make trouble for their governments has always been to lock them up. The claim to 'liberty and security'—in the direct sense of freedom from physical restrictions—has therefore always been in the forefront of the struggle for human rights. And so the Universal Declaration (Article 3), the CPR Covenant (Article 9(1)), the European and American Conventions (Articles 5(1) and 7(1) respectively), and the African Charter (Article 6) all declare that 'everyone has the right to liberty and security of person'.

As is generally the case, this is where the Universal Declaration stops. But the treaties, intended from the start to be legal documents, must necessarily go on to deal with the details. And such details are important, for this right cannot be absolute: if it were, no common criminal could ever be arrested. What follows in the treaties is therefore a precise code for what is and is not legitimate in the field of arrest and detention, designed to allow the ordinary criminal law to operate with the necessary safeguards, both for the community that needs to be protected from crime and for the arrested suspects in detention, without opening the door to abuse by oppressive regimes.

This code has five principal elements. No one shall be arrested or detained except on grounds, and by procedures, 'established by law'; when anyone is arrested, he must be told why; he must then be brought 'promptly' before a *judicial* officer, and either released or tried within a reasonable time; and he must always be entitled to test the legality of his detention by proceedings before a court.

Only the European Convention, in its Article 5(1), gives an exhaustive list of the 'grounds' for deprivation of liberty that may be 'established by law':

1. Imprisonment after conviction by a competent court;
2. Imprisonment for failure to comply with an order of a court;
3. Arrest on reasonable suspicion that the person has committed an offence, or where that is reasonably necessary to prevent him from doing so, or fleeing after he has done it;
4. The educational supervision of juveniles;
5. Preventing the spread of infectious diseases;
6. The detention of mental patients, alcoholics, drug addicts, or vagrants;
7. The detention of unlawful immigrants, or persons to be deported or extradited.

This Article has given rise to a great many cases before the Strasbourg institutions, and each of these 'grounds' has now been considered and interpreted there many times.

Like the right to life, respect for the right to liberty and security is an absolute and immediate obligation on the state parties to the treaties. But unlike the right to life, they are entitled to derogate from it, 'to the extent strictly required by the exigencies of the situation', in times of war or public emergency. On such occasions, therefore, they may detain people without charge or trial—but only where the circumstances 'strictly require' this.

Torture and ill-treatment

There can be no doubt that torture—the deliberate and wanton infliction of severe pain or suffering—is one of the foulest obscenities that human beings can perpetrate on each other. It becomes fouler still, if that is possible, when it is perpetrated as part of the official policy, and on the express orders, of a government whose main function is supposed to be looking after the welfare and security of its people. Yet the practice continues in many parts of the world; moreover, attempts are sometimes still made to justify it (though nowadays almost never by governments). The justification usually runs on something like the following lines:

'Suppose you know that some terrorists have planted a bomb some-where. You don't know where, but you do know that it is timed to go off six hours from now, and that when it does it will kill or maim many innocent people. Suppose at that point you catch one of the terrorists. Surely you are entitled to do everything you can to get him to tell you where that bomb is, so that you can save all those innocent victims, even if it means causing a guilty man some temporary pain?'

Leaving aside the fact that the mental scars of torture are dreadfully permanent, however temporary the physical pain may have been, this argument ignores at least four crucial factors:

1. You may *think* the man you have caught is a 'guilty' terrorist who knows where the bomb is, but you may well be wrong; if you are, you will be torturing an innocent person.
2. Confessions made under torture are seldom reliable; more often, the victim will say *anything* to make you stop.
3. Presumably, you are trying to protect the high values of your society from the evil people who are attacking them. But what kinds of values do you expect to develop in a society whose own government deliberately tortures its own people?
4. Once you accept—as you are doing here—that a good end will justify even the most evil means, where are you going to stop? How long will it be before you are locking up some of your own people in concentration camps, and putting others in front of the firing squads, for what you think is the benefit of the rest?

Whatever one may think of the morality of the matter, its *legality* is today no longer in any doubt. With one accord, without any kind of qualification, restriction, or limitation, and without the possibility of derogation even in times of war or public emer-gency, all the international human rights instruments un-equivocally declare that 'no one shall be subjected to torture or to cruel, inhuman or degrading treatment or punishment'. Note that here there is not even any mention of rights or freedoms: there is simply a total and absolute prohibition, and we have already seen in Chapter 7 that in *Filartiga* v. *Pena-Irala* an Amer-ican federal court has held that this prohibition has now become part of *customary* international law, so binding all nations and not only those that are parties to the treaties. As that court put it: 'The torturer has become—like the pirate and slave trader before him—*hostis humani generis*, an enemy of all mankind.'

Note also that the instruments prohibit, just as absolutely, not only torture but all 'cruel, inhuman or degrading treatment or punishment'—that is, no fewer than six other categories of ill-treatment. Most of the cases in this field that have gone to Strasbourg have been about the meaning of these words, and they have now been very extensively interpreted there. In the leading case of *Ireland* v. *United Kingdom*, for instance, the complaint was about the (largely psychological) methods of 'interrogation in depth' practised on suspected terrorists in Northern Ireland in 1971. The Commission concluded that these amounted to torture; the Court decided that their cruelty, and the intensity of suffering they inflicted, did not reach that level, but that they did amount to inhuman and degrading treatment.

In order to try to make these prohibitions more effective, a new Convention on the Elimination of Torture has been adopted by the UN, which will go so far as to make torture a 'crime under international law' triable anywhere, and not only in the country in which, or by or against whose nationals, it was committed. This will make it increasingly difficult for torturers to find safe havens for themselves, and so will operate as yet another disincentive to them.

Freedom of movement

For the oppressed individual, the ultimate escape is to leave the country, and try to settle elsewhere. For that reason, oppressive governments often try to prevent their disaffected citizens from emigrating, even at the cost of turning their whole country into a vast prison. The right to leave a country is therefore an important safeguard against oppression: so long as it remains available, the risk of a major outflow of refugees may limit the degree of oppression that a government is willing to impose.

The Universal Declaration therefore provides (Article 13(2)) that 'everyone has the right to leave any country, including his own . . .', and the treaties all repeat that provision—in the case of the European Convention in its Fourth Protocol (Article 2(2)). But now comes a difficulty: what about fugitives from justice? One could hardly allow every criminal, before or after arrest or conviction, to claim the right to leave the country and so escape the consequences of his crime. Similar problems could arise with spies, and perhaps in some other cases too. Here, therefore, we come across the first example of a typical 'restriction and limitation' clause. Having declared the general right, all the treaties go on to say something like this (the text quoted here is taken from the European Convention's Fourth Protocol, Article 2(3)):

'No restrictions shall be placed on the exercise of [this right] other than such as are in accordance with law and are necessary in a democratic society in the interests of national security or public safety, for the maintenance of public order, for the prevention of crime, for the protection of health or morals, or for the protection of the rights and freedoms of others.'

At first sight, this clause looks as if it could take away most of the original right. But, as we saw in Chapter 8, that is not in fact so: for any such restriction to be justifiable, the government concerned must show that the case falls strictly within the clause— that is, there must be a clear law about it, and that law must be *necessary*, in a democratic society, to protect one or more of the specific public interests listed in the clause. If the case does not fall squarely within those requirements, the restriction will be invalid, and the government will be in breach of its international legal obligations.

All the instruments also provide for freedom of movement, and free choice of residence, *within* a country, and for freedom to *enter* a country. But this last freedom is confined only to a country's nationals: none of these treaties puts any obligation on any government to admit even a single alien to its territory. That may seem harsh, especially on refugees, but it is the general law to which there are only a few local exceptions—such as the treaty establishing the European Economic Community which allows free movement of EEC nationals among all its member states.

However, this gap in human rights law provides the occasion for an interesting illustration of the ingenuity of which lawyers in general, and human rights lawyers in particular, are capable. In 1968, the government of the United Kingdom introduced new immigration controls which restricted the entry even of UK citizens if they had no 'close connection' with the UK. A number of UK citizens, of Asian origin and resident in East Africa, complained to the European Commission of Human Rights in Strasbourg. In fact, the UK had not ratified the Fourth Protocol, which protects the right of citizens to enter their own country. None the less, in the case of *Patel et al.* v. *United Kingdom*, the Commission upheld their complaint by a novel route: the immigration policy, it said, was racially discriminatory, and to be denied the right to enter your own country when others of a different race retain that right may constitute 'degrading treatment' within the meaning of Article 3 of the Convention itself, by which of course the UK *was* bound.

For freedom of movement too the state obligation is absolute and immediate, and this is another right from which states may derogate in times of war or public emergency—but again only 'to the extent strictly required by the exigencies of the situation'.

Asylum

Refugees from oppression (other than ordinary fugitives from justice) have a special call on the help of others, and conditions in the world today remain such that there are still very many of them. There is a special UN Convention Relating to the Status of Refugees which tries to soften the harshness of their fate, and a special UN agency—the UN High Commissioner for Refugees, based in Geneva—who works for their relief. Yet still, outside the Americas, no refugee has a formal *right* to be admitted to any other country. Though the Universal Declaration (Article 14(1)) says that 'everyone has the right to seek *and to enjoy* in other countries asylum from persecution', the American Convention (Article 22(7)) is the only treaty which expressly includes the right to 'be granted' asylum, as well as the right to seek it.

It is little use to have the right to seek what one cannot obtain. But here too, the European Commission has exercised its ingenuity. In August 1972, a Moroccan Air Force Lieutenant-Colonel flew to Gibraltar, immediately following an abortive attempt to assassinate the King of Morocco, and sought asylum. His request was refused, and on the following day he was sent home in a Moroccan Air Force plane, only to be summarily tried and shot by a firing-squad when he got there. His widow complained to Strasbourg (*Amekrane* v. *United Kingdom*), and once again the European Commission invoked Article 3 of the Convention: it declared the application admissible on the ground that to be sent to a country where you are liable to receive inhuman or degrading treatment or punishment may itself constitute a violation of the Convention. (This is technically called *refoulement*, and expressly prohibited only by Article 22(8) of the American Convention, and by the Convention on Refugees.) Following that decision, there was a 'friendly settlement' under which the UK government paid the widow and her children £37,500.

12

Food, shelter, health, and the family

Let us now suppose that Adam is alive, at liberty, unharmed, and more or less where he wants to be. The next needs of which he will then probably become aware are for food and shelter, and to remain in good health. He may also wish to marry and start a family, and to protect its weaker members. On all these things, the international code has something to say.

Standard of living

'Everyone', says the Universal Declaration in Article 25(1), 'has the right to a standard of living adequate for the health and well-being of himself and his family, including food, clothing, housing and medical care and necessary social services.' Certainly, the world would be a much better place if everyone had all these things: no one would dispute that people *ought* not to go hungry, cold, homeless, or sick. But can this properly be called a 'human' right? When such things happen to people, it is not always their government's fault, nor is their government always in a position to do anything about it. Many countries are still just desperately poor: in natural resources, human skills, available capital, and the organizing and managerial capacities that would be needed to put these things usefully together, even if they were all there. And many of these countries have far more mouths than they can feed, given their supply of fertile land and their pastoral and agricultural techniques. Simply declaring a general right of this kind cannot cure any of those ills.

What then is the mischief against which this provision is directed? The sad fact is that, beyond endemic poverty from natural causes, there is a great deal more that *is* avoidable. In many countries, wealth (and especially land), as well as political power, remains in the hands of such a minute and over-privileged fraction of the population that one does not need to be a communist, or even an egalitarian, to be outraged at the resulting extremes of wealth and poverty, both maintained by extreme exploitation. But moral outrage apart, such economic systems are also very inefficient: the ignorance, illiteracy, poverty, malnutrition, and disease of the rural peasantry and urban slum-dwellers are themselves major obstacles to production, and so to the improvement of everyone's living conditions. And there are other barriers too which it is within the power of many governments to dismantle: corruption; the maldistribution of aid of all kinds; the construction of grandiose monuments for the rulers, instead of the health, education, irrigation, or other projects which would do far more good; attempts to ape the 'developed' countries by ambitious schemes for industrialization which only result in depopulating the countryside and creating vast sprawls of urban slums . . .

One could easily continue that sad litany, but this is not the place for it. Nor are the over-concentration of economic and political power, and the other barriers to humane economic development, phenomena unique to 'capitalist' economies: there are just as many 'socialist' ones that demonstrate them quite as starkly. The simple point here is that where governments *can* do something to improve the standard of living of their people, they must do it without any of the discrimination which the international code expressly forbids, and in that sense a legal right to an adequate standard of living *can* be formulated.

When one turns, therefore, to the relevant treaties, one finds that all the state obligations under the ESCR Covenant (Article 2(1)) are relative and progressive: '. . . to the maximum of its *available resources*, with a view to achieving *progressively* the full realization of the rights recognized in the present Covenant by all *appropriate* means . . .'. Article 11(1) then formulates the right to an adequate standard of living in these words:

'The States Parties to the present Covenant recognize the right of everyone to an adequate standard of living for himself and his family, including adequate food, clothing and housing, and to the continuous improvement of living conditions. The States Parties will take appropriate steps to ensure the realization of this right, recognizing to this effect the essential importance of international co-operation based on free consent.'

There are no provisions in this Covenant for derogation in times of war or public emergency. But the most important aspect of all rights of this kind is the overriding non-discrimination

Article which governs these treaties: whatever a government does in the field of economic development, and however it goes about it, must be done for the benefit of *all* its people, and not just some favoured few at the expense of the human rights of the rest. This subject will be discussed further in the section on the 'right to development' in Chapter 18.

The European Social Charter (Article 4) also contains a requirement for a 'decent standard of living', but there it is placed in the context of fair pay for employed workers: see Chapter 13.

Health

The inclusion of 'health' and 'medical care' in Article 25(1) of the Universal Declaration has led to an Article each in the ESCR Covenant (Article 12), the European Social Charter (Article 11), and the African Charter (Article 16). All these recognize the right of everyone to the enjoyment of the 'highest' or 'best' *attainable* standard of health, physical and mental, and among the aspects singled out for special mention are infant mortality (which some might regard as an aspect of the right to life); environmental and industrial hygiene; epidemic, endemic, and occupational diseases; the development of medical services; and the encouragement of individual responsibility in matters of health. The relevant provisions in the European Social Charter have been considered by the Strasbourg Committee of Experts, which has laid down the minimum standards which the state parties to that treaty must observe in the health field if they are to be regarded as fulfilling their obligations.

Here too, of course, the real sting lies in the non-discrimination Article: whatever health care a nation *can* afford must not be reserved for those that happen to exercise political or economic power, or to be in favour with the nation's rulers.

Marriage and family

'Men and women of full age,' says Article 16(1) of the Universal Declaration, 'without any limitation due to race, nationality or religion, have the right to marry and found a family. They are entitled to equal rights as to marriage, during marriage and at its dissolution.' And in paragraph (2), the Article goes on: 'Marriage shall be entered into only with the free and full consent of the intending spouses.'

Here is a good example of a right that straddles the supposed distinction between civil and political rights on the one hand, and economic, social, and cultural ones on the other, for it reappears in *all* the relevant treaties: *both* the Covenants, the European Convention *and* the Social Charter, and both the American and the African treaties. Marriages and families are so fundamental to human existence that one simply cannot put the rights they entail into a single category of convenience. They involve civil status, economic relationships, social structures, and cultural customs and values.

In all these fields, of course, much of the world is still far from realizing the rights now declared in the international code. Quite apart from such iniquities as the prohibition of inter-racial marriages in some places, there are not yet many countries where women can truly be said to enjoy equal rights in relation to all the aspects of marriage. Indeed, in many places they are still regarded as chattels—first as their parents', and then as their husbands'—and their 'free and full consent' to marriage is a myth. Here, much still remains to be done, especially in those countries which have now ratified one or other of these treaties, and can therefore no longer defend such practices on the ground that, as sovereign states, they are entitled to maintain whatever national customs they please.

Mothers and children

Article 25(2) of the Universal Declaration tells us that 'motherhood and childhood are entitled to special care and assistance. All children, whether born in or out of wedlock, shall enjoy the same social protection.' Again, no doubt, a sentiment with which no one would wish to quarrel, but hardly a provision to which one could give legal effect without rather more particularity. And that particularity is supplied in good measure by the treaties. The CPR Covenant has Article 24, the ESCR Covenant Article 10, the American Convention Articles 17(5) and 19, the African Charter Article 18(3), and the European Social Charter no fewer than three Articles—7, 8, and 17—regulating in varying degrees of detail the kinds of protection their state parties must provide for mothers and children. This ranges from registration of births, through working conditions for women and paid maternity leave, to elaborate provisions to ensure that child labour will not be exploited, and that children's education will not be prejudiced by any work they do, within or outside the family.

In the context of the European Social Charter, the Strasbourg Committee of Experts has taken a great deal of trouble to interpret and apply these provisions, and has expressed its disapproval of a variety of practices which it has come across in the course of examining the state parties' 'country reports'—such as children working on their parents' farms to the prejudice of their school homework, or the dismissal of pregnant domestic servants to the prejudice of their entitlement to paid maternity leave. As a rule, such disapproval eventually leads to the abandonment of the practice concerned, though often only after the passage of some years.

13

Work, income, and property

The time may come, some prophets say, when everything that anyone could conceivably need—or even want—will flow in abundance from automated production lines requiring no more human labour than the push of the occasional button. Meanwhile, though, Adam must still earn his bread by the sweat of his brow. Even in the most technologically advanced countries, most people still have to do a good deal of work; in the less developed ones where most of the world's population lives, they will soon starve if they do not work very hard indeed on most days of the year. Work continues to be an essential part of the human condition—and one that gives rise to much conflict, for it also continues to be one of the most persistent occasions for the exploitation of human beings by their own kind.

And there lies the mischief. Clearly, people need to work in order to survive. It is a fact that work is more productive if it is organized, if there is a division of labour, and if capital equipment is used in a fruitful conjunction with it. But all these things can be abused and perverted in the naked pursuit of greed, and it is this which results in the gross exploitation of human beings in the course of the productive process which we still see in far too many places in the world.

The right to work

Article 23(1) of the Universal Declaration addresses this mischief with the lapidary statement that 'Everyone has the right to work.' Depending on their particular position, different people interpret that text very differently. To the socialist, it is an affirmation of Marxist doctrine: it tells the capitalist that he has no right to exploit the toiling masses by maintaining a pool of unemployment, and threatening to throw them into it if they refuse to do his bidding. To the liberal, it is the affirmation of individualism: the state may not prevent anyone from working if he so pleases, however much it may dislike him or what he does, says or believes. But both of these are thinking of work in an industrial setting: to the subsistence farmer, this text it is quite meaningless. For him, work is a daily necessity, not a right. If he does not tend his crops, there will simply be nothing to eat.

One must note, in all fairness, that the same Article goes on to declare a right 'to free choice of employment', though the language fails to make it clear whether this is a separate right, whether it explains the right to work, or whether the right to work includes it. Article 6(1) of the ESCR Covenant adopts the last of these solutions: 'The right to work', it says, '*includes* the right of everyone to the opportunity to gain his living by work which he freely chooses or accepts.' The other treaties that deal with this right have different emphases: Article 1 of the European Social Charter adopts the formulation 'Everyone shall have the opportunity to earn his living in an occupation freely entered upon'; Article 15 of the African Charter follows the Universal Declaration in stipulating that 'Every individual shall have the right to work', but stops at that point and makes no mention of any free choice. (Indeed, in Article 29(6) it goes on to declare that 'the individual shall . . . have the *duty* . . . to work to the best of his abilities and competence'.)

All this is rather unsatisfactory. Provisions intended to be legally binding should not be phrased with such inscrutable ambiguity, rendering them open to so many conflicting interpretations. The historical reason for this is of course well enough documented: in the euphoria that followed the Allied victories in 1945, the newly United Nations sincerely imagined that they could succeed, through their different economic routes, in finally banishing the curse of unemployment from the world, together with many of its other afflictions. Hence the unguarded optimism of the Universal Declaration. By the time the Covenants were being drafted, the cold war was in full spate, and their final formulation represented the result of many painful diplomatic compromises. Meanwhile, non-communist Europe, and now Africa, have gone their separate ways. This may not be the only blemish on the great edifice of the international code of human rights law, but it is certainly one of the most prominent. Perhaps its greatest demerit is that it misleads many perfectly well-meaning liberals into believing that the whole structure is a communist plot, and so opposing it when all their traditions should lead them to support it.

That may all be regrettable, but we now have to live with these provisions, and interpret them as best we can. In fact, there are only two competent international organs in this field, and both have begun to offer some interesting interpretations. The ILO Committee of Experts, advising ECOSOC as part of the supervision procedure under the ESCR Covenant (see Chapter 10), has expressed some views which, despite their diplomatic caution, are unlikely to find much favour in Marxist-Leninist circles. Among 'matters which may be relevant in considering how far a state party has made progress in achieving the observance of the provisions' of this Article, the Committee has said, are things like these:

The existence of a penal offence of 'leading a parasitic form of life', without any express limit to the scope of that offence;

The existence of model collective-farm rules under which a member may terminate his membership only with the consent of the management committee;

The existence of discrimination in employment, on the grounds of political activity which neither constitutes an activity against the security of the state, nor is incompatible with the requirements of the forms of the employment concerned.

Meanwhile, in Strasbourg, the European Committee of Experts has been saying the kinds of thing which are apt to raise the hackles of liberal *laissez-faire* enthusiasts:

If a state at any time abandoned the objective of full employment in favour of an economic system providing for a permanent pool of unemployment, it would be infringing its obligations under Article 1 of the Charter;

That Article requires the existence of a planned policy of employment, and special measures to help those who are at a disadvantage in seeking work.

The cross-fire of these two institutions, directed at different targets, has turned out to be remarkably symmetrical. It is as good an illustration as one can find of the value of official organs made up of unofficial—and therefore independent—individuals. There may be a wealth of distinguished academic literature discussing the tenable interpretations of the ambiguous 'right to work'. But meanwhile, the members of the competent institutions, sitting 'in their personal capacities', are quietly and pragmatically getting on with their job.

Slavery, servitude, and forced labour

The converse of 'free choice of employment', or 'work which he freely chooses or accepts', is slavery. That word is still apt to conjure up images of gangs of chained negroes working on American or West Indian plantations under their slavemasters' whips— something, we like to believe, that is now part of our world's discredited past, long since abolished and only of interest to students of social history. Alas, it is not so: in its protean forms, slavery and its allied practices survive to this day, like so many others of man's indefensible cruelties to his own kind. The provisions of the Slavery Convention, adopted in 1926 as the world's first true human rights treaty (see Chapter 4), are as important and relevant today as they were two generations ago.

This Convention defines slavery as 'the status or condition of a person over whom any or all of the powers attaching to the right of ownership are exercised'. But this is only the most extreme form of exploitation of the work of others. Alongside it, there is servitude, which includes customary practices like debt bondage, serfdom, the sale of wives as chattels, the inheritance of widows, and the sale of children for their work. All these things continue to go on in many parts of the world, entrenched there partly by local custom, but all too often by the economic necessity of the victims, who lack any effective protection by their governments.

Beyond that, there is the residual category called 'forced labour', defined by the International Labour Organization as 'all work or service which is exacted from any person under the menace of any penalty, and for which that person has not offered himself voluntarily'. Here one is approaching the margins of legitimacy. If one regards all work as something unpleasant which people would prefer not to do if they could avoid it, then all work is 'involuntary', and will only be performed if there is the 'menace' of some 'penalty'—like hunger, bankruptcy, or just shortage of money for minor pleasures. But that can surely not deprive the concept of 'forced labour' of *any* meaning, for far too much of it continues to be exacted, in one form or another, in far too many places, and the ILO continues to perform valuable work in defining its limits more precisely.

Of all these practices, slavery and servitude are forbidden not only by the two Slavery Conventions, but by all the relevant general human rights instruments—the Universal Declaration (Article 4), the CPR Covenant (Article 8), the European (Article 4) and American (Article 6) Conventions, and the African Charter (Article 5). And the prohibition, as in the case of torture, is absolute and unqualified: there are no restrictions or limitations on it, nor any scope for derogation even in times of war or public emergency.

But for the more marginal case of forced labour falling short of slavery or servitude, the position is rather different. Apart from two ILO Conventions (Nos. 29 and 105), the general human rights treaties also forbid it, but subject to some carefully drafted exceptions for:

work forming part of a sentence of imprisonment imposed by a competent court;

military service, or service performed in its place by recognized conscientious objectors;

services performed during national emergencies or calamities;

services which 'form part of normal civic obligations'.

The Strasbourg institutions have had quite a few occasions to consider the boundaries of these definitions. In *Iverson* v. *Norway*, for instance, the Commission rejected the complaint of a dentist who had been posted for two years to a remote and deprived part of his country, and it has also given short shrift to some German lawyers and notaries who complained of having to take part in legal aid schemes.

There is also a UN Convention for the Suppression of the Traffic in Persons and of the Exploitation of the Prostitution of Others, directed against the exploitation of both men and women for the purpose of sexual gratification to the profit of others.

Pay and conditions of work

In its Article 23, the Universal Declaration pronounces that 'Everyone has the right . . . to just and favourable conditions of work; everyone, without any discrimination, has the right to equal pay for equal work; everyone who works has the right to just and favourable remuneration ensuring for himself and his family an existence worthy of human dignity . . .' The ESCR Covenant follows this wording with a little expansion; the European Social Charter has its own formulation, in the same spirit, but (as usual) goes into rather greater detail.

At first sight, this looks like another of those unexceptionable sentiments incapable of precise definition, and therefore of legally binding quality. But that appearance is again deceptive. Behind those sonorous words there lies nearly three-quarters of a century's hard and detailed work, unremittingly and successfully carried out by the oldest of all these intergovernmental institutions, the International Labour Organization. Its origins go back to the worst of the 'bad old days' of the industrial revolution, when women were pulling wagons in coal-mines for a derisory pittance, and being poisoned in match factories. The need for reform was widely accepted, but the problem was the high cost of safety. Many enlightened manufacturers were quite willing to incur it, and their customers to have it passed on to them, but not if the only consequence was to make a free gift of the entire market to some foreign competitor who had no compunction about carrying on such practices, and thereby driving the enlightened manufacturers, and their workers, out of business and into bankruptcy and penury. The solution therefore lay in international agreements on minimum labour standards, and this was the task eventually assumed by the ILO.

Over the years, the ILO has constructed a substantial edifice of international standards in labour law, with over 150 conventions, ratified by many nations, regulating pay and conditions of work, and related matters such as occupational safety and health. And where the general human rights treaties call for 'just and favourable conditions of work', they are doing no more than pointing to these well-established specialized international standards, and calling on their state parties to adopt them if they have not already done so.

Rest and leisure

'Everyone has the right to rest and leisure, including reasonable limitation of working hours and periodic holidays with pay.' Thus

Article 24 of the Universal Declaration, only slightly expanded in the ESCR Covenant and the European Social Charter.

More than any other, this provision is apt to raise the hackles of some politicians, and even of some philosophers, who use it to ridicule and decry the whole policy of including 'economic and social' rights in the human rights catalogue. True, such criticisms only tend to be put forward in the prosperous industrial countries, where people nowadays are no longer likely to end up as discards on the labour scrap-heap through being prematurely worn out by their work. But the theoretical point which underlies them is that it is said to be difficult to derive a right to paid holidays from the classical 'natural rights' of Locke and Rousseau's time, which required others to do no more than refrain, without undue effort, from engaging in activities such as killing their fellows, or throwing them into jail. Paying people a full week's wages when they only work for forty or fifty hours may seem to some employers to be a sacrifice which society has no right to demand of them, and which cannot therefore fall into the category of a 'human' right for others.

Now it is true that this is a right which may be costly to fulfil, which is why its corresponding state obligation is relative and progressive, and not absolute and immediate—subject always, of course, to the overriding requirement of non-discrimination. But unless there are *international* standards about working hours and holidays, nations will continue to have a powerful incentive to compete with each other by seeing which of them can grind most production out of its workers. This is why, here again, the ILO has long since established such standards, and in fact all that these Articles do is to incorporate those standards into the appropriate human rights treaties. If Locke and Rousseau had lived in the times of Dickens and Tolstoy, or if they travelled widely in today's poorest countries, one wonders whether they would really have seen such insuperable difficulties in including such a right among their 'natural' rights. But whether they would or not, the right is now there, and a great many of the world's nations, both rich and poor, are now bound by international law to respect it.

Social security, assistance, and welfare

If you have work to do, and you can either use its product yourself or someone pays you a reasonable amount for the work or for the product, you may well be able to support yourself, and your family if you have one. But not everyone is so lucky. You may be sick, or disabled, or widowed, or too old to work. Your crops may fail; your suppliers or your customers may go bankrupt. If you are a wage-earner, you may simply find yourself unemployed. And all this may happen through no fault of your own. What then?

'Everyone, as a member of society,' says Article 22 of the Universal Declaration, 'has the right to social security . . .'—and, according to Article 25(1), 'the right to security in the event of unemployment, sickness, disability, widowhood, old age or other lack of livelihood in circumstances beyond his control.' For once, the ESCR Covenant actually abbreviates this, saying no more than that 'The States Parties . . . recognize the right of everyone to social security, including social insurance.' By contrast, the European Social Charter expands this simple right in no fewer that four Articles (12, 13, 14, and 15), with a wealth of detail. As always, there is a reason. Industrialized Europe can richly afford to look after its deprived members, and so has created a whole variety of schemes to that end: social security, social assistance, medical assistance, social welfare services, vocational training, rehabilitation, resettlement, and all the rest. At the other end of the spectrum, the world's poorest countries, for which the ESCR Covenant is the lowest common denominator, are lucky if they can afford even the most elementary social insurance.

But the main point is now well established: those who fall on hard times through any of the calamities that are apt to afflict mankind must not be allowed to perish without help. And that help is no longer a matter of discretionary charity: it is a *right*, exercisable against the state as representative of the whole community, which in its turn is under a duty to make whatever provision it can collectively afford—*without discrimination*. There, as ever, lies the sting.

Property

For John Locke, life, liberty, and property were the most sacred of all the Rights of Man. The leaders of the American revolution were at first inclined to follow him; but after much reflection they finally settled for life, liberty, and the pursuit of happiness.

Others have taken a different view: 'Property', said the early

French socialist Proudhon, 'is theft.' Evidently untroubled by that sweeping condemnation, Article 17 of the Universal Declaration pronounces that 'Everyone has the right to own property alone as well as in association with others', and goes on to add, in paragraph 2, that 'No one shall be *arbitrarily* deprived of his property.' In more muted fashion, the European and American instruments too declare such a right—and so, in the absolute form 'The right to property shall be guaranteed' does the African Charter. But not so either of the UN Covenants, which observe complete silence on the matter.

At first sight, that may seem odd. By and large, the general instruments tend to agree on things like these. They may differ in emphasis and detail, but on the whole they declare much the same rights in much the same terms. Why then this shyness about property at the UN? After all, everyone would like to have at least some of it—and one of the classical forms of oppression is to deprive people of it if you disapprove of them. The reason, of course, is again ideological. In the Marxist demonology, the property-owner is the wicked capitalist, exploiting the toiling masses and 'living by owning'. All productive property must therefore be vested only in the state, to use and dispose of in the collective interest, and if a capitalist's property is taken from him he deserves no compensation. But in the liberal ideology, the state is anathema, and the ability to acquire property is the principal incentive to thrift, hard work, responsibility, and the development of the individual's full potential. Europeans, Americans—and now, it seems, Africans—evidently prefer the latter view to the former, and therefore enshrine it as a universal (or at least a regional) human right. But a larger world that also includes the Soviet bloc and some other 'socialist' countries cannot agree so readily on such a formulation, and has therefore wisely agreed instead to remain silent on the matter.

Not that the 'right to own property' is at all unqualified in those treaties that deal with it. Quite the contrary: it is a great deal more qualified than most. Neither the European nor the American treaties even speak of 'ownership', but rather of 'use' and 'enjoyment'. And when it comes to deprivation of property, or control of its use, both they and the African Charter give the state and its public authorities far more scope for intervention than in the case of any of the other rights and freedoms, on grounds such as 'the public interest', 'the general interest', 'social interest', 'public need', and 'public utility', which are not to be found anywhere else in any human rights treaty. In sum, whatever the 'right to property' may be, it is more weakly protected than any other in these treaties.

So, just as there proves to be no support in the 'right to work' for the right-wing suspicion that all human rights are a communist plot, there is also none in the 'right to property' for the left-wing suspicion that the whole scheme is designed only to uphold the evils of capitalism.

14

Just laws and procedures

As we have seen in Part I, the concept of justice is deeply entwined in the fabric of human rights. It lies at the root of the idea of legitimacy, which in turn controls legality. One sees this perhaps most clearly in those parts of the international code that deal with laws and their administration, which in their turn are designed to encourage and procure the just conduct of all the members of a society, and to provide them with enforceable remedies against injustices perpetrated against them.

In a society that respects human rights under the rule of law, the individual is entitled to expect that the law will recognize him as having rights and obligations, and will treat him equally with all others, whoever he is and however powerful those others may be. He will likewise expect that any legal disputes in which he becomes involved—whether as a claimant or as a respondent to someone else's claim, and whether against another individual, or a corporation, or a trade union, or the state itself—will be adjudicated by fair procedures, in courts and by judges that are impartial and independent, and that he will there have equality of arms with his opponent, and such skilled legal assistance and representation as he may need.

Here, the mischief has been familiar enough for all too long. History abounds with examples of laws that have favoured one caste, or class, or some other privileged group at the expense of another; laws made with retroactive effect, often by incoming power-holders, to punish acts after the event which had been perfectly lawful when they were done; courts, judges, and lawyers cravenly subservient to the state, or the political party in power; the presumption that certain people are guilty, long before any evidence is produced to support it; trumped-up criminal charges against dissidents, perhaps supported by extorted or forged 'confessions'; rigged, secret, or 'show' trials, often before tribunals specially convened for the occasion, where the accused have no proper opportunity to defend themselves, and where everyone knows the verdict long before the trial even begins, and knows that it will be handed down regardless of any evidence called or any arguments put forward—in short, oppression and persecution conducted under the false cloak of legality. It is to these mischiefs that the provisions of the international code are directed. Although protection from them is potentially costly, the state obligations are all absolute and immediate.

Recognition and equality before the law

'Everyone', says the Universal Declaration in Article 6, 'has the right to recognition everywhere as a person before the law.' And it goes on, in the following Article, to say that 'All are equal before the law and are entitled without any discrimination to equal protection of the law'—propositions which are repeated, in almost identical language, in the CPR Covenant (Articles 14(1), 16, and 26), the American Convention (Articles 3 and 24), and the African Charter (Articles 3 and 5). Curiously, the European Convention omits them: perhaps its authors thought them too self-evident to be worth mentioning.

Students of American history will recognize that famous phrase about 'equal protection', for it comes from the much fought-over Fourteenth Amendment to the US Constitution, passed in the aftermath of the American civil war to ensure that the States of the vanquished Confederacy would not restore slavery by the back door through laws that discriminated against the recently emancipated negroes. It therefore forbids each State of the Union 'to deny to any person within its jurisdiction the equal protection of the laws'. But though it may have originated in North America, the phrase has since found its place in many other national constitutions. It has therefore received a wealth of interpretation, not only in the Supreme Court of the USA, but in those of several other countries, notably India.

Neither the CPR Covenant, nor the American Convention nor the African Charter, allow any derogation from this right, even in times of war or public emergency. Curiously, the European Convention does.

Retroactive laws

Here is what Article 11(2) of the Universal Declaration has to say on this subject:

'No one shall be held guilty of any penal offence on account of any act or omission which did not constitute a penal offence, under national or international law, at the time when it was committed. Nor shall a heavier penalty be imposed than the one that was applicable at the time the penal offfence was committed.'

All the treaties repeat these two provisions in much the same language: the CPR Covenant in Article 15, the European Convention in Article 7, the American Convention in Article 9, and the African Charter in Article 7(2). The Covenant and the American Convention add an additional provision saying that if, after the offence has been committed, the penalty for it is reduced, the offender must be given the benefit of the reduction.

There is now a fair amount of learning in the Strasbourg case law about these provisions. As there is a similar Article about 'ex post facto' laws in the American Constitution, there are also many decisions of the US Supreme Court in this field.

None of the treaties allow any derogation from this right in times of war or public emergency.

Fair trial

Article 10 of the Universal Declaration summarizes this concept as follows:

'Everyone is entitled in full equality to a fair and public hearing, by an independent and impartial tribunal, in the determination of his rights and obligations and of any criminal charge against him.'

Most of the general treaties repeat all that: the CPR Covenant in Article 14(1), the European Convention in Article 6(1), the American Convention in Article 8(1), and the African Charter in Articles 7(1) and 26. All of them make some additions: that the tribunal must be 'established by law' ('previously', cautions the American text), and 'competent' (though the European text omits this); and that the hearing must take place 'within a reasonable time' (this is one that the CPR Covenant leaves out at this point; it provides it elsewhere, in Article 9(3), but only for *detained* persons). The African Charter agrees with impartiality, independence, and a reasonable time, but does not say that the hearing need be either fair or public. As for publicity, the Covenant and the European Convention allow some limited exceptions (in matters concerning juveniles, for instance), and the American Convention requires it only for criminal trials.

These provisions have given rise to more litigation before the competent international institutions than almost any other part of the code, and as result there is now a wealth of interpretation of them to be found in the case reports of the European Commission and Court of Human Rights, and of the Inter-American Commission. In the leading case of *Golder* v. *United Kingdom*, for instance (the case of the prisoner who was not allowed to consult a lawyer in order to sue one of his warders for libel), the European Court derived from them a 'right of access to courts', which it expanded in *Airey* v. *Ireland* (the case of the poor wife trying to get a judicial separation from her husband) into a right to legal aid in important civil cases for people who need a lawyer but cannot afford one. There have also been many cases on the question of what constitutes a 'determination of . . . civil rights and obligations'—and, in particular, whether decisions by the public administration which may affect the rights and interests of individuals fall within this phrase. For it is increasingly being argued that a state which claims to observe and protect human rights under the rule of law should ensure that justice is dispensed not only in its law courts, but also when its officials are exercising discretionary powers.

The European institutions have also developed an important doctrine of 'equality of arms' in legal proceedings, especially criminal ones where the prosecution, representing the state, generally starts with great advantages.

Rights of the accused

Because of those advantages, the international code contains specific provisions enshrining special rights for people accused of criminal offences. Article 11(1) of the Universal Declaration, for example, says this:

'Everyone charged with a penal offence has the right to be presumed innocent until proved guilty according to law in a public trial at which he has had all the guarantees necessary for his defence.'

The treaties here simply repeat the presumption of innocence, without enlarging on it. But they all greatly enlarge 'the guarantees necessary for his defence' into full and detailed catalogues of the *minimum* rights which an accused person must be accorded. (The African Charter's provisions here are rather slighter than those of the others.) These include the right:

to be told, in detail, what he is charged with;

to have adequate time and facilities to prepare his defence;

to defend himself in person or by a lawyer of his own choice, for whom he need not pay if he cannot afford it;

to examine all the witnesses against him, and to have his own heard;

to have a free interpreter if he needs one;

not to have to give evidence against himself;

to appeal against conviction to a higher court;

not to be tried again for the same offence once he has been finally convicted or acquitted of it.

The exact scope of these rights, in a whole variety of different circumstances, and in the context of many different national systems of criminal procedure, has again given rise to a great many cases before the international institutions charged with interpreting and applying these treaties, and here again there is therefore now a great wealth of case-law. Indeed, within the European system several countries—particularly Germany and Austria—have had to make substantial changes in their criminal procedures, following decisions by the Strasbourg institutions, in order to remain in compliance with their obligations under this Article of the European Convention. This is one of the outstanding examples of how international human rights law can actually be made to *work*.

Miscarriages of justice

Because of human fallibility, even the best-designed systems of criminal justice can still occasionally go wrong, with the result that an innocent person is convicted. (This is of course one of the most powerful arguments against the irreversible death penalty.) For those cases, two of the treaties (the CPR Covenant in Article 14(6), and the American Convention in Article 10) provide that there must be a *legal* right to compensation, and not merely a discretionary one. This is one respect in which the United Kingdom has not yet brought its own laws into compliance with its international obligations, for such compensation is still a matter for the discretion of the Home Secretary, and even if there is a full pardon any compensation is only paid *ex gratia*.

15

Freedom of the mind

Man, the Bible tells us (in both Testaments), does not live by bread alone, 'but by every word that proceedeth out of the mouth of God'. It is certainly true that, once their bodily needs for food, water, shelter, and clothing have been satisfied, human beings soon begin to experience the needs of the emotional, mental, and spiritual faculties with which they are equipped—uniquely, we believe, among living things on this planet. These include the need to gratify our curiosity; to acquire information about our surroundings; to construct ordered systems of belief, religion, ideology, and ways of looking at the world; to exchange information, thoughts, and opinions with others; to learn from their experiences; and to take part in scientific, artistic, and other cultural endeavours. In all these things, human individuals display a powerful need for freedom of choice, autonomy, independence, and respect from others for their own integrity.

However—again uniquely among living things—these activities seem to provide human beings with yet more occasions for hostility towards each other. Not only are we apt to oppress, persecute, exploit, and deprive each other in the course of competition for material things, especially those that are in scarce supply; we are apt also to persecute others because they hold opinions, beliefs, or ideologies different from our own. There is hardly a religion or political ideology which has not at some time been persecuted—and yet, if it has succeeded in establishing itself in enough strength, it has not uncommonly then itself proceeded to persecute other religions or ideologies. Not content with trying to persuade others to our points of view by reason, persuasion, or example, we display a disturbing propensity for seeking to achieve that end by force, sometimes to the point of torture, murder, and even wholesale massacre.

As for the exchange of information, our curiosity about the affairs of others seems to be almost exactly matched by our secretiveness about our own. Governments especially like to operate behind a cloak of secrecy, broadcasting selected information about themselves in the form of political propaganda, but often quite paranoically sensitive about enquiries into their own conduct, let alone any criticism of it. Moreover, since those who oppose a government's policies must communicate with each other if their opposition is to be at all effective, governments have a natural interest in inhibiting such communications—and they often have the power to achieve that end.

Hence the mischief in this field which is still only too familiar all round the world: censorship of the press; the burning of books; state-controlled education and broadcasting; harassment of dissidents; imprisonment, and worse, for those who 'slander the state'; secret surveillance; tapping telephones and intercepting letters; and state control of science, the arts, and intellectual and cultural activity generally. It is against these that the relevant provisions of the international code are directed.

Thought, conscience, and religion

Article 18 of the Universal Declaration provides that

'Everyone has the right to freedom of thought, conscience and religion; this right includes freedom to change his religion or belief, and freedom, either alone or in community with others and in public or private, to manifest his religion or belief in teaching, practice, worship and observance.'

Three of the treaties—the CPR Covenant (Article 18), the European Convention (Article 9), and the American Convention (Article 12)—closely follow this wording, but go on to submit the *manifestation* of religion or beliefs to the usual limitations in the interests of public safety, order, health, or morals, or the protection of the rights and freedoms of others, so long as these are provided by law, and are 'necessary'—in the case of the European Convention only, 'in a democratic society'. The African Charter, in Article 8, is much more brief about all this.

In addition, Article 20(2) of the CPR Covenant provides that 'Any advocacy of . . . religious hatred that constitutes incitement to discrimination, hostility or violence shall be prohibited by law', and Article 27 says that, where a religious minority exists within a state, its members 'shall not be denied the right, in community with the other members of their group, to profess and practise their own religion' (see Chapter 18).

Behind those provisions, the struggles of centuries are still discernible. In Western Europe, during the Reformation and the Counter-Reformation, men and women were tortured, burnt at the stake, hanged, and beheaded for their opinions; even in the Age of Enlightenment which followed, 'free-thinkers' continued to suffer persecution in many places. Nor is all that yet behind us. In the United Kingdom, for example, the monarch to this day must be a Protestant and can only marry a Protestant, and it is only since 1974 that it has become possible for the Lord Chancellor to be a Roman Catholic. That only affects a few individuals; but far more pervasive religious discrimination, amounting in some places to outright persecution, still persists in many other parts of the world, and is in fact currently again increasing.

On this subject too, there is now a good deal of jurisprudence from Strasbourg—including, for example, the decision in *Arrowsmith* v. *United Kingdom* that the philosophy of pacifism falls within the ambit of the right to freedom of thought and conscience, and the decision in *X* v. *United Kingdom* that a Sikh may be required by law to wear a motor cycle crash-helmet for the protection of public health, even if that means that he must take off the turban which his religion requires him to wear. The Inter-American Commission has criticized a provision of the Nicaraguan Constitution, in the days of the Somoza regime, which prohibited political propaganda based on religious motives or beliefs, and criticisms from the pulpit of the government, the laws, or public officials.

The state obligation here is absolute and immediate, and only the European Convention allows any derogation in times of war or public emergency.

Exchange of information and ideas

Perhaps one of the most often quoted provisions of the Universal Declaration is Article 19:

'Everyone has the right to freedom of opinion and expression; this right includes freedom to hold opinions without interference and to seek, receive and impart information and ideas through any media and regardless of frontiers.'

The American Declaration puts it a little differently in its Article IV:

'Every person has the right to freedom of investigation, of opinion, and of the expression and dissemination of ideas, by any medium whatsoever.'

Here again, the wordings of the CPR Covenant (Article 19) and of the European and American Conventions (Articles 10 and 13 respectively) closely follow the Universal Declaration; but the Covenant and the American Convention both explain that 'through any media' means either orally, in writing or in print, in the form of art, or through any other medium of one's choice.

By contrast, Article 9 of the African Charter is very brief, saying only that 'Every individual shall have the right to receive information', and that 'Every individual shall have the right to express and disseminate his opinions *within the law*.'

In Europe, the struggle for 'freedom of speech' has gone on since at least the seventeenth century, at first of course closely allied to the struggle for freedom of religious belief. Its progression may be measured by the fact that the English Bill of Rights of 1688 only sought to protect parliamentarians, insisting 'that the freedom of speech and debate or proceedings *in Parliament* ought not to be impeached or questioned in any court or place *out of Parliament*'; while, by 1791, the very first Article of the US Bill of Rights—the famous First Amendment—was seeking to protect the general public *from* its parliamentarians, providing that '*Congress* shall make no law . . . abridging the freedom of speech, or of the press.'

But even though the state obligations about freedom of expression in today's international code are absolute and immediate, the protected freedom is far from absolute. For a start, it may be derogated from in times of war or other public emergency, albeit of course only to the extent strictly required by the exigencies of the situation. But it is also hedged around by limitations and restrictions—more of these, in the case of the European Convention, than for any of the other rights and freedoms it guarantees, for it adds four more to the usual catalogue of interests which laws, necessary in a democratic society, may seek to protect: territorial integrity, protection of the reputation of others, preventing the disclosure of information received in confidence, and maintaining the authority and impartiality of the judiciary. Only the American Convention explicitly prohibits 'prior censorship' (except for the sole purpose of regulating access to public entertainments for the moral protection of the young); but it adds, uniquely, an important paragraph:

'The right of expression may not be restricted by indirect methods or means, such as the abuse of government or private controls over news-print, radio broadcasting frequencies, or equipment used in the dissemination of information, or by any other means tending to impede the communication and circulation of ideas and opinions.'

On this subject, of course, there is a massive jurisprudence, not only from Strasbourg but from the supreme or constitutional courts of many nations—and pre-eminently from the US Supreme Court, which has been applying and interpreting the First Amendment for nigh on 200 years. Broadly speaking, this jurisprudence adds up to what one might today expect. The freedoms of speech, of expression, and of the Press constitute essential foundations of any free, open, and democratic society. They are needed in order to restrain the excesses of rulers by making their subjects aware of abuses, corruption, or incompetence, both in government and in other organizations; they serve to promote public debate about policies and issues that concern everyone, and so to arrive at peaceful resolutions of such issues; they serve to promote free and open competition between different ideas, philosophies, and political ideologies; and they are required for the intellectual and spiritual development of every individual. And in the two cases of *Handyside* v. *United Kingdom* and *Sunday Times* v. *United Kingdom*, the European Court of Human Rights reminded us again, as the US Supreme Court has often done before, that the freedom to communicate information and ideas is not confined to those that are favourably received, or regarded as inoffensive, or as a matter of indifference; but also to those that offend, shock, or disturb the state or any sector of the population.

As for the restrictions and limitations, these must be scrutinized with great care, and will only be allowed to prevail if, without them, the particular exercise of the freedom of expression under consideration could lead to some clear and imminent public danger—as in the often quoted example, given by the great US Supreme Court Justice Oliver Wendell Holmes in the famous case of *Schenck* v. *United States*, of the man who falsely shouts 'Fire!' in a theatre and causes a panic—or in order to safeguard the real concerns of national security, to compensate someone who has been unjustly defamed, or for one of the other reasons specifically mentioned in the treaty.

The European Convention's concern to protect 'the authority and impartiality of the judiciary' reflects the need for laws designed to prevent 'contempt of court', especially in the form of newspaper campaigns against a party to legal proceedings before there has been a trial. A jury in a criminal case, for example, might well be unfairly prejudiced against an accused if they had already read in their newspapers that he drinks, beats his wife, insults his neighbours, or has some past criminal convictions, even though these are quite irrelevant to the question of his present guilt. Nor will the headline 'Sex Maniac Arrested At Last', followed by the name and photograph of a current suspect, contribute to the fairness of his identification parades, or to the openness of his jury's minds in deciding whether he or someone else was the true culprit. However, in the *Sunday Times* case, the European Court of Human Rights has made it clear that the public has a right to know what happens in the courts, and the media have the task of imparting that information, so that any law of contempt of court must be strictly limited to what is necessary to avoid substantial risks of miscarriages of justice.

Here, by the way, is a right which at first sight looks as if it might be alienable, for it is obviously quite legitimate for someone to undertake to keep someone else's secrets, as for instance in the case of doctor and patient, or of one's employer's commercial affairs, or of military research. But the correct analysis is probably that such a voluntarily accepted restriction on one's freedom of expression falls under a specific exception, such as the one for 'the rights of others'.

Education and training

'Everyone', says Article 26 of the Universal Declaration, 'has the right to education', and goes on to require that elementary education shall be compulsory, and at least the elementary and fundamental stages of education shall be free. 'Technical and professional education shall be made generally available and higher education shall be made equally accessible to all on the basis of merit.' There follows an unexceptionable paragraph about the aims of education; finally, we are told that 'Parents have a prior right to choose the kind of education that shall be given to their children.'

For many of the world's poorer countries, this is a tall order—which is doubtless why the principal treaty provisions about education are to be found in Articles 13 and 14 of the ESCR Covenant and Articles 9 and 10 of the European Social Charter, which impose only the more relative and progressive obligations on their state parties, rather than the absolute and immediate ones of the CPR Covenant and the American Convention. (The only absolute and immediate obligation in this area is that of the European Convention's First Protocol, which stipulates that 'No person shall be denied the right to education.') But the provisions in these treaties are very detailed and specific, as can be seen by consulting them in the Appendix, especially if one bears in mind the over-riding non-discrimination provisions—designed to prevent, for instance, the admission to universities of the stupid and idle sons of the rich and powerful, while excluding from them the clever and ambitious daughters of the poor, or those whose skins are of the wrong colour, or whose parents' political beliefs or trade union activities have offended someone in a high place—as still happens in many parts of the world.

But the CPR Covenant and the American Convention are not entirely silent about education, for both of them—as well as the European Convention's First Protocol—have a provision giving parents the right to require their children to be educated in ac-cordance with their own convictions in the areas of religion, morality, or (in Europe) 'philosophy'. This is designed to limit the indoctrination in such areas which states might otherwise be tempted to carry on in their schools. The European institutions at Strasbourg have had occasion to apply this provision to such questions as the languages used in state schools (the *Belgian linguistic* case), sex education (the *Kjeldsen* case from Denmark), and corporal punishment (the *Campbell and Cosans* case from Scotland). Following the *Hartikainen* case before the Human Rights Committee, Finland changed its practices about religious education.

By way of footnote, the right to education seems to be the only human right which requires those who have it to be positively *compelled* to do something. Here, for once, there seems to be a real distinction between a right and a freedom.

Culture, arts, and science

'Everyone has the right', Article 27 of the Universal Declaration tells us, 'freely to participate in the cultural life of the community, to enjoy the arts and to share in scientific advancement and its benefits.' And everyone, it goes on, 'has the right to the protection of the moral and material interests resulting from any scientific, literary or artistic production of which he is the author'.

Unlike the right to education, it is not immediately obvious why these rights should only be the subject of relative and progressive state obligations, rather than absolute and immediate ones. After all, they only require states not to *prevent* their subjects from playing whatever part they wish in whatever culture, arts, and science there happen to be around, and to have in force the usual patent and copyright laws to ensure that people do not pirate other people's intellectual or artistic work for their own undeserved profit. However, apart from a brief mention in Article 17(2) of the African Charter, the only treaty provision which reflects this Article of the Universal Declaration is Article 15 of the ESCR Covenant, which adds a paragraph of major importance for all scientists and artists:

'The State Parties to the present Covenant undertake to respect the freedom indispensable for scientific research and creative activity.'

Truly, the sciences and the arts know no frontiers. But this is, so far, the only provision of binding international law which recognizes that fact.

Privacy, honour, and reputation

Article 12 of the Universal Declaration provides that

'No one shall be subjected to arbitrary interference with his privacy, home, family or correspondence, nor to attacks upon his honour and reputation. Everyone has the right to the protection of the law against such interference and attacks.'

For once, the treaties differ widely in the ways in which they transform these propositions into binding state obligations. Article 17 of the CPR Covenant closely follows the wording of the Declaration, only adding the word 'unlawful' twice: once to qualify the attacks, and again as an alternative to the 'arbitrary' interferences. Article 11 of the American Declaration adds dignity to honour and reputation, substitutes 'abusive' for the Covenant's first use of 'unlawful', and uniquely adds a right of public reply to inaccurate or offensive public statements. Article 8 of the European Convention follows quite a different route: without confining the matter to 'arbitrary', 'unlawful', or 'abusive' interferences, it first declares that 'Everyone has the right to respect for his private and family life, his home and his correspondence', but then proceeds to allow interferences *by public authorities*—but not, it seems, by anyone else, such as journalists in search of scandal—with the exercise of that right, in support of the usual legitimating values, to which it adds 'the economic well-being of the country' on this occasion.

The problem is indeed a difficult one, for in our modern technological age many matters which would have been regarded as infringements of the 'liberties of the subject' in the eighteenth century—such as searches and seizures of papers by the state's officials—are perceived in our own time as infringements of privacy, the word 'liberty' being nowadays more narrowly confined to *physical* freedom from arrest, imprisonment, or other restrictions on free movement.

Nor is that all. There are many matters over which I may wish to have my privacy respected—and, in the interests of my dignity, autonomy, and integrity in an ever more complex and bureaucratically regulated world, it is indeed important that this wish should be met whenever it can be. But it cannot always be—as, for example, where I wish to keep private the bombings or robberies I am planning, or the fraud I am perpetrating on the public, or the bribes I am taking, or my dog's attack of rabies, or my own attack of typhoid. As the European Convention rightly recognizes, there are occasions when privacy must give way to the interests of protecting others. This formulation is therefore in fact preferable to the use of words like 'arbitrary', 'unlawful', or 'abusive'; for 'arbitrary' only means wantonly and without regard to any rational rule, and 'unlawfully' is potentially circular, since it could allow a state to perpetrate the most pervasive and unnecessary infringements of privacy, provided only that it had first enacted a sufficiently wide-ranging or flexible law to cover them.

The European Convention, of course, only allows such interferences as are 'in accordance with the law', and 'necessary in a democratic society' in support of its protected values. This has been well illustrated by two cases about telephone tapping. In the *Klass* case from West Germany, the European Court of Human Rights, albeit with some reluctance, upheld the right of a state exposed to vicious attacks by terrorists to tap the telephones of suspects—but only because what the Court called 'this inherently menacing activity' was closely regulated by a German law which provided important safeguards for innocent people. But in the *Malone* case from the United Kingdom, the Court found that the English domestic law on this subject was 'somewhat obscure', and did not indicate with reasonable clarity the scope and manner of exercise of the discretion conferred on the public authorities to tap people's telephones. Accordingly, the 'minimum degree of legal protection to which citizens are entitled under the rule of law in a democratic society' was lacking, and the judgment went against the government.

This particular Article in the European Convention has proved a fruitful source for an expanding field of jurisprudence, being often invoked by complainants as an alternative to other Articles on which they found their main cases. In the course of determining these complaints, the Strasbourg institutions have given wide interpretations to all the principal concepts which this right protects—'private' and 'family' life, 'home', and 'correspondence'—and have developed the right of privacy into an important adjunct for the protection of the other Convention rights, in support of the principle of respect for the dignity, autonomy, independence, and integrity of the individual which underlies them all. The Council of Europe has also adopted a Convention for the Protection of Individuals with Regard to the Automatic Processing of Personal Data, which has put substantial pressures on its member states to enact their own laws for the control of computerized record-keeping, both by public authorities and by private companies.

The state obligation for this right is absolute and immediate, but derogation is allowed in times of war or public emergency.

16
Doing things together

There is very little that Adam could achieve on his own. Almost every activity, whether of work or play, needs the co-operation of others if it is to have any reasonable prospects of success. *Homo sapiens* is a highly co-operative species: indeed, this has been one of the main factors in its biological success. Not only has it learned how to *add* together the strength of individuals, as in a gang all pulling on the same rope, and so able to lift an object many times heavier than any of them; but it has learned how to *multiply* the different skills of different individuals, and so create new things which none of them could have created on their own.

In order that individuals can achieve their objectives, it is therefore essential that they should be free to get together, and organize themselves into groups—whether as families, villages, clubs, societies, partnerships, companies, trade unions, movements, parties, or indeed nations. In such associations lies strength, in far greater measure than the individuals who compose them would be able to deploy on their own. But that very strength can also pose a threat, for if it is directed *against* an individual he would, on his own, be quite powerless to resist it.

Governments are only too well aware of this. In order to enable individuals to further their objectives by associating with each other for *con*structive ends, they must facilitate the formation of such associations. But in order to protect individuals from associations that might pursue *de*structive ends, they must also be able to restrict their activities. The problem is obvious: how does one decide what is constructive and what is destructive, what should be facilitated and what should be restricted—and what should perhaps be forbidden altogether? Obviously, there must be laws against riots and lynchings: the extreme examples of a destructive association. Likewise, there must be laws against organized crime, protection rackets, and fraudulent company promoters—indeed, generally, against conspiracies to achieve unlawful objectives.

But what about political parties, formed in order to oust the present government from power—at the next election, or perhaps even before? Or trade unions, formed in order to force employers to improve the pay and working conditions of their employees, under the threat of strikes which will cut their revenues, and could put them out of business altogether if they do not give in to the workers' demands? Or cartels of businessmen, formed in order to keep up their prices to their customers? Are these—or should they be—unlawful objectives?

Here again lies the mischief. Governments in power have every incentive to reduce the strength of their political opponents, and one sure way of doing this is to prevent them from getting together with each other and organizing the opposition. That is why some countries exile their dissidents to their remote backwoods, and others have 'banning orders' which make it a criminal offence even to be in the presence of more than one other person at a time, let alone to speak to them. And governments may also favour one interest or another in the economic sphere. If they favour the consumer, they may prohibit monopolies and cartels. If they favour the producer, they may prohibit strikes, or even trade unions. And they may do that even if they claim to favour the workers; few countries that call themselves socialist today allow free trade unions.

Freedom of assembly

Clearly, no civilized or humane society can tolerate lynchings or riots. The individual must be free to go about his affairs in the streets and other public places, without fear of being attacked by a hostile crowd, or having his shop smashed or looted, or his house set on fire. But if that individual wishes to protest against something that is happening within his society—whether or not the government has anything to do with it—he must be free to do that too. One of the more effective ways of doing it is by a public demonstration—a mass meeting in a public place, or a march through the streets. Somewhere, therefore, one must draw the line between these two, and the obvious place to draw it is before there is any violence, or threat of violence—that is, so long as the crowd remains peaceful.

And so, Article 20(1) of the Universal Declaration provides that 'Everyone has the right to freedom of *peaceful* assembly...', and three of the relevant treaties repeat this. Article 15 of the

American Declaration for good measure adds 'without arms', but Article 11 of the African Charter for some reason leaves out the word 'peaceful'. Here again, the treaties need to go into greater detail than the Universal Declaration, if they are to work properly as legal texts. And so, as one might expect, they all add the now familiar paragraphs of restriction and limitation, allowing the state parties to restrict the exercise of this right—but only by laws which are necessary, in a democratic society, to protect one or more of the legitimating public interests—public order, public health, public morals, and so on. And the state obligation is absolute and immediate—though again, as one might expect, derogation is allowed in times of war or public emergency, but only 'to the extent strictly required by the exigencies of the situation'.

Freedom of association

The Universal Declaration simply adds 'and association' at the end of the Article in which it declares everyone's right to freedom of peaceful assembly, so treating these two rights or freedoms together. The European Convention, in Article 11, follows suit, but the CPR Covenant, the American Convention, and the African Charter all devote separate Articles to each of them. In fact, however, they make no great distinctions between them. The American Convention (in Article 16(1)) gives some examples of the purposes of association, such as 'ideological, religious, political, economic, labor, social, cultural, sports', but makes it clear that these are not intended to be exhaustive. The African Charter has a conventional restriction and limitation clause for the right of assembly, but none for the right of association: instead, it adds there the cryptic words 'provided that he abides by the law'.

But the Universal Declaration contains one other very important provision here. Doubtless recalling the pressures in totalitarian countries to join the ruling political party, or some of its offshoots, it adds: 'No one may be compelled to belong to an association.' Only the African Charter repeats this, but with the proviso 'Subject to the obligation of solidarity'—as to which, see Chapter 18. The CPR Covenant, and the European and American Conventions, do not.

Trade unions

Individuals who already have some power, political or economic, within their communities do not generally experience much difficulty in forming associations with each other. On the whole, they tend to support their existing social systems, and their governments will therefore have no immediate motive for restricting their freedom to associate. But the position is often different for those who have little or no power of their own—especially the very poor, in the shape of rural or industrial workers in societies in which they are grossly exploited. For them, the need to join together is paramount, as it will often provide the only means of improving their wretched position, by exercising collectively a degree of power in the pursuit of their individual interests which none of them could exercise singly, and which can only be exercised through a high degree of organization, and constant solidarity with each other in the face of oppression.

Trade unions have been the principal form of such associations, and over a period of more than a century they have achieved many remarkable successes for their members, though often at great cost. Indeed, but for them it is unlikely that the pay and conditions of workers, and the arrangements for their training, health, and safety, would have reached anything like their present levels in the developed countries—even if they still remain thoroughly inadequate elsewhere. In the course of that struggle, they have had to face much opposition—not only from the industrial employers and landowners whose economic interests they have opposed, but often also from governments who have aligned themselves with those interests. As a result, although in their beginnings they were concerned only with economic ends, they have often become, by necessity, involved in political matters also—so providing governments with a further motivation for restricting their activities.

All this is reflected in the international code. Article 23(4) of the Universal Declaration provides that 'Everyone has the right to form and to join trade unions for the protection of his interests', and four of the treaties repeat that provision in almost identical words. It is instructive to note that two of them—the CPR Covenant and the European Convention—are treaties that deal with 'civil and political' rights, while the other two—the ESCR Covenant and the European Social Charter—deal with 'econo-

mic, social and cultural' ones. Here then is another right or freedom which cannot be tidily placed in one of these categories
rather than another. (Though the American Convention and the
African Charter do not mention trade unions as such, the general
freedom of association which they protect presumably includes
them as a typical case.)

The ESCR Covenant draws a subtle but important distinction:
it declares a general right to 'form' trade unions, and then adds a
separate right to 'join *the* trade union *of his choice*, subject only
to the rules of the organization concerned'. This makes it clear—
and for some countries it needs to be made clear—that freedom
to join a trade union cannot be confined to a mere freedom
to join the single trade union established and controlled by the
employers, or by the government. Although this distinction is not
made in so many words in the European treaties, they have been
interpreted in the same sense by the Strasbourg institutions, which
have developed a rich jurisprudence on this subject, as well as
on 'the right to organize' and 'the right to bargain collectively',
respectively protected by Articles 5 and 6 of the European Social
Charter, which are based on the provisions of the relevant ILO
Conventions.

In the case of *Young, James and Webster* v. *United Kingdom*, the
European Court of Human Rights had occasion to consider a
converse violation of human rights in relation to trade unions,
namely one inflicted by a trade union itself, with the acquiescence
of the government which had omitted to have in force a law that
might have prevented the violation, or provided a remedy for it.
This was a case about a 'closed shop' in British Railways—that
is, a requirement imposed on an entire industry, by the collective
power of the dominant union in that industry, that only members
of that union were to be employed in it for certain kinds of
work. Accordingly, the individual worker in such a category was
deprived of any choice as to whether or not to join a union at all,
or whether to join one union or another: either he joined the
dominant union, or he could not work in the industry. We have
seen that the Universal Declaration says that 'No one may be
compelled to belong to an association', and that the ESCR
Covenant expressly gives freedom of choice between different
trade unions. But the European Convention, under which this
case came before the Strasbourg Court, does not say either of

these things in so many words. None the less, the Court ruled that an effective compulsion, on a worker already employed, to join a particular trade union under threat of the loss of his livelihood was not compatible with the *freedom* of association which the Convention requires. In failing to have appropriate legislation in force, the government had made itself responsible for the injury suffered by the applicants when their employer dismissed them because of the 'closed shop' agreement with the union—a good example of *Drittwirkung* (see Chapter 9). Accordingly, the judgment went against the government, which had to pay compensation to the applicants and was compelled to get the law appropriately changed. This case furnishes another example of how international human rights law can protect the weak from abuse of power by the strong—even where the strong happen to be an association of the weak, and operate in the private rather than the public sector.

As for the much discussed 'right to strike', only two of the general treaties mention it explicitly. (Two ILO Conventions deal with it in greater detail.) Article 8(1)(d) of the ESCR Covenant submits it to the ambiguous proviso 'that it is exercised in conformity with the laws of the particular country'; and Article 6(4) of the European Social Charter includes it as part of a 'right to collective action'—available, be it noted, to both workers *and* employers 'in cases of conflicts of interests'—but only 'subject to obligations that might arise out of collective agreements previously entered into'.

All the treaties accept that there may have to be restrictions on these rights in the case of the police, the armed forces, and civil servants, though the Committee of Experts in Strasbourg has been vigilant in not giving its approval to such restrictions if they go further than seems essential. As one might expect, the CPR Covenant and the European Convention both add one of their familiar clauses of restriction and limitation. And, again as one might expect, derogation from this group of rights is allowed in times of war or public emergency—except, oddly, under the ESCR Covenant, which has no derogation Article.

17

Democracy and public affairs

'Democracy', 'freedom', and 'respect for human rights' are often used as if they were synonyms for each other. But do they in fact mean the same thing? Is respect for human rights identical with freedom? Can either of them only flourish in a democracy? Does democratic government automatically guarantee freedom, or respect for human rights?

First, let us try to clarify our understanding of the term 'democracy'. We are still apt to use it with some vague connotation of the institutions of Athens around the time of Pericles, or of that memorable phrase of Abraham Lincoln's about 'government of the people, by the people, and for the people'. In fact, neither of these correspond at all accurately with any modern system of *representative* democratic government. Periclean Athens was governed by the entire assembly of its 'citizens', but those citizens constituted only part of the city state's population, the rest being women and slaves without a vote. And Lincoln's memorable phrase at Gettysburg was a splendid piece of rhetoric, but like all rhetoric it was some way from reality, for while the government of the people of the United States may have been conducted *for* them, it was certainly not conducted *by* them, but had for the past eighty-seven years been conducted by their elected representatives—or rather, by the representatives of those of them who were not negro slaves.

Besides, democracy has not always stood in such high esteem as it does today. Indeed, to some of the ancient Athenians it was a term of derision rather than praise, for to them *demos* meant the mob rather than the people, and in their eyes the connotation of democracy was therefore mob rule—as opposed to aristocracy which, literally, meant rule by the good, in the sense of those best fitted to rule by their education, judgment, altruism, nobility of mind, or whatever else was thought desirable.

Despite that, there are places in the world today where representative democracy works very well indeed. But those places are still comparatively few—for, in order to thrive, the democratic plant needs some rather special soil and some well-established roots. It needs a coherent nation with strong shared cultural traditions which will hold individuals and groups together even where their particular interests diverge. It needs the kind of political maturity born of a long common history, preferably including episodes of internal strife from which lessons are learnt that are not too quickly forgotten. It needs a high literacy rate, good media of communication, and comparative prosperity. It is greatly helped by geographic insulation, as by an English Channel, the Alps, or some great oceans. Not all these factors are absolutely essential, but they are highly desirable, and there are still only few places in the world whose soil seems to contain enough of them at the same time.

To return to the original question: even where there is democracy, will it guarantee freedom and respect for human rights? In order to answer that, it may help to look at some quite recent history. Take, for instance, Germany after 1933. It is at least arguable that what came to be called 'the Nazis'—and what called itself at the time the National Socialist German Workers' Party—first came to power in that country by constitutional, and so legitimate, means; and that it therefore represented, at least for some years, the democratically expressed will of the German people. Yet it was the very antithesis of freedom, and of respect for human rights: instead, it was the incarnation of the 'tyranny of the majority'. Conversely, it is at least possible to imagine Voltaire's 'enlightened despot'—a wholly benevolent Prince, not installed by anything even approaching free and fair elections, whose rule is founded on respect for freedom and the rights of his individual subjects. (Within the limits of the *mores* of his time and place, Federigo da Montefeltre, Duke of Urbino in the latter half of the fifteenth century, was one of the rare rulers who came quite close to that image.)

There is here a serious risk of confusion. *In theory*, the three concepts are independent of each other: neither democracy nor freedom is either a necessary or a sufficient condition for respect for human rights. Democracy *could* produce the tyranny of the majority: even under a secret ballot conducted on a basis of universal suffrage, a majority of white, Christian, or socialist voters could elect a government pledged to expel, or even to exterminate, all blacks, Jews, or capitalists. And 'freedom' *could* be interpreted as a licence to oppress, exploit, and deprive your poorest and weakest neighbours, if it is not a freedom limited by just laws.

But all that is only in theory. The practice looks rather different. On the whole, despots are *not* enlightened, but are only too apt to confirm Lord Acton's observation that power tends to corrupt, and that absolute power corrupts absolutely. On the whole, elected representatives are less prone to be corrupted by power, if that entails a real risk that the voters will throw them out of office next time. On the whole, therefore, democracy tends to march with respect for human rights, and respect for human rights tends to march with freedom under the law. But this does not mean that democracy will always, and everywhere, exclude tyranny, for the tyranny of the majority is not just a fantastic nightmare: it *can* happen, and it *has* happened, even in quite recent times. And so democracy is not, by itself, an absolute guarantee either of freedom, or of respect for human rights. That is, it is not a *sufficient* condition for either of these desirable objectives.

Is it then a *necessary* one? In theory, no—but in practice, very largely. It has, of course, some well-known demerits: contests on popularity rather than policies; the temptation, too seldom resisted, to promise the voters more than one can perform; cheap slanging-matches at election times; the cynical trading of principles for votes; short policy time-horizons always constrained by the next election; the built-in bias (admittedly shared by other systems too) in favour of power-hungry personalities avid for the public's adulation. But in a mature democratic system, its inherent merits will heavily outweigh these blemishes: the system of government by representatives of the people, freely and secretly elected by all of them at regular intervals, has a vastly better track record than any other in the promotion of both freedom and respect for human rights, each appropriately tempered by the other.

Here, the mischief is plain enough, and one has only to look around the world to see it in all its grimness: peoples governed by small cliques of men whose main concern seems to be to maintain their power in order to enjoy its fruits for themselves, and who cynically use all available means to that end, including the ruthless oppression and persecution of their opponents—at the expense of the people whose fate they have taken in their charge, and in apparent disregard of those people's interests or wishes.

The will of the people

Which is doubtless why the Universal Declaration says, in Article 21(3), that:

'The will of the people shall be the basis of the authority of government; this will shall be expressed in periodic and genuine elections which shall be by universal and equal suffrage and shall be held by secret vote or by equivalent free voting procedures.'

The first sentence here states the end, and the second the means. Now an election presupposes that some individuals will be chosen as the members of some public institution, and that 'the will of the people' will be expressed by that choice. But what institution is envisaged here? Looking at the Article, one might think it was the 'government'. But this is not the view taken by the treaties: Article 3 of the European Convention's First Protocol, for example, takes it to mean 'the legislature', which is not at all the same thing. (Europe, after all, still has several constitutional monarchies, whose government is at least formally conducted in the name of an individual chosen by heredity, and not by election.) The CPR Covenant (Article 25) and the American Convention (Article 23) leave the question quite open: looking carefully at their language, it remains a mystery who is to be elected to what. And the African Charter has nothing at all to say about 'the will of the people', or about elections.

Taking part in public affairs

The draftsmen of the treaties seem to have exhibited an understandable reluctance not to lay down too specific a set of rules for the governance of all nations, however different their political ideologies, economic systems, or historic or cultural traditions. After all, their concern was with the rights of *individuals*, and they therefore focused their efforts, quite properly, on the rights that those individuals should have in the management of the public affairs of their countries. And in this respect, they had some other precedents to follow, from the two earlier paragraphs of the same Article of the Universal Declaration:

'(1) Everyone has the right to take part in the government of his country, directly or through freely chosen representatives.

(2) Everyone has the right of equal access to public service in his country.'

The CPR Covenant, the American Convention, and the African Charter all follow the second of these precedents, more or less verbatim. But when it comes to the first, only the African Charter (in Article 13(1)) speaks of participating 'in the government of his country': the other two have both modified this to taking part 'in the conduct of public affairs'. And when it comes to elections, they make it clear that every *citizen* has the right both to stand for election and to vote—without any of the forbidden kinds of discrimination, but none the less subject to restrictions of a kind which the Covenant says must not be 'unreasonable', and for which Article 23(2) of the American Convention gives a catalogue of its own. These include, obviously, age, nationality, residence, and mental capacity—and, less obviously to democrats, language, education, criminal convictions, and 'civil capacity'. (The European Convention is silent on all this.) All these are of course absolute and immediate state obligations, but only the American Convention says that no derogation is allowed in times of war or public emergency.

The European Commission of Human Rights has had a fair number of cases arising from the dissatisfaction of people of different political persuasions with the electoral systems of their countries, including attacks (both dismissed) on the bicameral legislatures of Belgium and the United Kingdom—entirely non-elected in the case of the latter. And the Human Rights Committee and the Inter-American Commission have had occasion to condemn a number of political practices which they have found in various countries—including the institution of a Presidency-for-life in Haiti.

So where does all this leave the disputed relationship between democracy, freedom, and respect for human rights? Where the constitutional history of a nation begins with a successful rebellion against oppression, and the concurrent installation of a democratic system of government—as, pre-eminently, in the USA—its people tend to remain permanently imbued with the conviction that the three are inseparable. Even to a modern American, two centuries after those historic events, the proposition that freedom or respect for human rights could be maintained outside a fully democratic system of government is incomprehensible—indeed positively subversive. To him, as to many others raised in a strong democratic tradition, democracy is the only defensible end of all politics, and support for human rights is only one of several desirable means for achieving that end, rather than an end in itself.

Unfortunately, it has been the general experience both of colonization and decolonization that the democratic systems of Westminster, Capitol Hill, and even the Elysée do not always transplant successfully to countries with their own quite different traditions of culture, politics, economics, and the distribution of power—especially when they contain a motley assemblage of different peoples within an artificial set of frontiers originally drawn for them by colonial powers, which they cannot now risk changing. As a result, many of these countries have had to experiment with a variety of very different systems of government, not always to the taste of democrats. Admittedly, some of these experiments have produced appalling tyrannies, and gross violations of human rights. But some others have not: the correlation is by no means complete. It may be possible—though it would undoubtedly be difficult—to preserve human rights even in a one-party state, provided that it can instal appropriate institutions to that end—such as ombudsmen, and an open party structure accessible to all—which will perform the necessary functions that other kinds of checks and balances perform in democratic systems.

What then are the requirements of the international code about all this? On their proper construction, none of the treaties say anything about the precise system of government that any nation must have. True, they speak of genuine periodic elections, universal and equal suffrage, and a secret ballot. But that is only in the context of the right of individuals to take part in them without discrimination. It does not specify what those elections are to be *to*: that might indeed be the legislature, or the executive—but it might also be the council of tribal elders, or the praesidium of the local, regional, or national committee of the nation's single political party.

For the international code of human rights law, the end is the protection of human rights. The means for achieving that end—

including representative democracy, with its excellent track record where it is well established—are optional. What the treaties do require is that, in the conduct of public affairs and in the public service, as in all the other rights which they guarantee, all individuals shall be treated without discrimination. How that is achieved—whether by representative democracy or by any other system—they are content to leave to each nation for itself. It is therefore quite wrong to contend, as some do, that the code insists on imposing 'Western' or 'First World' structures of government on peoples who have different traditions, needs, and preferences of their own in these matters.

However, in just one respect the code does exhibit a subtle bias in favour of democracy, and that is in the area of what is legitimate in the way of limitations and exceptions—which, it will be recalled from Chapter 8, always need to be 'provided by law', and 'necessary' for the protection of one or other of some specified public values. But that word 'necessary' tends to attract the phrase 'in a democratic society'—almost always in the European and American Conventions, and in a few important places even in the UN Covenants: over the right of assembly, the right of association, trade unions, and when it is proper to keep the Press and the public out of the courts. At least for those things, then, the *universal* standard of what is 'necessary' is a democracy.

18

The rights of 'peoples'

So far, we have surveyed the rights of individuals, as they have grown up over the centuries in the struggle for human rights, and are now protected by the international code: first, the rights to be left alone, to live one's life as one pleases without interference by the state or its public authorities, unless one is doing demonstrable harm to others; and second, the rights to call on the state to intervene on one's behalf in order to redress injustices which one suffers without any fault of one's own, especially in the social and economic fields. These rights have recently come to be called 'first-generation' and 'second-generation' rights respectively, though that classification is probably no more useful than any other (see Chapter 8). But now, at the end of this survey, we must turn to look at a new set of rights, which their advocates call 'third-generation' or 'solidarity' rights. Most of these are still emerging concepts (rather than binding rules) in the field of human rights law—a field which is, happily, neither frozen nor set in concrete for all time, but continues to produce new growth.

Apart from being new, what these rights have in common is that it is sometimes difficult to see how they can be vested in, or exercised by, individuals. According to the classical theory, only the rights of human individuals can be 'human' rights; any rights belonging to entities of some other kind (such as states, churches, corporations, trade unions, and so forth) may be highly desirable, accepted, valid, and even enforceable—but, whatever else they may be, they cannot be *human* rights. If anyone then claims that rights like those of assembly and association, including trade union rights, are 'collective' rather than 'individual' rights, the short answer is that the language of the instruments does not support this claim, for they speak in all such instances of 'every-one', or 'every person', as the owner of the right. So, the right of association is a right of *individuals* to associate with other individuals: it is not a right that belongs to associations as sep-arate—and necessarily abstract—entities. In any case, just about every human right or freedom can in practice only be *exercised* in conjunction with other individuals, and there is no need to claim them unless there are other people who seek to deny them. Our allegorical Adam in Chapter 1 would have had no occasion to exercise any of his human rights or freedoms, nor to insist on their protection, until the arrival of Eve, Cain, and Abel, and the subsequent foundation of Adamsville.

Self-determination and liberation

All this seems to make good sense—until one looks at the very first Article of each of the two Covenants. 'All *peoples*', these both declare in identical words, 'have the right of self-determination.'

This language has a familiar ring, at all events to students of international affairs. It goes back to at least the UN Charter of 1945, which also speaks in its very first Article, where it declares the Organization's purposes, of the 'principle of equal rights and self-determination of peoples'. And the precise words of Article 1(1) of both the Covenants are to be found in Article 1 of the Declaration on the Granting of Independence to Colonial Countries and Peoples, adopted by the UN General Assembly in 1960. This provision therefore reflects the policy of de-colonization—one that is not only thoroughly laudable, but has proved immensely successful: today, there are hardly any colonies left in the world, and around two-thirds of the nearly 160 member states of the UN are ex-colonies which have achieved their independence since 1945.

But what kinds of *rights* are these? Since they are found in identical language in *both* Covenants, they are presumably both civil and political, *and* economic, social, and cultural. But are they 'human' rights? To whom do they belong? Against whom are they exercisable? At least that last question is answered in the Covenants themselves, for Article 1 stands alone in what is called Part I, and its third paragraph says that 'The States Parties . . . shall promote the realization of the right of self-determination . . .' Only after that do we come to Part II, where Article 2 imposes the state parties' obligations in respect of the various *individual* rights and freedoms recognized in the substantive Articles that follow in Part III.

Few today would deny that there ought to be a right of self-determination of peoples, or indeed that there is now such a right in international law. But who is it that *has* this right? We know what an individual is: you can see him or her in the street, or in the fields, or in prison, or in court, or in hospital, or in front of the firing-squad. But what is a people? A set of individuals, of course—it cannot be made up of anything else. But which of them? Who are the German, or the Jewish, or the Palestinian, or the Israeli 'people'? Can you be a German if you are a Jew? The question exercised many between 1933 and 1945, and the negative answer given to it by those who were then in power there caused unprecedented suffering, and cost around six million lives. Can you be a Palestinian if you are not an Israeli? That question is still exercising many today, and is meanwhile causing much suffering, and has already cost several thousand lives—and may yet cost far more.

What kind of a question is this, anyway? A real one, to which an answer could be found if only enough research were done on it? Or one of those which arises only from the language we use, and how we use that language to label things, and categorize them in ways that satisfy our love of tidiness—in which case it is unanswerable in the real world, since by changing our definitions we can always change the answer? Wisely perhaps, the Republic of India—with probably more 'peoples' within its national boundaries than any other nation state—has provided its own answer in a reservation made to both the Covenants: the right of self-determination, it declares, applies 'only to the peoples under foreign domination', and not 'to sovereign independent states or to a section of a people or nation—which is the essence of national integrity'.

The rights of 'peoples' raise an even more difficult problem, and in some ways an even more important one. 'It is expedient for us', Caiaphas the High Priest is reported to have said on an occasion that proved more memorable than he was to know, 'that one man should die for the people, and that the whole nation perish not.' Quite understandable, as a sentiment expressed by a senior administrator, charged with the care of an entire 'people' in difficult circumstances. Many of his successors in that profession have expressed it since, and all too many have put it into practice, sometimes at gigantic cost not just to one man, but to very many men and women—and all for the sake of the very 'people' to whom those men and women, and the administrators themselves, belonged. But is not that precisely the sentiment *against* which the entire canon of modern human rights law is meant to provide a protective bulwark? There are few atrocities which a sufficiently ingenious administrator could not excuse with some perfectly tenable 'reason of state': that there should 'perish not' the whole nation (on one occasion earlier this century called *das Reich*), or the one true faith, or the economy, or the pound, or the dollar—or, come to that, the toiling masses. How then can the rights of a 'people' ever form a part of *human* rights—that is, precisely the rights that the individual may invoke *against* the claims of those who exercise power over him, and which they only too often assert in the name of 'the people', or some other abstraction which they hope will legitimate what they do?

To this right of self-determination for peoples, Articles 19 and 20 of the new African Charter will add a few more rights when it comes into force: a right of equality, a right to existence, and a right to liberation, the last of which it expresses in these words:

'Colonized or oppressed peoples shall have the right to free themselves from the bonds of domination by resorting to any means recognized by the international community.'

Perhaps they shall, but this one surely cannot be a 'human' right. In fairness to the draftsmen of the African Charter, they did call it a Charter of Human *and Peoples'* Rights, and these Articles appear as part of a group which deals with the rights of peoples, as opposed to the earlier ones which deal with the rights of individuals. But all these Articles still form part of a single Chapter, headed 'Human and Peoples' Rights'.

Wealth, resources, and development

Having declared the right of self-determination of peoples, the next paragraph of Article 1 of both the Covenants goes on to say that 'All peoples may, for their own ends, freely dispose of their natural wealth and resources . . .', and this is referred to later as an 'inherent right' in Article 47 of the CPR Covenant, and Article 25 of the ESCR Covenant.

Here again, the sentiment is unexceptionable: as the Covenants both go on to say, 'In no case may a people be deprived of its own means of subsistence.' One could hardly maintain that

international law should not recognize such a right—and, through
the entry into force of the Covenants, it now does. But in all their
provisions other than this Article, these Covenants are treaties on
human rights, and it is difficult to see how this right can satisfy
the criteria of that special category of rights, since—excellent
though it is—it cannot belong to any identifiable individuals, nor
be exercisable against any readily identifiable entity.

Having expanded on this 'right to wealth and resources' in its
Article 21, the new African Charter goes on, in its next Article,
to provide that:

'(1) All peoples shall have the right to their economic, social and
cultural development with due regard to their freedom and identity and
in the equal enjoyment of the common heritage of mankind.
(2) States shall have the duty, individually or collectively, to ensure
the exercise of the right to development.'

This new 'right to development' is today one of the great growth
points—and one of the areas of hottest debate—in the field of
international law in general, and international human rights law
in particular. The mischief is clear to anyone who has ever visited
any of the poorer parts of the so-called Third World, in which
the majority of the planet's population lives, and there is no need
to describe here the wretched conditions of poverty, illiteracy,
disease, malnutrition, and often starvation which are endemic
there.

Clearly, the first duty of the governments of those countries
must be to try to do something to alleviate this suffering. But
they have the greatest difficulties, starting from where they are—
especially if the country is one of the 'emergent' ones, having
only recently achieved its independence from colonialism, with
its frontiers drawn by the ex-colonial powers, containing many
disparate 'peoples' with little sense of a common nationhood, no
economic infrastructure, let alone anything even resembling a
self-sufficient economy. It is perfectly understandable, therefore,
that such governments will assign the highest priority to economic
development.

Unfortunately, the pursuit of that desirable objective will be
beset with difficulties of every kind—not least the problem of
local tribes, castes, classes, and religions squabbling amongst
themselves, and offering powerful resistance to giving up old-

established habits, rituals, institutions, and power structures. Impatient governments will then be tempted to impose their development policies on their recalcitrant populations by a variety of means, not all of which will display an appropriate respect for human rights. Land reform and exchange control are one thing, since (as we have seen) the code is not very strong when it comes to the protection of property. But Press censorship, the direction of labour, and the prohibition of trade union activities are another, and unfortunately such measures are only too often apt to lead eventually to the forceful suppression of all dissent, and to end with re-education camps, 'disappearances', and firing-squads—all in the sacred name of development.

The problem, therefore, is how to reconcile development with respect for human rights, and here the key is whether the 'right to development' belongs only to states and to 'peoples', or also to individuals. If it can be expressed as a true *human* right vested in individuals, it can protect them from the ill-conceived ambitions of their rulers. But without that, it cannot. The solution can therefore only lie in the direction of defining *two* rights to development, one vested in individuals and the other in states—or, if one prefers, 'peoples'. If one defines development as a process designed, progressively, to create conditions in which *every* individual can enjoy, exercise, and utilize, under the rule of law, *all* his human rights—whether economic, social, cultural, civil, or political, for it has now long been accepted that these are all indivisible and interdependent—then the *individual's* right to development can be simply defined as his right to participate in, and benefit from, that process without any of the prohibited forms of discrimination. And, once a state can show that *this* is the kind of development it pursues, then it too can have a 'right to development' on the international plane, in the form of a right to call on other states for their help in pursuing its policies—so reflecting on the international plane the principle of non-discrimination which the human rights code already requires on the national one, and making the former depend on observance of the latter.

This is, in effect, the proposal which has recently been put before the international community by the International Commission of Jurists, and one can only hope that it will fall on fertile soil there.

International peace

Article 28 of the Universal Declaration says that

'Everyone is entitled to a social and international order in which the rights and freedoms set forth in this Declaration can be fully realized.'

So indeed they are, but here again it is difficult to see how one can vest a *legal* right to this effect in individuals, exercisable against their own governments, who may not be at all responsible for the international order, whatever power they may have over the social one. In fact, only Article 23 of the African Charter follows—and indeed expands—the broad sweep of this proposition; Article 20 of the CPR Covenant, and Article 13(5) of the American Convention, confine themselves to requiring the prohibition of propaganda for war, and of the advocacy of national, racial, or religious hatred that constitutes incitement to discrimination, hostility, or violence—which is something that governments do in fact have the power to prohibit, albeit at some cost to the freedom of expression which other Articles of the same treaties protect.

The environment

So far, the African Charter is alone in proclaiming this 'third-generation' right, when it says in Article 24 that 'All peoples shall have the right to a general satisfactory environment favourable to their development.' Such a right is indeed important, but here again it is difficult to see how individuals can assert it against states, and so how it can be satisfactorily classified as a *human* right. This is not to say that it should not exist, or that its more precise definition should not be pursued. Perhaps a solution may eventually be found on similar lines to the right to development, with which this right must be closely linked.

Indeed, if any of the new 'third-generation' or 'solidarity' rights are eventually to find their place in the universal canon of human rights, some formulations will have to be devised whereby each of them can be clearly seen to vest in individuals, to be exercisable by individuals, and to impose precise correlative duties on states— so that it can then be interpreted, applied, and enforced accordingly.

Minorities

Article 27 of the CPR Covenant, uniquely, provides as follows:

'In those states in which ethnic, religious or linguistic minorities exist, persons belonging to such minorities shall not be denied the right, in community with the other members of their group, to enjoy their own culture, to profess and practise their own religion, or to use their own language.'

Although the Universal Declaration provides no precedent for this, the provision is of great importance, for it offers a bridge between the rights of individuals and those of 'peoples'. Note that the right is *vested* in 'persons' who are members of the minority group, but that it can only be *exercised* 'in community with' the other members. It is therefore a true human right, notwithstanding that its exercise—like that of so many of the other human rights, such as those of assembly and association—can only be performed in common with others. So, if one likes, it can be viewed as attaching also to the abstract concept of the 'minority' to which all those members belong—but only because it belongs to each of them individually.

In the last analysis, all human rights exist for the benefit of individuals who are weak, and who need protection from oppression, persecution, exploitation, and deprivation by those who are strong. If their weakness derives (as it usually does) from some difference which distinguishes them from the dominant group they will see themselves, and be seen by their oppressors, as a minority, regardless of how many of them there are.

In that sense, therefore, all human rights exist for the protection of minorities. And that thought may provide a fitting conclusion to this book.

Appendix
The governing texts

The texts reprinted here cover only the substance of the nine *general* international human rights instruments, global and regional. The two Declarations are reproduced in full, but only the *substantive* material is reproduced from the treaties—that is, the Preambles and the Articles which spell out the rights, obligations, restrictions, and limitations. The Articles omitted relate largely to the *procedures* for ratification, supervision, etc.

The full texts of these instruments (other than the African Charter), and of many of the specialized ones, may be found in I. Brownlie, *Basic Documents on Human Rights* (2nd edn., Oxford, 1981), and the UN ones are also reproduced in the UN publication *Human Rights: A Compilation of International Instruments* (New York, 1983).

United Nations Charter

We the Peoples of the United Nations determined
to save succeeding generations from the scourge of war, which twice in
our lifetime has brought untold sorrow to mankind, and
to reaffirm faith in fundamental human rights, in the dignity and worth
of the human person, in the equal rights of men and women and of
nations large and small, and
to establish conditions under which justice and respect for the obligations arising from treaties and other sources of international law can
be maintained, and
to promote social progress and better standards of life in larger freedom,

>   *and for these ends*

to practise tolerance and live together in peace with one another as
good neighbours, and
to unite our strength to maintain international peace and security, and
to ensure, by the acceptance of principles and the institution of
methods, that armed force shall not be used, save in the common interest, and
to employ international machinery for the promotion of the economic
and social advancement of all peoples,

>   *have resolved to combine our efforts to accomplish these aims*

Accordingly, our respective Governments, through representatives
assembled in the city of San Francisco, who have exhibited their full
powers found to be in good and due form, have agreed to the present
Charter of the United Nations and do hereby establish an international
organization to be known as the United Nations.

Article 1

The Purposes of the United Nations are:
  1. To maintain international peace and security, and to that end: to
take effective collective measures for the prevention and removal of
threats to the peace, and for the suppression of acts of aggression or
other breaches of the peace, and to bring about by peaceful means, and
in conformity with the principles of justice and international law,
adjustment or settlement of international disputes or situations which
might lead to a breach of the peace;
  2. To develop friendly relations among nations based on respect for
the principle of equal rights and self-determination of peoples, and to
take other appropriate measures to strengthen universal peace;
  3. To achieve international co-operation in solving international
problems of an economic, social, cultural, or humanitarian character,
and in promoting and encouraging respect for human rights and for

fundamental freedoms for all without distinction as to race, sex, language, or religion; and

4. To be a centre for harmonizing the actions of nations in the attainment of these common ends.

. . . .

Article 55

With a view to the creation of conditions of stability and well-being which are necessary for peaceful and friendly relations among nations based on respect for the principle of equal rights and self-determination of peoples, the United Nations shall promote:

a. higher standards of living, full employment, and conditions of economic and social progress and development;

b. solutions of international economic, social, health, and related problems; and international cultural and educational co-operation; and

c. universal respect for, and observance of, human rights and fundamental freedoms for all without distinction as to race, sex, language, or religion.

Article 56

All Members pledge themselves to take joint and separate action in co-operation with the Organization for the achievement of the purposes set forth in Article 55.

. . . .

Universal Declaration of Human Rights

Whereas recognition of the inherent dignity and of the equal and inalienable rights of all members of the human family is the foundation of freedom, justice and peace in the world,

Whereas disregard and contempt for human rights have resulted in barbarous acts which have outraged the conscience of mankind, and the advent of a world in which human beings shall enjoy freedom of speech and belief and freedom from fear and want has been proclaimed as the highest aspiration of the common people,

Whereas it is essential, if man is not to be compelled to have recourse, as a last resort, to rebellion against tyranny and oppression, that human rights should be protected by the rule of law,

Whereas it is essential to promote the development of friendly relations between nations,

Whereas the peoples of the United Nations have in the Charter reaffirmed their faith in fundamental human rights, in the dignity and worth of the human person and in the equal rights of men and women and have determined to promote social progress and better standards of life in larger freedom,

Whereas Member States have pledged themselves to achieve, in cooperation with the United Nations, the promotion of universal respect for and observance of human rights and fundamental freedoms,

Whereas a common understanding of these rights and freedoms is of the greatest importance for the full realization of this pledge,

Now, therefore,

The General Assembly

Proclaims this Universal Declaration of Human Rights as a common standard of achievement for all peoples and all nations, to the end that every individual and every organ of society, keeping this Declaration constantly in mind, shall strive by teaching and education to promote respect for these rights and freedoms and by progressive measures, national and international, to secure their universal and effective recognition and observance, both among the peoples of Member States themselves and among the peoples of territories under their jurisdiction.

Article 1

All human beings are born free and equal in dignity and rights. They are endowed with reason and conscience and should act towards one another in a spirit of brotherhood.

Article 2

Everyone is entitled to all the rights and freedoms set forth in this Declaration, without distinction of any kind, such as race, colour, sex, language, religion, political or other opinion, national or social origin, property, birth or other status.

Furthermore, no distinction shall be made on the basis of the political, jurisdictional or international status of the country or territory to which a person belongs, whether it be independent, trust, non-self-governing or under any other limitation of sovereignty.

Article 3

Everyone has the right to life, liberty and security of person.

Article 4

No one shall be held in slavery or servitude; slavery and the slave trade shall be prohibited in all their forms.

Article 5

No one shall be subjected to torture or to cruel, inhuman or degrading treatment or punishment.

Article 6

Everyone has the right to recognition everywhere as a person before the law.

Article 7

All are equal before the law and are entitled without any discrimination to equal protection of the law. All are entitled to equal protection against any discrimination in violation of this Declaration and against any incitement to such discrimination.

Article 8

Everyone has the right to an effective remedy by the competent national tribunals for acts violating the fundamental rights granted him by the constitution or by law.

Article 9

No one shall be subjected to arbitrary arrest, detention or exile.

Article 10

Everyone is entitled in full equality to a fair and public hearing by an independent and impartial tribunal, in the determination of his rights and obligations and of any criminal charge against him.

Article 11

1. Everyone charged with a penal offence has the right to be presumed innocent until proved guilty according to law in a public trial at which he has had all the guarantees necessary for his defence.

2. No one shall be held guilty of any penal offence on account of any act or omission which did not constitute a penal offence, under national or international law, at the time when it was committed. Nor shall a heavier penalty be imposed than the one that was applicable at the time the penal offence was committed.

Article 12

No one shall be subjected to arbitrary interference with his privacy, family, home or correspondence, nor to attacks upon his honour and reputation. Everyone has the right to the protection of the law against such interference or attacks.

Article 13

1. Everyone has the right to freedom of movement and residence within the borders of each State.

2. Everyone has the right to leave any country, including his own, and to return to his country.

Article 14

1. Everyone has the right to seek and to enjoy in other countries asylum from persecution.

2. This right may not be invoked in the case of prosecutions genuinely arising from non-political crimes or from acts contrary to the purposes and principles of the United Nations.

Article 15

1. Everyone has the right to a nationality.

2. No one shall be arbitrarily deprived of his nationality nor denied the right to change his nationality.

Article 16

1. Men and women of full age, without any limitation due to race, nationality or religion, have the right to marry and to found a family. They are entitled to equal rights as to marriage, during marriage and at its dissolution.

2. Marriage shall be entered into only with the free and full consent of the intending spouses.

3. The family is the natural and fundamental group unit of society and is entitled to protection by society and the State.

Article 17

1. Everyone has the right to own property alone as well as in association with others.

2. No one shall be arbitrarily deprived of his property.

Article 18

Everyone has the right to freedom of thought, conscience and religion; this right includes freedom to change his religion or belief, and freedom, either alone or in community with others and in public or private, to manifest his religion or belief in teaching, practice, worship and observance.

Article 19

Everyone has the right to freedom of opinion and expression; this right includes freedom to hold opinions without interference and to seek, receive and impart information and ideas through any media and regardless of frontiers.

Article 20

1. Everyone has the right to freedom of peaceful assembly and association.

2. No one may be compelled to belong to an association.

Article 21

1. Everyone has the right to take part in the government of his country, directly or through freely chosen representatives.

2. Everyone has the right of equal access to public service in his country.

3. The will of the people shall be the basis of the authority of government; this will shall be expressed in periodic and genuine elections which shall be by universal and equal suffrage and shall be held by secret vote or by equivalent free voting procedures.

Article 22

Everyone, as a member of society, has the right to social security and is entitled to realization, through national effort and international co-operation and in accordance with the organization and resources of each State, of the economic, social and cultural rights indispensable for his dignity and the free development of his personality.

Article 23

1. Everyone has the right to work, to free choice of employment, to just and favourable conditions of work and to protection against unemployment.

2. Everyone, without any discrimination, has the right to equal pay for equal work.

3. Everyone who works has the right to just and favourable remuneration ensuring for himself and his family an existence worthy of human dignity, and supplemented, if necessary, by other means of social protection.

4. Everyone has the right to form and to join trade unions for the protection of his interests.

Article 24

Everyone has the right to rest and leisure, including reasonable limitation of working hours and periodic holidays with pay.

Article 25

1. Everyone has the right to a standard of living adequate for the health and well-being of himself and of his family, including food, clothing, housing and medical care and necessary social services, and the right to security in the event of unemployment, sickness, disability, widowhood, old age or other lack of livelihood in circumstances beyond his control.

2. Motherhood and childhood are entitled to special care and assistance. All children, whether born in or out of wedlock, shall enjoy the same social protection.

Article 26

1. Everyone has the right to education. Education shall be free, at least in the elementary and fundamental stages. Elementary education shall be compulsory. Technical and professional education shall be made generally available and higher education shall be equally accessible to all on the basis of merit.

2. Education shall be directed to the full development of the human personality and to the strengthening of respect for human rights and fundamental freedoms. It shall promote understanding, tolerance and friendship among all nations, racial or religious groups, and shall further the activities of the United Nations for the maintenance of peace.

3. Parents have a prior right to choose the kind of education that shall be given to their children.

Article 27

1. Everyone has the right freely to participate in the cultural life of the community, to enjoy the arts and to share in scientific advancement and its benefits.

2. Everyone has the right to the protection of the moral and material interests resulting from any scientific, literary or artistic production of which he is the author.

Article 28

Everyone is entitled to a social and international order in which the rights and freedoms set forth in this Declaration can be fully realized.

Article 29

1. Everyone has duties to the community in which alone the free and full development of his personality is possible.

2. In the exercise of his rights and freedoms, everyone shall be subject only to such limitations as are determined by law solely for the purpose of securing due recognition and respect for the rights and freedoms of others and of meeting the just requirements of morality, public order and the general welfare in a democratic society.

3. These rights and freedoms may in no case be exercised contrary to the purposes and principles of the United Nations.

Article 30

Nothing in this Declaration may be interpreted as implying for any State, group or person any right to engage in any activity or to perform any act aimed at the destruction of any of the rights and freedoms set forth herein.

International Covenant on Civil and Political Rights

Preamble

The States Parties to the present Covenant,

Considering that, in accordance with the principles proclaimed in the Charter of the United Nations, recognition of the inherent dignity and of the equal and inalienable rights of all members of the human family is the foundation of freedom, justice and peace in the world,

Recognizing that these rights derive from the inherent dignity of the human person,

Recognizing that, in accordance with the Universal Declaration of Human Rights, the ideal of free human beings enjoying civil and political freedom and freedom from fear and want can only be achieved if conditions are created whereby everyone may enjoy his civil and political rights, as well as his economic, social and cultural rights,

Considering the obligation of States under the Charter of the United Nations to promote universal respect for, and observance of, human rights and freedoms,

Realizing that the individual, having duties to other individuals and to the community to which he belongs, is under a responsibility to strive for the promotion and observance of the rights recognized in the present Covenant,

Agree upon the following articles:

PART I

Article 1

1. All peoples have the right of self-determination. By virtue of that right they freely determine their political status and freely pursue their economic, social and cultural development.

2. All peoples may, for their own ends, freely dispose of their natural wealth and resources without prejudice to any obligations arising out of international economic co-operation, based upon the principle of mutual benefit, and international law. In no case may a people be deprived of its own means of subsistence.

3. The States Parties to the present Covenant, including those having responsibility for the administration of Non-Self-Governing and Trust Territories, shall promote the realization of the right of self-determination, and shall respect that right, in conformity with the provisions of the Charter of the United Nations.

PART II

Article 2

1. Each State Party to the present Covenant undertakes to respect and to ensure to all individuals within its territory and subject to its jurisdiction the rights recognized in the present Covenant, without distinction of any kind, such as race, colour, sex, language, religion, political or other opinion, national or social origin, property, birth or other status.

2. Where not already provided for by existing legislative or other measures, each State Party to the present Covenant undertakes to take the necessary steps, in accordance with its constitutional processes and with the provisions of the present Covenant, to adopt such legislative or other measures as may be necessary to give effect to the rights recognized in the present Covenant.

3. Each State Party to the present Covenant undertakes:

(*a*) To ensure that any person whose rights or freedoms as herein recognized are violated shall have an effective remedy, notwithstanding that the violation has been committed by persons acting in an official capacity;

(*b*) To ensure that any person claiming such a remedy shall have his right thereto determined by competent judicial, administrative or legislative authorities, or by any other competent authority provided for by the legal system of the State, and to develop the possibilities of judicial remedy;

(*c*) To ensure that the competent authorities shall enforce such remedies when granted.

Article 3

The State Parties to the present Covenant undertake to ensure the equal right of men and women to the enjoyment of all civil and political rights set forth in the present Covenant.

Article 4

1. In time of public emergency which threatens the life of the nation and the existence of which is officially proclaimed, the States Parties to the present Covenant may take measures derogating from their obligations under the present Covenant to the extent strictly required by the exigencies of the situation, provided that such measures are not inconsistent with their other obligations under international law and do not involve discrimination solely on the ground of race, colour, sex, language, religion or social origin.

2. No derogation from articles 6, 7, 8 (paragraphs 1 and 2), 11, 15, 16 and 18 may be made under this provision.

3. Any State Party to the present Covenant availing itself of the right of derogation shall immediately inform the other States Parties to

the present Covenant, through the intermediary of the Secretary-General of the United Nations, of the provisions from which it has derogated and of the reasons by which it was actuated. A further communication shall be made, through the same intermediary, on the date on which it terminates such derogation.

Article 5

1. Nothing in the present Covenant may be interpreted as implying for any State, group or person any right to engage in any activity or perform any act aimed at the destruction of any of the rights and freedoms recognized herein or at their limitation to a greater extent than is provided for in the present Covenant.

2. There shall be no restriction upon or derogation from any of the fundamental human rights recognized or existing in any State Party to the present Covenant pursuant to law, conventions, regulations or custom on the pretext that the present Covenant does not recognize such rights or that it recognizes them to a lesser extent.

PART III

Article 6

1. Every human being has the inherent right to life. This right shall be protected by law. No one shall be arbitrarily deprived of his life.

2. In countries which have not abolished the death penalty, sentence of death may be imposed only for the most serious crimes in accordance with the law in force at the time of the commission of the crime and not contrary to the provisions of the present Covenant and to the Convention on the Prevention and Punishment of the Crime of Genocide. This penalty can only be carried out pursuant to a final judgement rendered by a competent court.

3. When deprivation of life constitutes the crime of genocide, it is understood that nothing in this article shall authorize any State Party to the present Covenant to derogate in any way from any obligation assumed under the provisions of the Convention on the Prevention and Punishment of the Crime of Genocide.

4. Anyone sentenced to death shall have the right to seek pardon or commutation of the sentence. Amnesty, pardon or commutation of the sentence of death may be granted in all cases.

5. Sentence of death shall not be imposed for crimes committed by persons below eighteen years of age and shall not be carried out on pregnant women.

6. Nothing in this article shall be invoked to delay or to prevent the abolition of capital punishment by any State Party to the present Covenant.

Article 7

No one shall be subjected to torture or to cruel, inhuman or degrading treatment or punishment. In particular, no one shall be subjected without his free consent to medical or scientific experimentation.

Article 8

1. No one shall be held in slavery; slavery and the slave-trade in all their forms shall be prohibited.

2. No one shall be held in servitude.

3. (*a*) No one shall be required to perform forced or compulsory labour;

(*b*) Paragraph 3 (*a*) shall not be held to preclude, in countries where imprisonment with hard labour may be imposed as a punishment for a crime, the performance of hard labour in pursuance of a sentence to such punishment by a competent court;

(*c*) For the purpose of this paragraph the term "forced or compulsory labour" shall not include:

   (i) Any work or service, not referred to in subparagraph (*b*), normally required of a person who is under detention in consequence of a lawful order of a court, or of a person during conditional release from such detention;

  (ii) Any service of a military character and, in countries where conscientious objection is recognized, any national service required by law of conscientious objectors;

 (iii) Any service exacted in cases of emergency or calamity threatening the life or well-being of the community;

 (iv) Any work or service which forms part of normal civil obligations.

Article 9

1. Everyone has the right to liberty and security of person. No one shall be subjected to arbitrary arrest or detention. No one shall be deprived of his liberty except on such grounds and in accordance with such procedure as are established by law.

2. Anyone who is arrested shall be informed, at the time of arrest, of the reasons for his arrest and shall be promptly informed of any charges against him.

3. Anyone arrested or detained on a criminal charge shall be brought promptly before a judge or other officer authorized by law to exercise judicial power and shall be entitled to trial within a reasonable time or to release. It shall not be the general rule that persons awaiting trial shall be detained in custody, but release may be subject to guarantees to appear for trial, at any other stage of the judicial proceedings, and, should occasion arise, for execution of the judgement.

4. Anyone who is deprived of his liberty by arrest or detention shall be entitled to take proceedings before a court, in order that that court

may decide without delay on the lawfulness of his detention and order his release if the detention is not lawful.

5. Anyone who has been the victim of unlawful arrest or detention shall have an enforceable right to compensation.

Article 10

1. All persons deprived of their liberty shall be treated with humanity and with respect for the inherent dignity of the human person.

2. (*a*) Accused persons shall, save in exceptional circumstances, be segregated from convicted persons and shall be subject to separate treatment appropriate to their status as unconvicted persons;

(*b*) Accused juvenile persons shall be separated from adults and brought as speedily as possible for adjudication.

3. The penitentiary system shall comprise treatment of prisoners the essential aim of which shall be their reformation and social rehabilitation. Juvenile offenders shall be segregated from adults and be accorded treatment appropriate to their age and legal status.

Article 11

No one shall be imprisoned merely on the ground of inability to fulfil a contractual obligation.

Article 12

1. Everyone lawfully within the territory of a State shall, within that territory, have the right to liberty of movement and freedom to choose his residence.

2. Everyone shall be free to leave any country, including his own.

3. The above-mentioned rights shall not be subject to any restrictions except those which are provided by law, are necessary to protect national security, public order (*ordre public*), public health or morals or the rights and freedoms of others, and are consistent with the other rights recognized in the present Covenant.

4. No one shall be arbitrarily deprived of the right to enter his own country.

Article 13

An alien lawfully in the territory of a State Party to the present Covenant may be expelled therefrom only in pursuance of a decision reached in accordance with law and shall, except where compelling reasons of national security otherwise require, be allowed to submit the reasons against his expulsion and to have his case reviewed by, and be represented for the purpose before, the competent authority or a person or persons especially designated by the competent authority.

Article 14

1. All persons shall be equal before the courts and tribunals. In the determination of any criminal charge against him, or of his rights and

obligations in a suit at law, everyone shall be entitled to a fair and public hearing by a competent, independent and impartial tribunal established by law. The Press and the public may be excluded from all or part of a trial for reasons of morals, public order (*ordre public*) or national security in a democratic society, or when the interest of the private lives of the parties so requires, or to the extent strictly necessary in the opinion of the court in special circumstances where publicity would prejudice the interests of justice; but any judgement rendered in a criminal case or in a suit at law shall be made public except where the interest of juvenile persons otherwise requires or the proceedings concern matrimonial disputes or the guardianship of children.

2. Everyone charged with a criminal offence shall have the right to be presumed innocent until proved guilty according to law.

3. In the determination of any criminal charge against him, everyone shall be entitled to the following minimum guarantees, in full equality:

(*a*) To be informed promptly and in detail in a language which he understands of the nature and cause of the charge against him;

(*b*) To have adequate time and facilities for the preparation of his defence and to communicate with counsel of his own choosing;

(*c*) To be tried without undue delay;

(*d*) To be tried in his presence, and to defend himself in person or through legal assistance of his own choosing; to be informed, if he does not have legal assistance, of this right; and to have legal assistance assigned to him, in any case where the interests of justice so require, and without payment by him in any such case if he does not have sufficient means to pay for it;

(*e*) To examine, or have examined, the witnesses against him and to obtain the attendance and examination of witnesses on his behalf under the same conditions as witnesses against him;

(*f*) To have the free assistance of an interpreter if he cannot understand or speak the language used in court;

(*g*) Not to be compelled to testify against himself or to confess guilt.

4. In the case of juvenile persons, the procedure shall be such as will take account of their age and the desirability of promoting their rehabilitation.

5. Everyone convicted of a crime shall have the right to his conviction and sentence being reviewed by a higher tribunal according to law.

6. When a person has by a final decision been convicted of a criminal offence and when subsequently his conviction has been reversed or he has been pardoned on the ground that a new or newly discovered fact shows conclusively that there has been a miscarriage of justice, the person who has suffered punishment as a result of such conviction shall be compensated according to law, unless it is proved that the non-disclosure of the unknown fact in time is wholly or partly attributable to him.

7. No one shall be liable to be tried or punished again for an offence for which he has already been finally convicted or acquitted in accordance with the law and penal procedure of each country.

Article 15

1. No one shall be held guilty of any criminal offence on account of any act or omission which did not constitute a criminal offence, under national or international law, at the time when it was committed. Nor shall a heavier penalty be imposed than the one that was applicable at the time when the criminal offence was committed. If, subsequent to the commission of the offence, provision is made by law for the imposition of the lighter penalty, the offender shall benefit thereby.

2. Nothing in this article shall prejudice the trial and punishment of any person for any act or omission which, at the time when it was committed, was criminal according to the general principles of law recognized by the community of nations.

Article 16

Everyone shall have the right to recognition everywhere as a person before the law.

Article 17

1. No one shall be subjected to arbitrary or unlawful interference with his privacy, family, home or correspondence, nor to unlawful attacks on his honour and reputation.

2. Everyone has the right to the protection of the law against such interference or attacks.

Article 18

1. Everyone shall have the right to freedom of thought, conscience and religion. This right shall include freedom to have or to adopt a religion or belief of his choice, and freedom, either individually or in community with others and in public or private, to manifest his religion or belief in worship, observance, practice and teaching.

2. No one shall be subject to coercion which would impair his freedom to have or to adopt a religion or belief of his choice.

3. Freedom to manifest one's religion or beliefs may be subject only to such limitations as are prescribed by law and are necessary to protect public safety, order, health, or morals or the fundamental rights and freedoms of others.

4. The States Parties to the present Covenant undertake to have respect for the liberty of parents and, when applicable, legal guardians to ensure the religious and moral education of their children in conformity with their own convictions.

Article 19

1. Everyone shall have the right to hold opinions without interference.

2. Everyone shall have the right to freedom of expression; this right shall include freedom to seek, receive and impart information and ideas of all kinds, regardless of frontiers, either orally, in writing or in print, in the form of art, or through any other media of his choice.

3. The exercise of the rights provided for in paragraph 2 of this article carries with it special duties and responsibilities. It may therefore be subject to certain restrictions, but these shall only be such as are provided by law and are necessary:

(*a*) For respect of the rights or reputations of others;

(*b*) For the protection of national security or of public order (*ordre public*), or of public health or morals.

Article 20

1. Any propaganda for war shall be prohibited by law.

2. Any advocacy of national, racial or religious hatred that constitutes incitement to discrimination, hostility or violence shall be prohibited by law.

Article 21

The right of peaceful assembly shall be recognized. No restrictions may be placed on the exercise of this right other than those imposed in conformity with the law and which are necessary in a democratic society in the interests of national security or public safety, public order (*ordre public*), the protection of public health or morals or the protection of the rights and freedoms of others.

Article 22

1. Everyone shall have the right to freedom of association with others, including the right to form and join trade unions for the protection of his interests.

2. No restrictions may be placed on the exercise of this right other than those which are prescribed by law and which are necessary in a democratic society in the interests of national security or public safety, public order (*ordre public*), the protection of public health or morals or the protection of the rights and freedoms of others. This article shall not prevent the imposition of lawful restrictions on members of the armed forces and of the police in their exercise of this right.

3. Nothing in this article shall authorize States Parties to the International Labour Organisation Convention of 1948 concerning Freedom of Association and Protection of the Right to Organize to take legislative measures which would prejudice, or to apply the law in such a manner as to prejudice, the guarantees provided for in that Convention.

Article 23

1. The family is the natural and fundamental group unit of society and is entitled to protection by society and the State.

2. The right of men and women of marriageable age to marry and to found a family shall be recognized.

3. No marriage shall be entered into without the free and full consent of the intending spouses.

4. States Parties to the present Covenant shall take appropriate steps to ensure equality of rights and responsibilities of spouses as to marriage, during marriage and at its dissolution. In the case of dissolution, provision shall be made for the necessary protection of any children.

Article 24

1. Every child shall have, without any discrimination as to race, colour, sex, language, religion, national or social origin, property or birth, the right to such measures of protection as are required by his status as a minor, on the part of his family, society and the State.

2. Every child shall be registered immediately after birth and shall have a name.

3. Every child has the right to acquire a nationality.

Article 25

Every citizen shall have the right and the opportunity, without any of the distinctions mentioned in article 2 and without unreasonable restrictions:

(*a*) To take part in the conduct of public affairs, directly or through freely chosen representatives;

(*b*) To vote and to be elected at genuine periodic elections which shall be by universal and equal suffrage and shall be held by secret ballot, guaranteeing the free expression of the will of the electors;

(*c*) To have access, on general terms of equality, to public service in his country.

Article 26

All persons are equal before the law and are entitled without any discrimination to the equal protection of the law. In this respect, the law shall prohibit any discrimination and guarantee to all persons equal and effective protection against discrimination on any ground such as race, colour, sex, language, religion, political or other opinion, national or social origin, property, birth or other status.

Article 27

In those States in which ethnic, religious or linguistic minorities exist, persons belonging to such minorities shall not be denied the right, in community with the other members of their group, to enjoy their own culture, to profess and practise their own religion, or to use their own language.

Article 47

Nothing in the present Covenant shall be interpreted as impairing the inherent right of all peoples to enjoy and utilize fully and freely their natural wealth and resources.

International Covenant on Economic, Social and Cultural Rights

PREAMBLE

The States Parties to the present Covenant,

Considering that, in accordance with the principles proclaimed in the Charter of the United Nations, recognition of the inherent dignity and of the equal and inalienable rights of all members of the human family is the foundation of freedom, justice and peace in the world,

Recognizing that these rights derive from the inherent dignity of the human person,

Recognizing that, in accordance with the Universal Declaration of Human Rights, the ideal of free human beings enjoying freedom from fear and want can only be achieved if conditions are created whereby everyone may enjoy his economic, social and cultural rights, as well as his civil and political rights,

Considering the obligation of States under the Charter of the United Nations to promote universal respect for, and observance of, human rights and freedoms,

Realizing that the individual, having duties to other individuals and to the community to which he belongs, is under a responsibility to strive for the promotion and observance of the rights recognized in the present Covenant,

Agree upon the following articles:

PART I

Article 1

1. All peoples have the right of self-determination. By virtue of that right they freely determine their political status and freely pursue their economic, social and cultural development.

2. All peoples may, for their own ends, freely dispose of their natural wealth and resources without prejudice to any obligations arising out of international economic co-operation, based upon the principle of mutual benefit, and international law. In no case may a people be deprived of its own means of subsistence.

3. The States Parties to the present Covenant, including those having responsibility for the administration of Non-Self-Governing and Trust Territories, shall promote the realization of the right of self-determination, and shall respect that right, in conformity with the provisions of the Charter of the United Nations.

Part II

Article 2

1. Each State Party to the present Covenant undertakes to take steps, individually and through international assistance and co-operation, especially economic and technical, to the maximum of its available resources, with a view to achieving progressively the full realization of the rights recognized in the present Covenant by all appropriate means, including particularly the adoption of legislative measures.

2. The States Parties to the present Covenant undertake to guarantee that the rights enunciated in the present Covenant will be exercised without discrimination of any kind as to race, colour, sex, language, religion, political or other opinion, national or social origin, property, birth or other status.

3. Developing countries, with due regard to human rights and their national economy, may determine to what extent they would guarantee the economic rights recognized in the present Covenant to non-nationals.

Article 3

The States Parties to the present Covenant undertake to ensure the equal right of men and women to the enjoyment of all economic, social and cultural rights set forth in the present Covenant.

Article 4

The States Parties to the present Covenant recognize that, in the enjoyment of those rights provided by the State in conformity with the present Covenant, the State may subject such rights only to such limitations as are determined by law only in so far as this may be compatible with the nature of these rights and solely for the purpose of promoting the general welfare in a democratic society.

Article 5

1. Nothing in the present Covenant may be interpreted as implying for any State, group or person any right to engage in any activity or to perform any act aimed at the destruction of any of the rights or freedoms recognized herein, or at their limitation to a greater extent than is provided for in the present Covenant.

2. No restriction upon or derogation from any of the fundamental human rights recognized or existing in any country in virtue of law, conventions, regulations or custom shall be admitted on the pretext that the present Covenant does not recognize such rights or that it recognizes them to a lesser extent.

Part III

Article 6

1. The States Parties to the present Covenant recognize the right to work, which includes the right of everyone to the opportunity to gain his living by work which he freely chooses or accepts, and will take appropriate steps to safeguard this right.

2. The steps to be taken by a State Party to the present Covenant to achieve the full realization of this right shall include technical and vocational guidance and training programmes, policies and techniques to achieve steady economic, social and cultural development and full and productive employment under conditions safeguarding fundamental political and economic freedoms to the individual.

Article 7

The States Parties to the present Covenant recognize the right of everyone to the enjoyment of just and favourable conditions of work which ensure, in particular:

(*a*) Remuneration which provides all workers, as a minimum, with:

   (i) Fair wages and equal remuneration for work of equal value without distinction of any kind, in particular women being guaranteed conditions of work not inferior to those enjoyed by men, with equal pay for equal work;

 (ii) A decent living for themselves and their families in accordance with the provisions of the present Covenant;

(*b*) Safe and healthy working conditions;

(*c*) Equal opportunity for everyone to be promoted in his employment to an appropriate higher level, subject to no considerations other than those of seniority and competence;

(*d*) Rest, leisure and reasonable limitation of working hours and periodic holidays with pay, as well as remuneration for public holidays.

Article 8

1. The States Parties to the present Covenant undertake to ensure:

(*a*) The right of everyone to form trade unions and join the trade union of his choice, subject only to the rules of the organization concerned, for the promotion and protection of his economic and social interests. No restrictions may be placed on the exercise of this right other than those prescribed by law and which are necessary in a democratic society in the interests of national security or public order or for the protection of the rights and freedoms of others;

(*b*) The right of trade unions to establish national federations or confederations and the right of the latter to form or join international trade-union organizations;

(*c*) The right of trade unions to function freely subject to no limitations other than those prescribed by law and which are necessary in a democratic society in the interests of national security or public order or for the protection of the rights and freedoms of others;

(*d*) The right to strike, provided that it is exercised in conformity with the laws of the particular country.

2. This article shall not prevent the imposition of lawful restrictions on the exercise of these rights by members of the armed forces or of the police or of the administration of the State.

3. Nothing in this article shall authorize States Parties to the International Labour Organisation Convention of 1948 concerning Freedom of Association and Protection of the Right to Organize to take legislative measures which would prejudice, or apply the law in such a manner as would prejudice, the guarantees provided for in that Convention.

Article 9

The States Parties to the present Covenant recognize the right of everyone to social security, including social insurance.

Article 10

The States Parties to the present Covenant recognize that:

1. The widest possible protection and assistance should be accorded to the family, which is the natural and fundamental group unit of society, particularly for its establishment and while it is responsible for the care and education of dependent children. Marriage must be entered into with the free consent of the intending spouses.

2. Special protection should be accorded to mothers during a reasonable period before and after childbirth. During such period working mothers should be accorded paid leave or leave with adequate social security benefits.

3. Special measures of protection and assistance should be taken on behalf of all children and young persons without any discrimination for reasons of parentage or other conditions. Children and young persons should be protected from economic and social exploitation. Their employment in work harmful to their morals or health or dangerous to life or likely to hamper their normal development should be punishable by law. States should also set age limits below which the paid employment of child labour should be prohibited and punishable by law.

Article 11

1. The States Parties to the present Covenant recognize the right of everyone to an adequate standard of living for himself and his family, including adequate food, clothing and housing, and to the continuous improvement of living conditions. The States Parties will take appropriate steps to ensure the realization of this right, recognizing to this effect the essential importance of international co-operation based on free consent.

2. The States Parties to the present Covenant, recognizing the fundamental right of everyone to be free from hunger, shall take, individually and through international co-operation, the measures, including specific programmes, which are needed:

(*a*) To improve methods of production, conservation and distribution of food by making full use of technical and scientific knowledge, by disseminating knowledge of the principles of nutrition and by developing or reforming agrarian systems in such a way as to achieve the most efficient development and utilization of natural resources;

(*b*) Taking into account the problems of both food-importing and food-exporting countries, to ensure an equitable distribution of world food supplies in relation to need.

Article 12

1. The States Parties to the present Covenant recognize the right of everyone to the enjoyment of the highest attainable standard of physical and mental health.

2. The steps to be taken by the States Parties to the present Covenant to achieve the full realization of this right shall include those necessary for:

(*a*) The provision for the reduction of the stillbirth-rate and of infant mortality and for the healthy development of the child;

(*b*) The improvement of all aspects of environmental and industrial hygiene;

(*c*) The prevention, treatment and control of epidemic, endemic, occupational and other diseases;

(*d*) The creation of conditions which would assure to all medical service and medical attention in the event of sickness.

Article 13

1. The States Parties to the present Covenant recognize the right of everyone to education. They agree that education shall be directed to the full development of the human personality and the sense of its dignity, and shall strengthen the respect for human rights and fundamental freedoms. They further agree that education shall enable all persons to participate effectively in a free society, promote understanding, tolerance and friendship among all nations and all racial, ethnic or religious groups, and further the activities of the United Nations for the maintenance of peace.

2. The States Parties to the present Covenant recognize that, with a view to achieving the full realization of this right:

(*a*) Primary education shall be compulsory and available free to all;

(*b*) Secondary education in its different forms, including technical and vocational secondary education, shall be made generally available and accessible to all by every appropriate means, and in particular by the progressive introduction of free education;

(*c*) Higher education shall be made equally accessible to all, on the basis of capacity, by every appropriate means, and in particular by the progressive introduction of free education;

(*d*) Fundamental education shall be encouraged or intensified as far as possible for those persons who have not received or completed the whole period of their primary education;

(*e*) The development of a system of schools at all levels shall be actively pursued, an adequate fellowship system shall be established, and the material conditions of teaching staff shall be continuously improved.

3. The States Parties to the present Covenant undertake to have respect for the liberty of parents and, when applicable, legal guardians to choose for their children schools, other than those established by the public authorities, which conform to such minimum educational standards as may be laid down or approved by the State and to ensure the religious and moral education of their children in conformity with their own convictions.

4. No part of this article shall be construed so as to interfere with the liberty of individuals and bodies to establish and direct educational institutions, subject always to the observance of the principles set forth in paragraph 1 of this article and to the requirement that the education given in such institutions shall conform to such minimum standards as may be laid down by the State.

Article 14

Each State Party to the present Covenant which, at the time of becoming a Party, has not been able to secure in its metropolitan territory or other territories under its jurisdiction compulsory primary education, free of charge, undertakes, within two years, to work out and adopt a detailed plan of action for the progressive implementation, within a reasonable number of years, to be fixed in the plan, of the principle of compulsory education free of charge for all.

Article 15

1. The States Parties to the present Covenant recognize the right of everyone:

(*a*) To take part in cultural life;

(*b*) To enjoy the benefits of scientific progress and its applications;

(*c*) To benefit from the protection of the moral and material interests resulting from any scientific, literary or artistic production of which he is the author.

2. The steps to be taken by the States Parties to the present Covenant to achieve the full realization of this right shall include those necessary for the conservation, the development and the diffusion of science and culture.

3. The States Parties to the present Covenant undertake to respect the freedom indispensable for scientific research and creative activity.

4. The States Parties to the present Covenant recognize the benefits to be derived from the encouragement and development of international contacts and co-operation in the scientific and cultural fields.

.   .   .   .

Article 25

Nothing in the present Covenant shall be interpreted as impairing the inherent rights of all peoples to enjoy and utilize fully and freely their natural wealth and resources.

.   .   .   .

European Convention for the Protection of Human Rights and Fundamental Freedoms

The Governments signatory hereto, being Members of the Council of Europe,

Considering the Universal Declaration of Human Rights proclaimed by the General Assembly of the United Nations on 10 December 1948;

Considering that this Declaration aims at securing the universal and effective recognition and observance of the Rights therein declared;

Considering that the aim of the Council of Europe is the achievement of greater unity between its Members and that one of the methods by which that aim is to be pursued is the maintenance and further realization of Human Rights and Fundamental Freedoms;

Reaffirming their profound belief in those Fundamental Freedoms which are the foundation of justice and peace in the world and are best maintained on the one hand by an effective political democracy and on the other by a common understanding and observance of the Human Rights upon which they depend;

Being resolved, as the Governments of European countries which are likeminded and have a common heritage of political traditions, ideals, freedom and the rule of law to take the first steps for the collective enforcement of certain of the Rights stated in the Universal Declaration;

Have agreed as follows:

Article 1

The High Contracting Parties shall secure to everyone within their jurisdiction the rights and freedoms defined in Section I of this Convention.

SECTION I

Article 2

1. Everyone's right to life shall be protected by law. No one shall be deprived of his life intentionally save in the execution of a sentence of a court following his conviction of a crime for which this penalty is provided by law.

2. Deprivation of life shall not be regarded as inflicted in contravention of this Article when it results from the use of force which is no more than absolutely necessary:

   (*a*) in defence of any person from unlawful violence;
   (*b*) in order to effect a lawful arrest or to prevent the escape of a person lawfully detained;
   (*c*) in action lawfully taken for the purpose of quelling a riot or insurrection.

Article 3

No one shall be subjected to torture or to inhuman or degrading treatment or punishment.

Article 4

1. No one shall be held in slavery or servitude.
2. No one shall be required to perform forced or compulsory labour.
3. For the purpose of this Article the term 'forced or compulsory labour' shall not include:
   (*a*) any work required to be done in the ordinary course of detention imposed according to the provisions of Article 5 of this Convention or during conditional release from such detention;
   (*b*) any service of a military character or, in case of conscientious objectors in countries where they are recognized, service exacted instead of compulsory military service;
   (*c*) any service exacted in case of an emergency or calamity threatening the life or well-being of the community;
   (*d*) any work or service which forms part of normal civic obligations.

Article 5

1. Everyone has the right to liberty and security of person.
   No one shall be deprived of his liberty save in the following cases and in accordance with a procedure prescribed by law;
   (*a*) the lawful detention of a person after conviction by a competent court;
   (*b*) the lawful arrest or detention of a person for non-compliance with the lawful order of a court or in order to secure the fulfilment of any obligation prescribed by law;
   (*c*) the lawful arrest or detention of a person effected for the purpose of bringing him before the competent legal authority on reasonable suspicion of having committed an offence or when it is reasonably considered necessary to prevent his committing an offence or fleeing after having done so;
   (*d*) the detention of a minor by lawful order for the purpose of educational supervision or his lawful detention for the purpose of bringing him before the competent legal authority;
   (*e*) the lawful detention of persons for the prevention of the spreading of infectious diseases, of persons of unsound mind, alcoholics or drug addicts, or vagrants;
   (*f*) the lawful arrest or detention of a person to prevent his effecting an unauthorized entry into the country or of a person against whom action is being taken with a view to deportation or extradition.

2. Everyone who is arrested shall be informed promptly, in a language which he understands, of the reasons for his arrest and of any charge against him.

3. Everyone arrested or detained in accordance with the provisions of paragraph 1 (*c*) of this Article shall be brought promptly before a judge or other officer authorized by law to exercise judicial power and shall be entitled to trial within a reasonable time or to release pending trial. Release may be conditioned by guarantees to appear for trial.

4. Everyone who is deprived of his liberty by arrest or detention shall be entitled to take proceedings by which the lawfulness of his detention shall be decided speedily by a court and his release ordered if the detention is not lawful.

5. Everyone who has been the victim of arrest or detention in contravention of the provisions of this Article shall have an enforceable right to compensation.

Article 6

1. In the determination of his civil rights and obligations or of any criminal charge against him, everyone is entitled to a fair and public hearing within a reasonable time by an independent and impartial tribunal established by law. Judgement shall be pronounced publicly but the press and public may be excluded from all or part of the trial in the interest of morals, public order or national security in a democratic society, where the interest of juveniles or the protection of the private life of the parties so require, or to the extent strictly necessary in the opinion of the court in special circumstances where publicity would prejudice the interests of justice.

2. Everyone charged with a criminal offence shall be presumed innocent until proved guilty according to law.

3. Everyone charged with a criminal offence has the following minimum rights:

- (*a*) to be informed promptly, in a language which he understands and in detail, of the nature and cause of the accusation against him;
- (*b*) to have adequate time and facilities for the preparation of his defence;
- (*c*) to defend himself in person or through legal assistance of his own choosing or, if he has not sufficient means to pay for legal assistance, to be given it free when the interests of justice so require;
- (*d*) to examine or have examined witnesses against him and to obtain the attendance and examination of witnesses on his behalf under the same conditions as witnesses against him;
- (*e*) to have the free assistance of an interpreter if he cannot understand or speak the language used in court.

Article 7

1. No one shall be held guilty of any criminal offence on account of any act or omission which did not constitute a criminal offence under national or international law at the time when it was committed. Nor shall a heavier penalty be imposed than the one that was applicable at the time the criminal offence was committed.

2. This Article shall not prejudice the trial and punishment of any person for any act or omission which, at the time when it was committed, was criminal according to the general principles of law recognized by civilized nations.

Article 8

1. Everyone has the right to respect for his private and family life, his home and his correspondence.

2. There shall be no interference by a public authority with the exercise of this right except such as is in accordance with the law and is necessary in a democratic society in the interests of national security, public safety or the economic well-being of the country, for the prevention of disorder or crime, for the protection of health or morals, or for the protection of the rights and freedoms of others.

Article 9

1. Everyone has the right to freedom of thought, conscience and religion; this right includes freedom to change his religion or belief, and freedom, either alone or in community with others and in public or private, to manifest his religion or belief, in worship, teaching, practice and observance.

2. Freedom to manifest one's religion or beliefs shall be subject only to such limitations as are prescribed by law and are necessary in a democratic society in the interests of public safety, for the protection of public order, health or morals, or for the protection of the rights and freedoms of others.

Article 10

1. Everyone has the right to freedom of expression. This right shall include freedom to hold opinions and to receive and impart information and ideas without interference by public authority and regardless of frontiers. This Article shall not prevent States from requiring the licensing of broadcasting, television or cinema enterprises.

2. The exercise of these freedoms, since it carries with it duties and responsibilities, may be subject to such formalities, conditions, restrictions or penalties as are prescribed by law and are necessary in a democratic society in the interests of national security, territorial integrity or public safety, for the prevention of disorder or crime, for the protection of health or morals, for the protection of the reputation or

rights of others, for preventing the disclosure of information received in confidence, or for maintaining the authority and impartiality of the judiciary.

Article 11

1. Everyone has the right to freedom of peaceful assembly and to freedom of association with others, including the right to form and to join trade unions for the protection of his interests.
2. No restrictions shall be placed on the exercise of these rights other than such as are prescribed by law and are necessary in a democratic society in the interests of national security or public safety, for the prevention of disorder or crime, for the protection of health or morals or for the protection of the rights and freedoms of others. This Article shall not prevent the imposition of lawful restrictions on the exercise of these rights by members of the armed forces, of the police or of the administration of the State.

Article 12

Men and women of marriageable age have the right to marry and to found a family, according to the national laws governing the exercise of this right.

Article 13

Everyone whose rights and freedoms as set forth in this Convention are violated shall have an effective remedy before a national authority notwithstanding that the violation has been committed by persons acting in an official capacity.

Article 14

The enjoyment of the rights and freedoms set forth in this Convention shall be secured without discrimination on any ground such as sex, race, colour, language, religion, political or other opinion, national or social origin, association with a national minority, property, birth or other status.

Article 15

1. In time of war or other public emergency threatening the life of the nation any High Contracting Party may take measures derogating from its obligations under this Convention to the extent strictly required by the exigencies of the situation, provided that such measures are not inconsistent with its other obligations under international law.
2. No derogation from Article 2, except in respect of deaths resulting from lawful acts of war, or from Articles 3, 4 (paragraph 1) and 7 shall be made under this provision.
3. Any High Contracting Party availing itself of this right of derogation shall keep the Secretary-General of the Council of Europe fully

informed of the measures which it has taken and the reasons therefor. It shall also inform the Secretary-General of the Council of Europe when such measures have ceased to operate and the provisions of the Convention are again being fully executed.

Article 16

Nothing in Articles 10, 11, and 14 shall be regarded as preventing the High Contracting Parties from imposing restrictions on the political activity of aliens.

Article 17

Nothing in this Convention may be interpreted as implying for any State, group or person any right to engage in any activity or perform any act aimed at the destruction of any of the rights and freedoms set forth herein or at their limitation to a greater extent than is provided for in the Convention.

Article 18

The restrictions permitted under this Convention to the said rights and freedoms shall not be applied for any purpose other than those for which they have been prescribed.

. . . .

PROTOCOL 1—ENFORCEMENT OF CERTAIN RIGHTS AND FREEDOMS NOT INCLUDED IN SECTION I OF THE CONVENTION

The Governments signatory hereto, being Members of the Council of Europe,

Being resolved to take steps to ensure the collective enforcement of certain rights and freedoms other than those already included in Section I of the Convention for the Protection of Human Rights and Fundamental Freedoms signed at Rome on 4th November, 1950 (hereinafter referred to as 'the Convention'),

Have agreed as follows:

Article 1

Every natural or legal person is entitled to the peaceful enjoyment of his possessions. No one shall be deprived of his possessions except in the public interest and subject to the conditions provided for by law and by the general principles of international law.

The preceding provisions shall not, however, in any way impair the right of a State to enforce such laws as it deems necessary to control the use of property in accordance with the general interest or to secure the payment of taxes or other contributions or penalties.

Article 2

No person shall be denied the right to education. In the exercise of any functions which it assumes in relation to education and to teaching, the State shall respect the right of parents to ensure such education and teaching in conformity with their own religious and philosophical convictions.

Article 3

The High Contracting Parties undertake to hold free elections at reasonable intervals by secret ballot, under conditions which will ensure the free expression of the opinion of the people in the choice of the legislature.

. . . .

PROTOCOL 4—PROTECTING CERTAIN ADDITIONAL RIGHTS

The Governments signatory hereto, being Members of the Council of Europe,

Being resolved to take steps to ensure the collective enforcement of certain rights and freedoms other than those already included in Section I of the Convention for the Protection of Human Rights and Fundamental Freedoms signed at Rome on 4 November 1950 (hereinafter referred to as 'the Convention') and in Articles 1 to 3 of the First Protocol to the Convention, signed at Paris on 20 March 1952,

Have agreed as follows:

Article 1

No one shall be deprived of his liberty merely on the ground of inability to fulfil a contractual obligation.

Article 2

1. Everyone lawfully within the territory of a State shall, within that territory, have the right to liberty of movement and freedom to choose his residence.
2. Everyone shall be free to leave any country, including his own.
3. No restrictions shall be placed on the exercise of these rights other than such as are in accordance with law and are necessary in a democratic society in the interests of national security or public safety, for the maintenance of 'ordre public', for the prevention of crime or for the protection of the rights and freedoms of others.
4. The rights set forth in paragraph 1 may also be subject, in particular areas, to restrictions imposed in accordance with law and justified by the public interest in a democratic society.

Article 3

1. No one shall be expelled, by means either of an individual or of a collective measure, from the territory of the State of which he is a national.

2. No one shall be deprived of the right to enter the territory of the State of which he is a national.

Article 4

Collective expulsion of aliens is prohibited.

European Social Charter

The Governments signatory hereto, being Members of the Council of Europe,

Considering that the aim of the Council of Europe is the achievement of greater unity between its Members for the purpose of safeguarding and realizing the ideals and principles which are their common heritage and of facilitating their economic and social progress, in particular by the maintenance and further realization of human rights and fundamental freedoms;

Considering that in the European Convention for the Protection of Human Rights and Fundamental Freedoms signed at Rome on 4th November 1950, and the Protocol thereto signed at Paris on 20th March 1952, the member States of the Council of Europe agreed to secure to their populations the civil and political rights and freedoms therein specified;

Considering that the enjoyment of social rights should be secured without discrimination on grounds of race, colour, sex, religion, political opinion, national extraction or social origin;

Being resolved to make every effort in common to improve the standard of living and to promote the social well-being of both their urban and rural populations by means of appropriate institutions and action,

Have agreed as follows:

PART I

The Contracting Parties accept as the aim of their policy, to be pursued by all appropriate means, both national and international in character, the attainment of conditions in which the following rights and principles may be effectively realized:

(1) Everyone shall have the opportunity to earn his living in an occupation freely entered upon.

(2) All workers have the right to just conditions of work.

(3) All workers have the right to safe and healthy working conditions.

(4) All workers have the right to a fair remuneration sufficient for a decent standard of living for themselves and their families.

(5) All workers and employers have the right to freedom of association in national or international organizations for the protection of their economic and social interests.

(6) All workers and employers have the right to bargain collectively.

(7) Children and young persons have the right to a special protec-

tion against the physical and moral hazards to which they are exposed.

(8) Employed women, in case of maternity, and other employed women as appropriate, have the right to a special protection in their work.

(9) Everyone has the right to appropriate facilities for vocational guidance with a view to helping him choose an occupation suited to his personal aptitude and interests.

(10) Everyone has the right to appropriate facilities for vocational training.

(11) Everyone has the right to benefit from any measures enabling him to enjoy the highest possible standard of health attainable.

(12) All workers and their dependants have the right to social security.

(13) Anyone without adequate resources has the right to social and medical assistance.

(14) Everyone has the right to benefit from social welfare services.

(15) Disabled persons have the right to vocational training, rehabilitation and resettlement, whatever the origin and nature of their disability.

(16) The family as a fundamental unit of society has the right to appropriate social, legal and economic protection to ensure its full development.

(17) Mothers and children, irrespective of marital status and family relations, have the right to appropriate social and economic protection.

(18) The nationals of any one of the Contracting Parties have the right to engage in any gainful occupation in the territory of any one of the others on a footing of equality with the nationals of the latter, subject to restrictions based on cogent economic or social reasons.

(19) Migrant workers who are nationals of a Contracting Party and their families have the right to protection and assistance in the territory of any other Contracting Party.

Part II

The Contracting Parties undertake, as provided for in Part III, to consider themselves bound by the obligations laid down in the following Articles and paragraphs.

Article 1—The Right to Work

With a view to ensuring the effective exercise of the right to work, the Contracting Parties undertake:

(1) to accept as one of their primary aims and responsibilities the achievement and maintenance of as high and stable a level of

employment as possible, with a view to the attainment of full employment;

(2) to protect effectively the right of the worker to earn his living in an occupation freely entered upon;

(3) to establish or maintain free employment services for all workers;

(4) to provide or promote appropriate vocational guidance, training and rehabilitation.

Article 2—The Right to Just Conditions of Work

With a view to ensuring the effective exercise of the right to just conditions of work, the Contracting Parties undertake:

(1) to provide for reasonable daily and weekly working hours, the working week to be progressively reduced to the extent that the increase of productivity and other relevant factors permit;

(2) to provide for public holidays with pay;

(3) to provide for a minimum of two weeks' annual holiday with pay;

(4) to provide for additional paid holidays or reduced working hours for workers engaged in dangerous or unhealthy occupations as prescribed;

(5) to ensure a weekly rest period which shall, as far as possible, coincide with the day recognized by tradition or custom in the country or region concerned as a day of rest.

Article 3—The Right to Safe and Healthy Working Conditions

With a view to ensuring the effective exercise of the right to safe and healthy working conditons, the Contracting Parties undertake:

(1) to issue safety and health regulations;

(2) to provide for the enforcement of such regulations by measures of supervision;

(3) to consult, as appropriate, employers' and workers' organizations on measures intended to improve industrial safety and health.

Article 4—The Right to a Fair Remuneration

With a view to ensuring the effective exercise of the right to a fair remuneration, the Contracting Parties undertake:

(1) to recognize the right of workers to a remuneration such as will give them and their families a decent standard of living;

(2) to recognize the right of workers to an increased rate of remuneration for overtime work, subject to exceptions in particular cases;

(3) to recognize the right of men and women workers to equal pay for work of equal value;

(4) to recognize the right of all workers to a reasonable period of notice for termination of employment;

(5) to permit deductions from wages only under conditions and to the extent prescribed by national laws or regulations or fixed by collective agreements or arbitration awards.

The exercise of these rights shall be achieved by freely concluded collective agreements, by statutory wage-fixing machinery, or by other means appropriate to national conditions.

Article 5—The Right to Organize

With a view to ensuring or promoting the freedom of workers and employers to form local, national or international organizations for the protection of their economic and social interests and to join those organizations, the Contracting Parties undertake that national law shall not be such as to impair, nor shall it be so applied as to impair, this freedom. The extent to which the guarantees provided for in this Article shall apply to the police shall be determined by national laws or regulations. The principle governing the application to the members of the armed forces of these guarantees and the extent to which they shall apply to persons in this category shall equally be determined by national laws or regulations.

Article 6—The Right to Bargain Collectively

With a view to ensuring the effective exercise of the right to bargain collectively, the Contracting Parties undertake:

(1) to promote joint consultation between workers and employers;

(2) to promote, where necessary and appropriate, machinery for voluntary negotiations between employers or employers' organizations and workers' organizations, with a view to the regulation of terms and conditions of employment by means of collective agreements;

(3) to promote the establishment and use of appropriate machinery for conciliation and voluntary arbitration for the settlement of labour disputes;

and recognize:

(4) the right of workers and employers to collective action in cases of conflicts of interest, including the right to strike, subject to obligations that might arise out of collective agreements previously entered into.

Article 7—The Right of Children and Young Persons to Protection

With a view to ensuring the effective exercise of the right of children and young persons to protection, the Contracting Parties undertake:

(1) to provide that the minimum age of admission to employment shall be 15 years, subject to exceptions for children employed

in prescribed light work without harm to their health, morals or education;

(2) to provide that a higher minimum age of admission to employment shall be fixed with respect to prescribed occupations regarded as dangerous or unhealthy;

(3) to provide that persons who are still subject to compulsory education shall not be employed in such work as would deprive them of the full benefit of their education;

(4) to provide that the working hours of persons under 16 years of age shall be limited in accordance with the needs of their development, and particularly with their need for vocational training;

(5) to recognize the right of young workers and apprentices to a fair wage or other appropriate allowances;

(6) to provide that the time spent by young persons in vocational training during the normal working hours with the consent of the employer shall be treated as forming part of the working day;

(7) to provide that employed persons of under 18 years of age shall be entitled to not less than three weeks' annual holiday with pay;

(8) to provide that persons under 18 years of age shall not be employed in night work with the exception of certain occupations provided for by national laws or regulations;

(9) to provide that persons under 18 years of age employed in occupations prescribed by national laws or regulations shall be subject to regular medical control;

(10) to ensure special protection against physical and moral dangers to which children and young persons are exposed, and particularly against those resulting directly or indirectly from their work.

Article 8—The Right of Employed Women to Protection

With a view to ensuring the effective exercise of the right of employed women to protection, the Contracting Parties undertake:

(1) to provide either by paid leave, by adequate social security benefits or by benefits from public funds, for women to take leave before and after childbirth up to a total of at least 12 weeks;

(2) to consider it as unlawful for an employer to give a woman notice of dismissal during her absence on maternity leave or to give her notice of dismissal at such a time that the notice would expire during such absence;

(3) to provide that mothers who are nursing their infants shall be entitled to sufficient time off for this purpose;

(4) (*a*) to regulate the employment of women workers on night work in industrial employment;

    (*b*) to prohibit the employment of women workers in underground mining, and, as appropriate, on all other work which is unsuitable for them by reason of its dangerous, unhealthy, or arduous nature.

Article 9—*The Right to Vocational Guidance*

With a view to ensuring the effective exercise of the right to vocational guidance, the Contracting Parties undertake to provide or promote, as necessary, a service which will assist all persons, including the handicapped, to solve problems related to occupational choice and progress, with due regard to the individual's characteristics and their relation to occupational opportunity: this assistance should be available free of charge, both to young persons, including school children, and to adults.

Article 10—*The Right to Vocational Training*

With a view to ensuring the effective exercise of the right to vocational training, the Contracting Parties undertake:

(1) to provide or promote, as necessary, the technical and vocational training of all persons, including the handicapped, in consultation with employers' and workers' organizations, and to grant facilities for access to higher technical and university education, based solely on individual aptitude;

(2) to provide or promote a system of apprenticeship and other systematic arrangements for training young boys and girls in their various employments;

(3) to provide or promote, as necessary:

    (*a*) adequate and readily available training facilities for adult workers;

    (*b*) special facilities for the re-training of adult workers needed as a result of technological developments or new trends in employment;

(4) to encourage the full utilization of the facilities provided by appropriate measures such as:

    (*a*) reducing or abolishing any fees or charges;

    (*b*) granting financial assistance in appropriate cases;

    (*c*) including in the normal working hours time spent on supplementary training taken by the worker, at the request of his employer, during employment;

    (*d*) ensuring, through adequate supervision, in consultation with the employers' and workers' organizations, the efficiency of apprenticeship and other training arrangements for young workers, and the adequate protection of young workers generally.

Article 11—The Right to Protection of Health

With a view to ensuring the effective exercise of the right to protection of health, the Contracting Parties undertake, either directly or in co-operation with public or private organizations, to take appropriate measures designed *inter alia*:

(1) to remove as far as possible the causes of ill-health;
(2) to provide advisory and educational facilities for the promotion of health and the encouragement of individual responsibility in matters of health;
(3) to prevent as far as possible epidemic, endemic and other diseases.

Article 12—The Right to Social Security

With a view to ensuring the effective exercise of the right to social security, the Contracting Parties undertake:

(1) to establish or maintain a system of social security;
(2) to maintain the social security system at a satisfactory level at least equal to that required for ratification of International Labour Convention (No. 102) Concerning Minimum Standards of Social Security;
(3) to endeavour to raise progressively the system of social security to a higher level;
(4) to take steps, by the conclusion of appropriate bilateral and multilateral agreements, or by other means, and subject to the conditions laid down in such agreements, in order to ensure:
   (a) equal treatment with their own nationals of the nationals of other Contracting Parties in respect of social security rights, including the retention of benefits arising out of social security legislation, whatever movements the persons protected may undertake between the territories of the Contracting Parties;
   (b) the granting, maintenance and resumption of social security rights by such means as the accumulation of insurance or employment periods completed under the legislation of each of the Contracting Parties.

Article 13—The Right to Social and Medical Assistance

With a view to ensuring the effective exercise of the right to social and medical assistance, the Contracting Parties undertake:

(1) to ensure that any person who is without adequate resources and who is unable to secure such resources either by his own efforts or from other sources, in particular by benefits under a social security scheme, be granted adequate assistance, and, in case of sickness, the care necessitated by his condition;
(2) to ensure that persons receiving such assistance shall not, for

that reason, suffer from a diminution of their political or social rights;

(3) to provide that everyone may receive by appropriate public or private services such advice and personal help as may be required to prevent, to remove, or to alleviate personal or family want;

(4) to apply the provisions referred to in paragraphs 1, 2 and 3 of this Article on an equal footing with their nationals to nationals of other Contracting Parties lawfully within their territories, in accordance with their obligations under the European Convention on Social and Medical Assistance, signed at Paris on 11th December 1953.

Article 14—The Right to Benefit from Social Welfare Services

With a view to ensuring the effective exercise of the right to benefit from social welfare services, the Contracting Parties undertake:

(1) to promote or provide services which, by using methods of social work, would contribute to the welfare and development of both individuals and groups in the community, and to their adjustment to the social environment;

(2) to encourage the participation of individuals and voluntary or other organizations in the establishment and maintenance of such services.

Article 15—The Right of Physically or Mentally Disabled Persons to Vocational Training, Rehabilitation and Social Resettlement

With a view to ensuring the effective exercise of the right of the physically or mentally disabled to vocational training, rehabilitation and resettlement, the Contracting Parties undertake:

(1) to take adequate measures for the provision of training facilities, including, where necessary, specialized institutions, public or private;

(2) to take adequate measures for the placing of disabled persons in employment, such as specialized placing services, facilities for sheltered employment and measures to encourage employers to admit disabled persons to employment.

Article 16—The Right of the Family to Social, Legal and Economic Protection

With a view to ensuring the necessary conditions for the full development of the family, which is a fundamental unit of society, the Contracting Parties undertake to promote the economic, legal and social protection of family life by such means as social and family benefits, fiscal arrangements, provision of family housing, benefits for the newly married, and other appropriate means.

Article 17—The Right of Mothers and Children to Social and Economic Protection

With a view to ensuring the effective exercise of the right of mothers and children to social and economic protection, the Contracting Parties will take all appropriate and necessary measures to that end, including the establishment or maintenance of appropriate institutions or services.

Article 18—The Right to Engage in a Gainful Occupation in the Territory of Other Contracting Parties

With a view to ensuring the effective exercise of the right to engage in a gainful occupation in the territory of any other Contracting Party, the Contracting Parties undertake:
  (1) to apply existing regulations in a spirit of liberality;
  (2) to simplify existing formalities and to reduce or abolish chancery dues and other charges payable by foreign workers or their employers;
  (3) to liberalize, individually or collectively, regulations governing the employment of foreign workers;
and recognize:
  (4) the right of their nationals to leave the country to engage in a gainful occupation in the territories of the other Contracting Parties.

Article 19—The Right of Migrant Workers and their Families to Protection and Assistance

With a view to ensuring the effective exercise of the right of migrant workers and their families to protection and assistance in the territory of any other Contracting Party, the Contracting Parties undertake:
  (1) to maintain or to satisfy themselves that there are maintained adequate and free services to assist such workers, particularly in obtaining accurate information, and to take all appropriate steps, so far as national laws and regulations permit, against misleading propaganda relating to emigration and immigration;
  (2) to adopt appropriate measures within their own jurisdiction to facilitate the departure, journey and reception of such workers and their families, and to provide, within their own jurisdiction, appropriate services for health, medical attention and good hygienic conditions during the journey;
  (3) to promote co-operation, as appropriate, between social services, public and private, in emigration and immigration countries;
  (4) to secure for such workers lawfully within their territories, insofar as such matters are regulated by law or regulations or are subject to the control of administrative authorities,

treatment not less favourable than that of their own nationals in respect of the following matters:

  (*a*) remuneration and other employment and working conditions;
  (*b*) membership of trade unions and enjoyment of the benefits of collective bargaining;
  (*c*) accommodation;

 (5) to secure for such workers lawfully within their territories treatment not less favourable than that of their own nationals with regard to employment taxes, dues or contributions payable in respect of employed persons;
 (6) to facilitate as far as possible the reunion of the family of a foreign worker permitted to establish himself in the territory;
 (7) to secure for such workers lawfully within their territories treatment not less favourable than that of their own nationals in respect of legal proceedings relating to matters referred to in this Article;
 (8) to secure that such workers lawfully residing within their territories àre not expelled unless they endanger national security or offend against public interest or morality;
 (9) to permit, within legal limits, the transfer of such parts of the earnings and savings of such workers as they may desire;
 (10) to extend the protection and assistance provided for in this Article to self-employed migrants insofar as such measures apply.

PART III

Article 20—Undertakings

1. Each of the Contracting Parties undertakes:
  (*a*) to consider Part I of this Charter as a declaration of the aims which it will pursue by all appropriate means, as stated in the introductory paragraph of that Part;
  (*b*) to consider itself bound by at least five of the following Articles of Part II of this Charter: Articles 1, 5, 6, 12, 13, 16 and 19;
  (*c*) in addition to the Articles selected by it in accordance with the preceding sub-paragraph, to consider itself bound by such a number of Articles or numbered paragraphs of Part II of the Charter as it may select, provided that the total number of Articles or numbered paragraphs by which it is bound is not less than 10 Articles or 45 numbered paragraphs.

2. The Articles or paragraphs selected in accordance with sub-paragraphs (*b*) and (*c*) of paragraph 1 of this Article shall be notified to the Secretary-General of the Council of Europe at the time when the instrument of ratification or approval of the Contracting Party concerned is deposited.

3. Any Contracting Party may, at a later date, declare by notification to the Secretary-General that it considers itself bound by any Articles or any numbered paragraphs of Part II of the Charter which it has not already accepted under the terms of paragraph 1 of this Article. Such undertakings subsequently given shall be deemed to be an integral part of the ratification or approval, and shall have the same effect as from the thirtieth day after the date of the notification.

4. The Secretary-General shall communicate to all the signatory Governments and to the Director-General of the International Labour Office any notification which he shall have received pursuant to this Part of the Charter.

5. Each Contracting Party shall maintain a system of labour inspection appropriate to national conditions.

. . . .

PART V

Article 30—Derogations in time of War or Public Emergency
1. In time of war or other public emergency threatening the life of the nation any Contracting Party may take measures derogating from its obligation under this Charter to the extent strictly required by the exigencies of the situation, provided that such measures are not inconsistent with its other obligations under international law.

2. Any Contracting Party which has availed itself of this right of derogation shall, within a reasonable lapse of time, keep the Secretary-General of the Council of Europe fully informed of the measures taken and of the reasons therefor. It shall likewise inform the Secretary-General when such measures have ceased to operate and the provisions of the Charter which it has accepted are again being fully executed.

3. The Secretary-General shall in turn inform other Contracting Parties and the Director-General of the International Labour Office of all communications received in accordance with paragraph 2 of this article.

Article 31—Restrictions
1. The rights and principles set forth in Part I when effectively realized, and their effective exercise as provided for in Part II, shall not be subject to any restrictions or limitations not specified in those Parts, except such as are prescribed by law and are necessary in a democratic society for the protection of the rights and freedoms of others or for the protection of public interest, national security, public health, or morals.

2. The restrictions permitted under this Charter to the rights and obligations set forth herein shall not be applied for any purpose other than that for which they have been prescribed.

. . . .

American Declaration of the Rights and Duties of Man

Whereas:

The American peoples have acknowledged the dignity of the individual, and their national constitutions recognize that juridical and political institutions, which regulate life in human society, have as their principal aim the protection of the essential rights of man and the creation of circumstances that will permit him to achieve spiritual and material progress and attain happiness;

The American States have on repeated occasions recognized that the essential rights of man are not derived from the fact that he is a national of a certain state, but are based upon attributes of his human personality;

The international protection of the rights of man should be the principal guide of an evolving American law;

The affirmation of essential human rights by the American States together with the guarantees given by the internal régimes of the states establish the initial system of protection considered by the American States as being suited to the present social and juridical conditions, not without a recognition on their part that they should increasingly strengthen that system in the international field as conditions become more favourable,

The Ninth International Conference of American States

Agrees

To adopt the following

AMERICAN DECLARATION OF THE RIGHTS AND DUTIES OF MAN

PREAMBLE

All men are born free and equal, in dignity and in rights, and, being endowed by nature with reason and conscience, they should conduct themselves as brothers one to another.

The fulfillment of duty by each individual is a prerequisite to the rights of all. Rights and duties are interrelated in every social and political activity of man. While rights exalt individual liberty, duties express the dignity of that liberty.

Duties of a juridical nature presuppose others of a moral nature which support them in principle and constitute their basis.

Inasmuch as spiritual development is the supreme end of human existence and the highest expression thereof, it is the duty of man to serve that end with all his strength and resources.

Since culture is the highest social and historical expression of that spiritual development, it is the duty of man to preserve, practise and foster culture by every means within his power.

And, since moral conduct constitutes the noblest flowering of culture, it is the duty of every man always to hold it in high respect.

CHAPTER ONE—RIGHTS

Article I

Every human being has the right to life, liberty and the security of his person.

Article II

All persons are equal before the law and have the rights and duties established in this Declaration, without distinction as to race, sex, language, creed or any other factor.

Article III

Every person has the right freely to profess a religious faith, and to manifest and practise it both in public and in private.

Article IV

Every person has the right to freedom of investigation, of opinion, and of the expression and dissemination of ideas, by any medium whatsoever.

Article V

Every person has the right to the protection of the law against abusive attacks upon his honor, his reputation, and his private and family life.

Article VI

Every person has the right to establish a family, the basic element of society, and to receive protection therefor.

Article VII

All women, during pregnancy and the nursing period, and all children have the right to special protection, care and aid.

Article VIII

Every person has the right to fix his residence within the territory of the state of which he is a national, to move about freely within such territory, and not to leave it except by his own will.

Article IX

Every person has the right to the inviolability of his home.

Article X

Every person has the right to the inviolability and transmission of his correspondence.

Article XI

Every person has the right to the preservation of his health through sanitary and social measures relating to food, clothing, housing and medical care, to the extent permitted by public and community resources.

Article XII

Every person has the right to an education, which should be based on the principles of liberty, morality and human solidarity.

Likewise every person has the right to an education that will prepare him to attain a decent life, to raise his standard of living, and to be a useful member of society.

The right to an education includes the right to equality of opportunity in every case, in accordance with natural talents, merit and the desire to utilize the resources that the state or the community is in a position to provide.

Every person has the right to receive, free, at least a primary education.

Article XIII

Every person has the right to take part in the cultural life of the community, to enjoy the arts, and to participate in the benefits that result from intellectual progress, especially scientific discoveries.

He likewise has the right to the protection of his moral and material interests as regards his inventions or any literary, scientific or artistic works of which he is the author.

Article XIV

Every person has the right to work, under proper conditions, and to follow his vocation freely, in so far as existing conditions of employment permit.

Every person who works has the right to receive such remuneration as will, in proportion to his capacity and skill, assure him a standard of living suitable for himself and for his family.

Article XV

Every person has the right to leisure time, to wholesome recreation, and to the opportunity for advantageous use of his free time to his spiritual, cultural and physical benefit.

Article XVI

Every person has the right to social security which will protect him from the consequences of unemployment, old age, and any disabilities arising from causes beyond his control that make it physically or mentally impossible for him to earn a living.

Article XVII

Every person has the right to be recognized everywhere as a person having rights and obligations, and to enjoy the basic civil rights.

Article XVIII

Every person may resort to the courts to ensure respect for his legal rights. There should likewise be available to him a simple, brief procedure whereby the courts will protect him from acts of authority that, to his prejudice, violate any fundamental constitutional rights.

Article XIX

Every person has the right to the nationality to which he is entitled by law and to change it, if he so wishes, for the nationality of any other country that is willing to grant it to him.

Article XX

Every person having legal capacity is entitled to participate in the government of his country, directly or through his representatives, and to take part in popular elections, which shall be by secret ballot, and shall be honest, periodic and free.

Article XXI

Every person has the right to assemble peaceably with others in a formal public meeting or an informal gathering, in connection with matters of common interest of any nature.

Article XXII

Every person has the right to associate with others to promote, exercise and protect his legitimate interests of a political, economic, religious, social, cultural, professional, labor union or other nature.

Article XXIII

Every person has a right to own such private property as meets the essential needs of decent living and helps to maintain the dignity of the individual and of the home.

Article XXIV

Every person has the right to submit respectful petitions to any competent authority, for reasons of either general or private interest, and the right to obtain a prompt decision thereon.

Article XXV

No person may be deprived of his liberty except in the cases and according to the procedures established by pre-existing law.

No person may be deprived of liberty for nonfulfillment of obligations of a purely civil character.

Every individual who has been deprived of his liberty has the right to have the legality of his detention ascertained without delay by a court, and the right to be tried without undue delay, or otherwise to be released. He also has the right to humane treatment during the time he is in custody.

Article XXVI

Every accused person is presumed to be innocent until proved guilty.

Every person accused of an offense has the right to be given an impartial and public hearing, and to be tried by courts previously established in accordance with pre-existing laws, and not to receive cruel, infamous or unusual punishment.

Article XXVII

Every person has the right, in case of pursuit not resulting from ordinary crimes, to seek and receive asylum in foreign territory, in accordance with the laws of each country and with international agreements.

Article XXVIII

The rights of man are limited by the rights of others, by the security of all, and by the just demands of the general welfare and the advancement of democracy.

CHAPTER TWO—DUTIES

Article XXIX

It is the duty of the individual so to conduct himself in relation to others that each and every one may fully form and develop his personality.

Article XXX

It is the duty of every person to aid, support, educate and protect his minor children, and it is the duty of children to honor their parents always and to aid, support and protect them when they need it.

Article XXXI

It is the duty of every person to acquire at least an elementary education.

Article XXXII

It is the duty of every person to vote in the popular elections of the country of which he is a national, when he is legally capable of doing so.

Article XXXIII

It is the duty of every person to obey the law and other legitimate commands of the authorities of his country and those of the country in which he may be.

Article XXXIV

It is the duty of every able-bodied person to render whatever civil and military service his country may require for its defense and preservation, and, in case of public disaster, to render such services as may be in his power.

It is likewise his duty to hold any public office to which he may be elected by popular vote in the state of which he is a national.

Article XXXV

It is the duty of every person to cooperate with the state and the community with respect to social security and welfare, in accordance with his ability and with existing circumstances.

Article XXXVI

It is the duty of every person to pay the taxes established by law for the support of public services.

Article XXXVII

It is the duty of every person to work, as far as his capacity and possibilities permit, in order to obtain the means of livelihood or to benefit his community.

Article XXXVIII

It is the duty of every person to refrain from taking part in political activities that, according to law, are reserved exclusively to the citizens of the state in which he is an alien.

American Convention on Human Rights

Preamble

The American states signatory to the present Convention,

Reaffirming their intention to consolidate in this hemisphere, within the framework of democratic institutions, a system of personal liberty and social justice based on respect for the essential rights of man;

Recognizing that the essential rights of man are not derived from one's being a national of a certain state, but are based upon attributes of the human personality, and that they therefore justify international protection in the form of a convention reinforcing or complementing the protection provided by the domestic law of the American states;

Considering that these principles have been set forth in the Charter of the Organization of American States, in the American Declaration of the Rights and Duties of Man, and in the Universal Declaration of Human Rights, and that they have been reaffirmed and refined in other international instruments, worldwide as well as regional in scope;

Reiterating that, in accordance with the Universal Declaration of Human Rights, the ideal of free men enjoying freedom from fear and want can be achieved only if conditions are created whereby everyone may enjoy his economic, social, and cultural rights, as well as his civil and political rights; and

Considering that the Third Special Inter-American Conference (Buenos Aires, 1967) approved the incorporation into the Charter of the Organization itself of broader standards with respect to economic, social, and educational rights and resolved that an inter-American convention on human rights should determine the structure, competence, and procedure of the organs responsible for these matters,

Have agreed upon the following:

PART I—STATE OBLIGATIONS AND RIGHTS PROTECTED

Chapter I—General Obligations

Article 1—Obligation to Respect Rights

1. The States Parties to this Convention undertake to respect the rights and freedoms recognized herein and to ensure to all persons subject to their jurisdiction the free and full exercise of those rights and freedoms, without any discrimination for reasons of race, color, sex, language, religion, political or other opinion, national or social origin, economic status, birth, or any other social condition.

2. For the purposes of this Convention, 'person' means every human being.

Article 2—*Domestic Legal Effects*

Where the exercise of any of the rights or freedoms referred to in Article 1 is not already ensured by legislative or other provisions, the States Parties undertake to adopt, in accordance with their constitutional processes and the provisions of this Convention, such legislative or other measures as may be necessary to give effect to those rights or freedoms.

CHAPTER II—CIVIL AND POLITICAL RIGHTS

Article 3—*Right to Juridical Personality*

Every person has the right to recognition as a person before the law.

Article 4—*Right to Life*

1. Every person has the right to have his life respected. This right shall be protected by law, and, in general, from the moment of conception. No one shall be arbitrarily deprived of his life.

2. In countries that have not abolished the death penalty, it may be imposed only for the most serious crimes and pursuant to a final judgment rendered by a competent court and in accordance with a law establishing such punishment, enacted prior to the commission of the crime. The application of such punishment shall not be extended to crimes to which it does not presently apply.

3. The death penalty shall not be reestablished in states that have abolished it.

4. In no case shall capital punishment be inflicted for political offenses or related common crimes.

5. Capital punishment shall not be imposed upon persons who, at the time the crime was committed, were under 18 years of age or over 70 years of age; nor shall it be applied to pregnant women.

6. Every person condemned to death shall have the right to apply for amnesty, pardon, or commutation of sentence, which may be granted in all cases. Capital punishment shall not be imposed while such a petition is pending decision by the competent authority.

Article 5—*Right to Humane Treatment*

1. Every person has the right to have his physical, mental, and moral integrity respected.

2. No one shall be subjected to torture or to cruel, inhuman, or degrading punishment or treatment. All persons deprived of their liberty shall be treated with respect for the inherent dignity of the human person.

3. Punishment shall not be extended to any person other than the criminal.

4. Accused persons shall, save in exceptional circumstances, be segregated from convicted persons, and shall be subject to separate treatment appropriate to their status as unconvicted persons.

5. Minors while subject to criminal proceedings shall be separated from adults and brought before specialized tribunals, as speedily as possible, so that they may be treated in accordance with their status as minors.

6. Punishments consisting of deprivation of liberty shall have as an essential aim the reform and social readaptation of the prisoners.

Article 6—Freedom from Slavery

1. No one shall be subject to slavery or to involuntary servitude, which are prohibited in all their forms, as are the slave trade and traffic in women.

2. No one shall be required to perform forced or compulsory labor. This provision shall not be interpreted to mean that, in those countries in which the penalty established for certain crimes is deprivation of liberty at forced labor, the carrying out of such a sentence imposed by a competent court is prohibited. Forced labor shall not adversely affect the dignity or the physical or intellectual capacity of the prisoner.

3. For the purposes of this article the following do not constitute forced or compulsory labor:

(*a*) work or service normally required of a person imprisoned in execution of a sentence or formal decision passed by the competent judicial authority. Such work or service shall be carried out under the supervision and control of public authorities, and any persons performing such work or service shall not be placed at the disposal of any private party, company, or juridical person;

(*b*) military service and, in countries in which conscientious objectors are recognized, national service that the law may provide for in lieu of military service;

(*c*) service exacted in time of danger or calamity that threatens the existence or the well-being of the community; or

(*d*) work or service that forms part of normal civic obligations.

Article 7—Right to Personal Liberty

1. Every person has the right to personal liberty and security.

2. No one shall be deprived of his physical liberty except for the reasons and under the conditions established beforehand by the constitution of the State Party concerned or by a law established pursuant thereto.

3. No one shall be subject to arbitrary arrest or imprisonment.

4. Anyone who is detained shall be informed of the reasons for his detention and shall be promptly notified of the charge or charges against him.

5. Any person detained shall be brought promptly before a judge or other officer authorized by law to exercise judicial power and shall be entitled to trial within a reasonable time or to be released without prejudice to the continuation of the proceedings. His release may be subject to guarantees to assure his appearance for trial.

6. Anyone who is deprived of his liberty shall be entitled to recourse to a competent court, in order that the court may decide without delay on the lawfulness of his arrest or detention and order his release if the arrest or detention is unlawful. In States Parties whose laws provide that anyone who believes himself to be threatened with deprivation of his liberty is entitled to recourse to a competent court in order that it may decide on the lawfulness of such threat, this remedy may not be restricted or abolished. The interested party or another person in his behalf is entitled to seek these remedies.

7. No one shall be detained for debt. This principle shall not limit the orders of a competent judicial authority issued for nonfulfillment of duties of support.

Article 8—Right to a Fair Trial

1. Every person has the right to a hearing, with due guarantees and within a reasonable time, by a competent, independent, and impartial tribunal, previously established by law, in the substantiation of any accusation of a criminal nature made against him or for the determination of his rights and obligations of a civil, labor, fiscal, or any other nature.

2. Every person accused of a criminal offense has the right to be presumed innocent so long as his guilt has not been proven according to law. During the proceedings, every person is entitled, with full equality, to the following minimum guarantees:

    (*a*) the right of the accused to be assisted without charge by a translator or interpreter, if he does not understand or does not speak the language of the tribunal or court;

    (*b*) prior notification in detail to the accused of the charges against him;

    (*c*) adequate time and means for the preparation of his defense;

    (*d*) the right of the accused to defend himself personally or to be assisted by legal counsel of his own choosing, and to communicate freely and privately with his counsel;

    (*e*) the inalienable right to be assisted by counsel provided by the state, paid or not as the domestic law provides, if the accused does not defend himself personally or engage his own counsel within the time period established by law;

    (*f*) the right of the defense to examine witnesses present in the court and to obtain the appearance, as witnesses, of experts or other persons who may throw light on the facts;

(*g*) the right not to be compelled to be a witness against himself or to plead guilty; and

(*h*) the right to appeal the judgment to a higher court.

3. A confession of guilt by the accused shall be valid only if it is made without coercion of any kind.

4. An accused person acquitted by a nonappealable judgment shall not be subjected to a new trial for the same cause.

5. Criminal proceedings shall be public, except insofar as may be necessary to protect the interests of justice.

Article 9—Freedom from Ex Post Facto Laws

No one shall be convicted of any act or omission that did not constitute a criminal offense, under the applicable law, at the time it was committed. A heavier penalty shall not be imposed than the one that was applicable at the time the criminal offense was committed. If subsequent to the commission of the offense the law provides for the imposition of a lighter punishment, the guilty person shall benefit therefrom.

Article 10—Right to Compensation

Every person has the right to be compensated in accordance with the law in the event he has been sentenced by a final judgment through a miscarriage of justice.

Article 11—Right to Privacy

1. Everyone has the right to have his honor respected and his dignity recognized.

2. No one may be the object of arbitrary or abusive interference with his private life, his family, his home, or his correspondence, or of unlawful attacks on his honor or reputation.

3. Everyone has the right to the protection of the law against such interference or attacks.

Article 12—Freedom of Conscience and Religion

1. Everyone has the right to freedom of conscience and of religion. This includes freedom to maintain or to change one's religion or beliefs, and freedom to profess or disseminate one's religion or beliefs either individually or together with others, in public or in private.

2. No one shall be subject to restrictions that might impair his freedom to maintain or to change his religion or beliefs.

3. Freedom to manifest one's religion and beliefs may be subject only to the limitations prescribed by law that are necessary to protect public safety, order, health or morals, or the rights or freedoms of others.

4. Parents or guardians, as the case may be, have the right to provide for the religious and moral education of their children or wards that is in accord with their own convictions.

Article 13—Freedom of Thought and Expression

1. Everyone shall have the right to freedom of thought and expression. This right shall include freedom to seek, receive, and impart information and ideas of all kinds, regardless of frontiers, either orally, in writing, in print, in the form of art, or through any other medium of one's choice.

2. The exercise of the right provided for in the foregoing paragraph shall not be subject to prior censorship but shall be subject to subsequent imposition of liability, which shall be expressly established by law to the extent necessary in order to ensure:

(*a*) respect for the rights or reputations of others; or

(*b*) the protection of national security, public order, or public health or morals.

3. The right of expression may not be restricted by indirect methods or means, such as the abuse of government or private controls over newsprint, radio broadcasting frequencies, or equipment used in the dissemination of information, or by any other means tending to impede the communication and circulation of ideas and opinions.

4. Notwithstanding the provisions of paragraph 2 above, public entertainments may be subject by law to prior censorship for the sole purpose of regulating access to them for the moral protection of childhood and adolescence.

5. Any propaganda for war and any advocacy of national, racial, or religious hatred that constitute incitements to lawless violence or to any other similar illegal action against any person or group of persons on any grounds including those of race, color, religion, language, or national origin shall be considered as offenses punishable by law.

Article 14—Right of Reply

1. Anyone injured by inaccurate or offensive statements or ideas disseminated to the public in general by a legally regulated medium of communication has the right to reply or make a correction using the same communications outlet, under such conditions as the law may establish.

2. The correction or reply shall not in any case remit other legal liabilities that may have been incurred.

3. For the effective protection of honor and reputation, every publisher, and every newspaper, motion picture, radio, and television company, shall have a person responsible, who is not protected by immunities or special privileges.

Article 15—Right of Assembly

The right of peaceful assembly, without arms, is recognized. No restrictions may be placed on the exercise of this right other than those imposed in conformity with the law and necessary in a democratic society in the interest of national security, public safety or public order, or to protect public health or morals or the rights or freedoms of others.

Article 16—Freedom of Association

1. Everyone has the right to associate freely for ideological, religious, political, economic, labor, social, cultural, sports or other purposes.

2. The exercise of this right shall be subject only to such restrictions established by law as may be necessary in a democratic society, in the interest of national security, public safety or public order, or to protect public health or morals or the rights and freedoms of others.

3. The provisions of this article do not bar the imposition of legal restrictions, including even deprivation of the exercise of the right of association, on members of the armed forces and the police.

Article 17—Rights of the Family

1. The family is the natural and fundamental group unit of society and is entitled to protection by society and the State.

2. The right of men and women of marriageable age to marry and to raise a family shall be recognized, if they meet the conditions required by domestic laws, insofar as such conditions do not affect the principle of nondiscrimination established in this Convention.

3. No marriage shall be entered into without the free and full consent of the intending spouses.

4. The States Parties shall take appropriate steps to ensure the equality of rights and the adequate balancing of responsibilities of the spouses as to marriage, during marriage, and in the event of its dissolution. In case of dissolution, provision shall be made for the necessary protection of any children solely on the basis of their own best interests.

5. The law shall recognize equal rights for chidren born out of wedlock and those born in wedlock.

Article 18—Right to a Name

Every person has the right to a given name and to the surnames of his parents or that of one of them. The law shall regulate the manner in which this right shall be ensured for all, by the use of assumed names if necessary.

Article 19—Rights of the Child

Every minor child has the right to the measures of protection required by his condition as a minor on the part of his family, society, and the State.

Article 20—Right to Nationality

1. Every person has the right to a nationality.

2. Every person has the right to the nationality of the state in whose territory he was born if he does not have the right to any other nationality.

3. No one shall be arbitrarily deprived of his nationality or of the right to change it.

Article 21—Right to Property

1. Everyone has the right to the use and enjoyment of his property. The law may subordinate such use and enjoyment to the interest of society.

2. No one shall be deprived of his property except upon payment of just compensation, for reasons of public utility or social interest, and in the cases and according to the forms established by law.

3. Usury and any other form of exploitation of man by man shall be prohibited by law.

Article 22—Freedom of Movement and Residence

1. Every person lawfully in the territory of a State Party has the right to move about in it and to reside in it subject to the provisions of the law.

2. Every person has the right to leave any country freely, including his own.

3. The exercise of the foregoing rights may be restricted only pursuant to a law to the extent necessary in a democratic society to prevent crime or to protect national security, public safety, public order, public morals, public health, or the rights or freedoms of others.

4. The exercise of the rights recognized in paragraph 1 may also be restricted by law in designated zones for reasons of public interest.

5. No one can be expelled from the territory of the state of which he is a national or be deprived of the right to enter it.

6. An alien lawfully in the territory of a State Party to this Convention may be expelled from it only pursuant to a decision reached in accordance with law.

7. Every person has the right to seek and be granted asylum in a foreign territory, in accordance with the legislation of the state and international conventions, in the event he is being pursued for political offenses or related common crimes.

8. In no case may an alien be deported or returned to a country, regardless of whether or not it is his country of origin, if in that country his right to life or personal freedom is in danger of being violated because of his race, nationality, religion, social status, or political opinions.

9. The collective expulsion of aliens is prohibited.

Article 23—Right to Participate in Government

  1. Every citizen shall enjoy the following rights and opportunities:

    (*a*) to take part in the conduct of public affairs, directly or through freely chosen representatives;

    (*b*) to vote and to be elected in genuine periodic elections, which shall be by universal and equal suffrage and by secret ballot that guarantees the free expression of the will of the voters; and

    (*c*) to have access, under general conditions of equality, to the public service of his country.

  2. The law may regulate the exercise of the rights and opportunities referred to in the preceding paragraph only on the basis of age, nationality, residence, language, education, civil and mental capacity, or sentencing by a competent court in criminal proceedings.

Article 24—Right to Equal Protection

All persons are equal before the law. Consequently, they are entitled, without discrimination, to equal protection of the law.

Article 25—Right to Judicial Protection

  1. Everyone has the right to simple and prompt recourse, or any other effective recourse, to a competent court or tribunal for protection against acts that violate his fundamental rights recognized by the constitution or laws of the state concerned or by this Convention, even though such violation may have been committed by persons acting in the course of their official duties.

  2. The States Parties undertake:

    (*a*) to ensure that any person claiming such remedy shall have his rights determined by the competent authority provided for by the legal system of the state;

    (*b*) to develop the possibilities of judicial remedy; and

    (*c*) to ensure that the competent authorities shall enforce such remedies when granted.

CHAPTER III—ECONOMIC, SOCIAL, AND CULTURAL RIGHTS

Article 26—Progressive Development

The States Parties undertake to adopt measures, both internally and through international cooperation, especially those of an economic and technical nature, with a view to achieving progressively, by legislation or other appropriate means, the full realization of the rights implicit in the economic, social, educational, scientific, and cultural standards set forth in the Charter of the Organization of American States as amended by the Protocol of Buenos Aires.

CHAPTER IV—SUSPENSION OF GUARANTEES, INTERPRETATION, AND
APPLICATION

Article 27—Suspension of Guarantees

1. In time of war, public danger, or other emergency that threatens
the independence or security of a State Party, it may take measures
derogating from its obligations under the present Convention to the
extent and for the period of time strictly required by the exigencies of
the situation, provided that such measures are not inconsistent with its
other obligations under international law and do not involve discrimination on the ground of race, color, sex, language, religion, or social
origin.

2. The foregoing provision does not authorize any suspension of the
following articles: Article 3 (Right to Juridical Personality), Article 4
(Right to Life), Article 5 (Right to Humane Treatment), Article 6
(Freedom from Slavery), Article 9 (Freedom from Ex Post Facto
Laws), Article 12 (Freedom of Conscience and Religion), Article 17
(Rights of the Family), Article 18 (Right to a Name), Article 19
(Rights of the Child), Article 20 (Right to Nationality), and Article 23
(Right to Participate in Government), or of the judicial guarantees
essential for the protection of such rights.

3. Any State Party availing itself of the right of suspension shall
immediately inform the other States Parties, through the Secretary
General of the Organization of American States, of the provisions
the application of which it has suspended, the reasons that gave rise
to the suspension, and the date set for the termination of such
suspension.

.   .   .   .

Article 29—Restrictions Regarding Interpretation

No provision of this Convention shall be interpreted as:

   (*a*) permitting any State Party, group, or person to suppress the
        enjoyment or exercise of the rights and freedoms recognized in
        this Convention or to restrict them to a greater extent than is
        provided for herein;
   (*b*) restricting the enjoyment or exercise of any right or freedom
        recognized by virtue of the laws of any State Party or by virtue
        of another convention to which one of the said states is a party;
   (*c*) precluding other rights or guarantees that are inherent in the
        human personality or derived from representative democracy
        as a form of government; or
   (*d*) excluding or limiting the effect that the American Declaration
        of the Rights and Duties of Man and other international acts of
        the same nature may have.

Article 30—Scope of Restrictions

The restrictions that, pursuant to this Convention, may be placed on the enjoyment or exercise of the rights or freedoms recognized herein may not be applied except in accordance with the laws enacted for reasons of general interest and in accordance with the purpose for which such restrictions have been established.

. . . .

CHAPTER V—PERSONAL RESPONSIBILITIES

Article 32—Relationship between Duties and Rights

1. Every person has responsibilities to his family, his community, and mankind.

2. The rights of each person are limited by the rights of others, by the security of all, and by the just demands of the general welfare, in a democratic society.

. . . .

African Charter on Human and Peoples' Rights

The African States members of the Organization of African Unity, parties to the present Convention entitled "African Charter on Human and Peoples' Rights",

Recalling Decision 115 (XVI) of the Assembly of Heads of State and Government at its Sixteenth Ordinary Session held in Monrovia, Liberia, from 17 to 20 July 1979 on the preparation of "a preliminary draft on an African Charter on Human and Peoples' Rights providing *inter alia* for the establishment of bodies to promote and protect human and peoples' rights";

Considering the Charter of the Organization of African Unity, which stipulates that "freedom, equality, justice and dignity are essential objectives for the achievement of the legitimate aspirations of the African peoples";

Reaffirming the pledge they solemnly made in Article 2 of the said Charter to eradicate all forms of colonialism from Africa and to promote international cooperation having due regard to the Charter of the United Nations and the Universal Declaration of Human Rights;

Taking into consideration the virtues of their historical tradition and the values of African civilization which should inspire and characterize their reflection on the concept of human and peoples' rights;

Recognizing on the one hand, that fundamental human rights stem from the attributes of human beings, which justifies their national and international protection and on the other hand that the reality and respect of peoples' rights should necessarily guarantee human rights;

Considering that the enjoyment of rights and freedoms also implies the performance of duties on the part of everyone;

Convinced that it is henceforth essential to pay particular attention to the right to development and that civil and political rights cannot be dissociated from economic, social and cultural rights in their conception as well as universality and that the satisfaction of economic, social and cultural rights is a guarantee for the enjoyment of civil and political rights;

Conscious of their duty to achieve the total liberation of Africa, the peoples of which are still struggling for their dignity and genuine independence, and undertaking to eliminate colonialism, neo-colonialism, apartheid, zionism and to dismantle aggressive foreign military bases and all forms of discrimination, particularly those based on race, ethnic group, colour, sex, language, religion or political opinion;

Reaffirming their adherence to the principles of human and peoples' rights and freedoms contained in the declarations, conventions and other instruments adopted by the Organization of African Unity, the Movement of Non-Aligned Countries and the United Nations;

Firmly convinced of the duty to promote and protect human and peoples' rights and freedoms taking into account the importance traditionally attached to these rights and freedoms in Africa;

Have agreed as follows:

PART I—RIGHTS AND DUTIES

CHAPTER I—HUMAN AND PEOPLES' RIGHTS

Article 1

The Member States of the Organization of African Unity parties to the present Charter shall recognize the rights, duties and freedoms enshrined in this Charter and shall undertake to adopt legislative or other measures to give effect to them.

Article 2

Every individual shall be entitled to the enjoyment of the rights and freedoms recognized and guaranteed in the present Charter without distinction of any kind such as race, ethnic group, colour, sex, language, religion, political or any other opinion, national and social origin, fortune, birth or other status.

Article 3

1. Every individual shall be equal before the law.
2. Every individual shall be entitled to equal protection of the law.

Article 4

Human beings are inviolable. Every human being shall be entitled to respect for his life and the integrity of his person. No one may be arbitrarily deprived of this right.

Article 5

Every individual shall have the right to the respect of the dignity inherent in a human being and to the recognition of his legal status. All forms of exploitation and degradation of man, particularly slavery, slave trade, torture, cruel, inhuman or degrading punishment and treatment, shall be prohibited.

Article 6

Every individual shall have the right to liberty and to the security of his person. No one may be deprived of his freedom except for reasons and conditions previously laid down by law. In particular, no one may be arbitrarily arrested or detained.

Article 7

1. Every individual shall have the right to have his cause heard. This comprises:
   (a) the right to an appeal to competent national organs against acts violating his fundamental rights as recognized and guaranteed by conventions, laws, regulations and customs in force;
   (b) the right to be presumed innocent until proved guilty by a competent court or tribunal;
   (c) the right to defence, including the right to be defended by counsel of his choice;
   (d) the right to be tried within a reasonable time by an impartial court or tribunal.
2. No one may be condemned for an act or omission which did not constitute a legally punishable offence at the time it was committed. No penalty may be inflicted for an offence for which no provision was made at the time it was committed. Punishment is personal and can be imposed only on the offender.

Article 8

Freedom of conscience, the profession and free practice of religion, shall be guaranteed. No one may, subject to law and order, be submitted to measures restricting the exercise of these freedoms.

Article 9

1. Every individual shall have the right to receive information.
2. Every individual shall have the right to express and disseminate his opinions within the law.

Article 10

1. Every individual shall have the right to free association provided that he abides by the law.
2. Subject to the obligation of solidarity provided for in Article 29 no one may be compelled to join an association.

Article 11

Every individual shall have the right to assemble freely with others. The exercise of this right shall be subject only to necessary restrictions provided for by law, in particular those enacted in the interests of national security, safety, health, ethics and the rights and freedoms of others.

Article 12

1. Every individual shall have the right to freedom of movement and residence within the borders of a State provided he abides by the law.

2. Every individual shall have the right to leave any country including his own, and to return to his country. This right may only be subject to restrictions provided for by law for the protection of national security, law and order, public health or morality.
3. Every individual shall have the right, when persecuted, to seek and obtain asylum in other countries in accordance with the laws of those countries and international conventions.
4. A non-national legally admitted in a territory of a State Party to the present Charter, may only be expelled from it by virtue of a decision taken in accordance with the law.
5. The mass expulsion of non-nationals shall be prohibited. Mass expulsion shall be that which is aimed at national, racial, ethnic or religious groups.

Article 13

1. Every citizen shall have the right to freely participate in the government of his country, either directly or through freely chosen representatives, in accordance with the provisions of the law.
2. Every citizen shall have the right of equal access to the public service of his country.
3. Every individual shall have the right of access to public property and services, in strict equality of all persons before the law.

Article 14

The right to property shall be guaranteed. It may only be encroached upon in the interest of public need or in the general interest of the community and in accordance with the provisions of appropriate laws.

Article 15

Every individual shall have the right to work under equitable and satisfactory conditions and shall receive equal pay for equal work.

Article 16

1. Every individual shall have the right to enjoy the best attainable state of physical and mental health.
2. States Parties to the present Charter shall take the necessary measures to protect the health of their people and to ensure that they receive medical attention when they are sick.

Article 17

1. Every individual shall have the right to education.
2. Every individual may freely take part in the cultural life of his community.
3. The promotion and protection of morals and traditional values recognized by the community shall be the duty of the State.

Article 18

1. The family shall be the natural unit and basis of society. It shall be protected by the State.
2. The State shall have the duty to assist the family which is the custodian of morals and traditional values recognized by the community.
3. The State shall ensure the elimination of every discrimination against women and also ensure the protection of the rights of the woman and the child as stipulated in international declarations and conventions.
4. The aged and the disabled shall also have the right to special measures of protection in keeping with their physical or moral needs.

Article 19

All peoples shall be equal; they shall enjoy the same respect and shall have the same rights. Nothing shall justify the domination of a people by another.

Article 20

1. All peoples shall have the right to existence. They shall have the unquestionable and inalienable right to self-determination. They shall freely determine their political status and shall pursue their economic and social development according to the policy they have freely chosen.
2. Colonized or oppressed peoples shall have the right to free themselves from the bonds of domination by resorting to any means recognized by the international community.
3. All peoples shall have the right to the assistance of the States Parties to the present Charter in their liberation struggle against foreign domination, be it political, economic or cultural.

Article 21

1. All peoples shall freely dispose of their wealth and natural resources. This right shall be exercised in the exclusive interest of the people. In no case shall a people be deprived of it.
2. In case of spoliation the dispossessed people shall have the right to the lawful recovery of its property as well as to an adequate compensation.
3. The free disposal of wealth and natural resources shall be exercised without prejudice to the obligation of promoting international economic cooperation based on mutual respect, equitable exchange and the principles of international law.
4. States Parties to the present Charter shall individually and collectively exercise the right to free disposal of their wealth and natural resources with a view to strengthening African unity and solidarity.

5. States Parties to the present Charter shall undertake to eliminate all forms of foreign economic exploitation particularly that practised by international monopolies so as to enable their peoples to fully benefit from the advantages derived from their national resources.

Article 22

1. All peoples shall have the right to their economic, social and cultural development with due regard to their freedom and identity and in the equal enjoyment of the common heritage of mankind.
2. States shall have the duty, individually or collectively, to ensure the exercise of the right to development.

Article 23

1. All peoples shall have the right to national and international peace and security. The principles of solidarity and friendly relations implicitly affirmed by the Charter of the United Nations and re-affirmed by that of the Organization of African Unity shall govern relations between States.
2. For the purpose of strengthening peace, solidarity and friendly relations, States parties to the present Charter shall ensure that:
    (a) any individual enjoying the right of asylum under Article 12 of the present Charter shall not engage in subversive activities against his country of origin or any other State Party to the present Charter;
    (b) their territories shall not be used as bases for subversive or terrorist activities against the people of any other State Party to the present Charter.

Article 24

All peoples shall have the right to a general satisfactory environment favourable to their development.

Article 25

States Parties to the present Charter shall have the duty to promote and ensure through teaching, education and publication, the respect of the rights and freedoms contained in the present Charter and to see to it that these freedoms and rights as well as corresponding obligations and duties are understood.

Article 26

States Parties to the present Charter shall have the duty to guarantee the independence of the Courts and shall allow the establishment and improvement of appropriate national institutions entrusted with the promotion and protection of the rights and freedoms guaranteed by the present Charter.

Chapter II—Duties

Article 27

1. Every individual shall have duties towards his family and society, the State and other legally recognized communities and the international community.
2. The rights and freedoms of each individual shall be exercised with due regard to the rights of others, collective security, morality and common interest.

Article 28

Every individual shall have the duty to respect and consider his fellow beings without discrimination, and to maintain relations aimed at promoting, safeguarding and reinforcing mutual respect and tolerance.

Article 29

The individual shall also have the duty:

1. To preserve the harmonious development of the family and to work for the cohesion and respect of the family, to respect his parents at all times, to maintain them in case of need;
2. To serve his national community by placing his physical and intellectual abilities at its service;
3. Not to compromise the security of the State whose national or resident he is;
4. To preserve and strengthen social and national solidarity, particularly when the latter is threatened;
5. To preserve and strengthen the national independence and the territorial integrity of his country and to contribute to its defence in accordance with the law;
6. To work to the best of his abilities and competence, and to pay taxes imposed by law in the interest of the society;
7. To preserve and strengthen positive African cultural values in his relations with other members of the society, in the spirit of tolerance, dialogue and consultation and, in general, to contribute to the promotion of the moral well-being of society;
8. To contribute to the best of his abilities, at all times and at all levels, to the promotion and achievement of African unity.

Table of Instruments

	Year of adoption	Year of entry into force	Number of state parties on 1 Jan. 84
Global			
United Nations Charter	1945	1945	158
Universal Declaration of Human Rights	1948		
International Covenant on Economic, Social and Cultural Rights	1966	1976	80
International Covenant on Civil and Political Rights	1966	1976	77
Optional Protocol thereto	1966	1976	31
Regional			
Council of Europe Convention for the Protection of Human Rights and Fundamental Freedoms	1950	1953	21
First Protocol thereto	1952	1954	21
Fourth Protocol thereto	1963	1968	13
European Social Charter	1961	1965	13
American Declaration of the Rights and Duties of Man	1948		
American Convention on Human Rights	1969	1978	17
African Charter on Human and Peoples' Rights	1981		
Specialized			
Convention on the Prevention and Punishment of the Crime of Genocide	1948	1951	92
International Convention on the Suppression and Punishment of the Crime of Apartheid	1973	1976	77
Convention on the Elimination of all Forms of Racial Discrimination	1965	1969	122
Convention Relating to the Status of Refugees	1951	1954	94
Convention Relating to the Status of Stateless Persons	1954	1960	34

	Year of adoption	Year of entry into force	Number of state parties on 1 Jan. 84
Convention on the Reduction of Statelessness	1961	1975	12
Convention on the Elimination of all Forms of Discrimination against Women	1979	1981	53
Convention on the Political Rights of Women	1952	1954	91
Convention on the Nationality of Married Women	1957	1958	54
Convention on Consent to Marriage, Minimum Age for Marriage and Registration of Marriages	1962	1964	34
Convention against Discrimination in Education	1960	1962 ⎫	73
Protocol thereto	1962	1968 ⎭	
Slavery Convention (as amended by 1953 Protocol)	1926	1927	79
Supplementary Convention on the Abolition of Slavery, the Slave Trade, and Institutions and Practices similar to Slavery	1956	1957	98
Convention for the Suppression of the Traffic in Persons and of the Exploitation of the Prostitution of Others	1949	1951	56
Convention on the International Right of Correction	1952	1962	11
ILO			
Convention concerning Forced Labour	1930	1932	128
Convention concerning Freedom of Association and Protection of the Right to Organize	1948	1950	97
Convention concerning the Application of the Principles of the Right to Organize and to Bargain Collectively	1949	1951	113
Convention concerning Equal Remuneration for Men and Women Workers for Work of Equal Value	1951	1953	105

	Year of adoption	Year of entry into force	Number of state parties on 1 Jan. 84
Convention concerning the Abolition of Forced Labour	1957	1959	109
Convention concerning Discrimination in Respect of Employment and Occupation	1958	1960	106
Convention concerning Employment Policy	1964	1966	69
Convention concerning Protection and Facilities to be Afforded to Workers' Representatives in the Undertaking	1971	1973	41

Table of states bound by the general treaties[a]

(on 1 Jan. 1984)

State	UN Charter	CPR Covenant	ESCR Covenant	European Convention	European Social Charter	American Convention
Afghanistan	★	★	★			
Albania	★					
Algeria	★					
Angola	★					
Antigua and Barbuda	★					
Argentina	★					
Australia	★	★	★			
Austria	★	★	★	★	★	
Bahamas	★					
Bahrain	★					
Bangladesh	★					
Barbados	★	★[b]	★			★
Belgium	★	★	★	★		
Belize	★					
Benin	★					
Bhutan	★					
Bolivia	★	★[b]	★			★
Botswana	★					
Brazil	★					
Bulgaria	★	★	★			
Burma	★					
Burundi	★					
Byelorussian SSR	★	★	★			
Canada	★	★[b]	★			
Cape Verde	★					
Central African Republic	★	★[b]	★			
Chad	★					
Chile	★	★	★			
China	★					
Colombia	★	★[b]	★			★
Comoros	★					
Congo	★	★[b]	★			
Costa Rica	★	★[b]	★			★
Cuba	★					
Cyprus	★	★	★	★	★	
Czechoslovakia	★	★	★			
Democratic Kampuchea	★					

[a] Whether by ratification or accession; and subject to any reservations duly notified.
[b] Also bound by the Optional Protocol.

State	UN Charter	CPR Covenant	ESCR Covenant	European Convention	European Social Charter	American Convention
Democratic Yemen	★					
Denmark	★	★[b]	★	★	★	
Djibouti	★					
Dominica	★					
Dominican Republic	★	★[b]	★			★
Ecuador	★	★[b]	★			★
Egypt	★	★	★			
El Salvador	★	★	★			★
Equatorial Guinea	★					
Ethiopia	★					
Fiji	★					
Finland	★	★[b]	★			
France	★	★	★	★	★	
Gabon	★	★	★			
Gambia	★	★	★			
German Democratic Republic	★	★	★			
German Federal Republic	★	★	★	★	★	
Ghana	★					
Greece	★			★		
Grenada	★					★
Guatemala	★					★
Guinea	★	★	★			
Guinea-Bissau	★					
Guyana	★	★	★			
Haiti	★					★
Honduras	★		★			★
Hungary	★	★	★			
Iceland	★	★[b]	★	★	★	
India	★	★	★			
Indonesia	★					
Iran	★	★	★			
Iraq	★	★	★			
Ireland	★			★	★	
Israel	★					
Italy	★	★[b]	★	★	★	
Ivory Coast	★					
Jamaica	★	★[b]	★			★
Japan	★	★	★			
Jordan	★	★	★			
Kenya	★	★	★			
Korean Democratic Republic		★	★			
Kuwait	★					
Lao Democratic Republic	★					
Lebanon	★	★	★			
Lesotho	★					

State	UN Charter	CPR Covenant	ESCR Covenant	European Convention	European Social Charter	American Convention
Liberia	★					
Libyan Arab Jamahiriya	★	★	★			
Liechtenstein				★		
Luxembourg	★	★[b]	★	★		
Madagascar	★	★[b]	★			
Malawi	★					
Malaysia	★					
Maldives	★					
Mali	★	★	★			
Malta	★			★		
Mauritania	★					
Mauritius	★	★[b]	★			
Mexico	★	★	★			★
Mongolia	★	★	★			
Morocco	★	★	★			
Mozambique	★					
Nepal	★					
Netherlands	★	★[b]	★	★	★	
New Zealand	★	★	★			
Nicaragua	★	★[b]	★			★
Niger	★					
Nigeria	★					
Norway	★	★[b]	★	★	★	
Oman	★					
Pakistan	★					
Panama	★	★[b]	★			★
Papua New Guinea	★					
Paraguay	★					
Peru	★	★[b]	★			★
Philippines	★		★			
Poland	★	★	★			
Portugal	★	★[b]	★	★		
Qatar	★					
Romania	★	★	★			
Rwanda	★	★	★			
St Christopher and Nevis	★					
St Lucia	★					
St Vincent and Grenadines	★	★[b]	★			
Samoa	★					
São Tomé and Principe	★					
Saudi Arabia	★					
Senegal	★	★[b]	★			
Seychelles	★					
Sierra Leone	★					
Singapore	★					
Solomon Islands	★		★			
Somalia	★					
South Africa	★					
Spain	★	★	★	★	★	

States bound by the general treaties

State	UN Charter	CPR Covenant	ESCR Covenant	European Convention	European Social Charter	American Convention
Sri Lanka	★	★	★			
Sudan	★					
Suriname	★	★[b]	★			
Swaziland	★					
Sweden	★	★[b]	★	★	★	
Switzerland				★		
Syrian Arab Republic	★	★	★			
Thailand	★					
Togo	★					
Trinidad and Tobago	★	★[b]	★			
Tunisia	★	★	★			
Turkey	★			★		
Uganda	★					
Ukrainian SSR	★	★	★			
United Arab Emirates	★					
United Kingdom	★	★	★	★	★	
United Republic of Cameroon	★					
United Republic of Tanzania	★	★	★			
Upper Volta	★					
Uruguay	★	★[b]	★			
USA	★					
USSR	★	★	★			
Vanuatu	★					
Venezuela	★	★[b]	★			★
Vietnam	★	★	★			
Yemen	★					
Yugoslavia	★	★	★			
Zaire	★	★[b]	★			
Zambia	★					
Zimbabwe	★					

Table of cases cited

International Court of Justice

Barcelona Traction case	ICJ 1970, 4
Genocide Convention case	ICJ 1951, 15
Iranian Hostages case	ICJ 1980, 4

Human Rights Committee

Aumeeruddy-Cziffra v. *Mauritius*	HRC 36, 134
Hartikainen v. *Finland*	HRC 36, 147
Lovelace v. *Canada*	HRC 36, 166

European Court of Human Rights

Airey v. *Ireland*	2 EHRR 305
Belgian linguistic case	1 EHRR 252
Campbell and Cosans v. *UK*	4 EHRR 293
Golder v. *UK*	1 EHRR 524
Handyside v. *UK*	1 EHRR 737
Ireland v. *UK*	2 EHRR 25
Kjeldsen et al. v. *Denmark*	1 EHRR 711
Klass v. *Federal Republic of Germany*	2 EHRR 214
Malone v. *United Kingdom*	Judgment: 2 August 1984
Sunday Times v. *UK*	2 EHRR 245
Young, James and Webster v. *UK*	4 EHRR 38

European Commission of Human Rights

Amekrane v. *UK*	YB 16, 356
Arrowsmith v. *UK*	3 EHRR 218
Denmark et al. v. *Greece*	YB 12 *bis*
Iversen v. *Norway*	YB 6, 278
Patel et al. v. *UK*	3 EHRR 76
X v. *UK* (Application No. 7992/77)	DR 14, 234

England

Sommersett's case	20 State Trials 1

USA

Filartiga v. *Pena-Irala*	630 F.(2nd) 876

Schenck v. *US*   249 US 47

Upper Silesian Arbitral Tribunal
Steiner and Gross v. *The Polish State*   4 Annual Digest
                                                            (1927–8), Cases
                                                            Nos. 188 and 287

ABBREVIATIONS
Decisions and Reports of the European Com-
    mission of Human Rights   DR
European Human Rights Reports   EHRR
Federal Reporter, Second Series   F.(2nd)
Reports of the Human Rights Committee to
    the UN General Assembly   HRC
Reports of the International Court of Justice   ICJ
United States Reports   US
Yearbook of the European Convention on
    Human Rights   YB

Further reading

Part I

A self-contained and reasonably concise discussion of the main theories of political philosophy which underlie today's notions of human rights can be found in Jerome J. Shestack's 'The Jurisprudence of Human Rights', the third chapter of T. Meron (ed.), *Human Rights in International Law: Legal and Policy Issues* (2 vols., Oxford, 1984). For a full understanding of these theories, there is no ultimate substitute for the great classics of the past, such as Plato's *Republic*, Aristotle's *Politics*, Machiavelli's *The Prince* (preferably balanced by Castiglione's *The Courtier*), More's *Utopia*, Hobbes's *Leviathan*, Locke's *Treatise on Government*, Rousseau's *The Social Contract*, Montesquieu's *The Spirit of Laws*, Marx's *Capital*, and J. S. Mill's *Essay on Liberty*. But for those with less time, Sabine's *A History of Political Theory* will provide a sound and reliable guide. D. D. Raphael (ed.), *Political Theory and the Rights of Man* (London, 1967), and A. Gewirth, *Human Rights* (Chicago, 1982), are also recommended.

Among the modern books on the concepts of justice and rights, the most recent and substantial are J. Rawls, *A Theory of Justice* (Oxford, 1972); B. Barry, *The Liberal Theory of Justice* (Oxford, 1973); R. Nozick, *Anarchy, State and Utopia* (Oxford, 1974); D. Miller, *Social Justice* (Oxford, 1976); R. Dworkin, *Taking Rights Seriously* (London, 1976); C. Fried, *Right and Wrong* (Cambridge, Mass., 1978); J. R. Lucas, *On Justice* (Oxford, 1980); and J. Feinberg, *Rights, Justice and the Bounds of Liberty* (Princeton, 1980). The positivist view was perhaps most comprehensively argued in H. Kelsen, *What is Justice?* (Berkeley, 1960).

S. E. Finer's *Five Constitutions* (Harmondsworth, 1979) is indispensable for an understanding of the role (and limitations) of constitutions in this field, and includes texts dating from 1787 (USA) to 1977 (USSR). B. Schwarz, *The Great Rights of Mankind* (New York, 1977) lucidly describes how the seminal US Bill of Rights of 1791 was drafted and adopted.

The contemporary literature on the problems of human rights is immense, and four books written at different times, and from different perspectives, must suffice here as samples. H. Lauterpacht's *International Law and Human Rights*, first published in 1950 when the only binding treaty even mentioning human rights was the young UN Charter, shows the cautious delight of a great international lawyer of the classical school at this wondrous new seedling in his garden. M. Cranston's *What are Human Rights?* (London, 1973) displays some irritation at its rapid growth, and some evident worries that it might become a weed. L. Henkin's *The Rights of Man Today* (London, 1978) looks back at its achievements, and forward to its future, from a viewpoint of guarded optimism. Finally, Meron's two volumes mentioned above (1984) provide a comprehensive review of the current state of the discussion.

Part II

Among the standard textbooks on international law, the most suitable for general use are D. P. O'Connell, *International Law* (2 vols., London, 1970); I. Brownlie, *Principles of Public International Law* (3rd edn., Oxford, 1979); and D. J. Harris, *Cases and Materials on International Law* (3rd edn., London, 1983). The full texts of the general international human rights instruments (other than the African Charter), including all their procedural Articles, can be found in I. Brownlie, *Basic Documents on Human Rights* (2nd edn., Oxford, 1981), as can many of the specialized instruments. Those promoted by the United Nations are also reprinted in the UN publication *Human Rights: A Compilation of International Instruments* (New York, 1983).

The 'civil and political' part of the European system is described in J. E. S. Fawcett, *The Application of the European Convention on Human Rights* (Oxford, 1969); F. G. Jacobs, *The European Convention on Human Rights* (Oxford, 1975); and A. H. Robertson, *Human Rights in Europe* (2nd edn., Manchester, 1977). A wider field is covered in A. H. Robertson, *Human Rights in the World* (2nd edn., Manchester, 1984).

Non-discrimination is discussed more fully in W. McKean, *Equality and Discrimination under International Law* (Oxford, 1983). Derogation is the subject of the International Commission of Jurists' comprehensive study *States of Emergency: Their Impact on Human Rights* (Geneva, 1983).

The available international remedies are described and discussed in detail in H. Hannum (ed.), *Guide to International Human Rights Practice* (Philadelphia, 1984).

Part III

A much fuller treatment of the substantive law about each of these rights—that is, the relevant texts of all the general international instruments, and the extensive case-law of the competent independent international and national institutions—can be found in P. Sieghart, *The International Law of Human Rights* (Oxford, 1983). There is an important discussion of the emergent 'right to development' in the International Commission of Jurists' *Development, Human Rights and the Rule of Law* (Oxford, 1981).

Index of names

Subject index